PINKY PROMISES

MAX JESTER

authorHOUSE®

AuthorHouse™
1663 Liberty Drive
Bloomington, IN 47403
www.authorhouse.com
Phone: 833-262-8899

Published by AuthorHouse   09/14/2021

ISBN: 978-1-6655-3634-9 (sc)
ISBN: 978-1-6655-3633-2 (hc)
ISBN: 978-1-6655-3632-5 (e)

Library of Congress Control Number: 2021917502

CONTENTS

PREFACE

Hello, I'm Pinky. That's the name my ancestors gave me so the costume fits appropriately. I can assure you the name *Pinky* was earned one tourniquet at a time. There is a reason for it. Groomed for all to see, this is my life. I didn't ask to be here, but I'm still standing. It's fairly obvious. Many watched for themselves. I'm the man in the box, the unicorn, if you understand as I do. Groomed to be entertaining for all to see, I've been blessed to call this amazing life mine again. Privacy is a *right*, not a privilege. I'm not entitled to either. The real question is "How did I know?" Because I'm supposed to be blind, right? These are my memoirs. This is my life and how, after I took it back from my captors to give it to my King where it belongs, I promised my King, that I would write down what I learned for others to gain understanding from what I've lived through. Consider it a pinky promise. Because, well, I am fairly well known, aren't I?

This memoir is a pinky promise to my creator. It's what He commanded me to do a long time ago to set myself free for His glory, not my own. I'm fairly certain I'm not the only one. I am thankful I am still standing, still smiling, with the sun on my face, fully alive and awake now. It's written that when you put all your faith and hope in the Lord, you will not perish but have everlasting life. Without the Holy Spirit's discernment, I would not be able to share this testimony.

Jesus Christ is truly the only way to receive salvation and forgiveness. I now know that much is gained and much is lost when going through the refiner's fire. It is when you keep having a good attitude by always looking for the silver lining, keeping a smile on your face even though you're surrounded by your enemies on all sides—that's when the Lord is able to use your faith and perform miracles.

I know it is well. He makes it possible for the meek to overcome strongholds with simple faith. I am so far from perfect. I am only a sinner saved by the grace of God. I'm Pinky, and this is the story from my eyes. I grew up in a box, and it wasn't until later that I knew. I didn't even know I was groomed to be a source of entertainment for all the world to see. Many of you reading this saw it for yourself, my life unfolding right before your very eyes. I know it won't ever be the same as what's on the screen, because after all, everything you see on a screen has been edited. Most aren't privy enough to understand how entertainment works. Maybe you know who I am. Maybe you've seen me in real life. So, what is that? Is there such a thing as reality entertainment? Or is it simply rage? I couldn't tell you, but my life hasn't been all bad. There were some good moments. I honestly didn't know my free will was undoubtedly being removed slowly but surely, only to be replaced with a demonic stronghold by way of scripted lies, control, and manipulation. Many of you think or want to believe the story and the events are too far out there to be real, that maybe it is a mental thing or something. But honestly that is the enemy's goal and only defense. Being great at lies and manipulation, that's his calling card. Some may think that there is no way possible to deceive on such a large scale. But when you understand there are actions and motives, you may fully open your eyes to the truth that lies beneath the surface. And you may have seen it before. The Lord loves forgiveness. It's the opposite of our flesh that holds on to people who can't let go.

As I'm writing this book, I've tried all other ways I know to explain, and I'm fully aware that it's going to cost me my life. I'm only compelled because I know that my life is not my own. It's my creator's life that He planned for me. I'm lucky enough to enjoy every day and be thankful for His goodness. Every day is a blessing, good, bad, ugly. It is still an amazing day. For I know today is the day the Lord has made, and I will rejoice and be glad in it.

CHAPTER 1

Mirth

"A little more sleep and a little more slumber, and poverty comes up like the flies." As usual, I'm up early, before dawn. He commands it. I'm looking forward to today and everything it has for me. I have been dreaming of this for a long time. Today is the day the Lord has made. I will rejoice and be glad in it. I slowly sit and take in the coolness of the morning. The sun is coming up over the oak-tree-crested hills in the distance, which becomes a canvas framed by an old rustic-looking privacy fence on the left. It's been falling down for years and needs to be replaced, but it is quite relaxing to stare at. In my solitude, I've grown accustomed to years of the same scenery. And how it lends bliss to a tired soul, when the divine artist is present to make it all look new again.

I'm watching my master paint a living story. Starting in the darkness, He brings first the light. And He uses the horizon as His palette of colors. Today, I'm treated with high clouds on the horizon. I first notice the red sky in the morning—and I'm reminded, "Sailor, take warning." I'm seeing the beautiful change that's taking place. It looks as though the sky is on fire and melting together with beautiful blues and pinks that look so dynamic in that moment. It's when the darkness is overtaken by the light that I find again my favorite portion of the day.

I try to spend the first few moments of the day with my father in heaven. It's my selfish time with Him alone. It's like I'm captivated by His ever-changing beauty, which I can't help but be in deep silence about as I listen to everything around me. For He has complete dominion over the beasts of the field and the birds of the air. It's easy to see. I'm so energized by His hand on my life and the visual affirmation I get daily because of our time together. I sit and watch again as another symphony on the horizon plays out in perfect harmony, as if it's a majestic show that's been put on for only me and purely my enjoyment.

It's a blessing to see the handiwork of my father. In that morning, at that moment, I'm overjoyed at the amazing honor that's bestowed on me, while incredibly humbled at the same time. That feeling of presence is always so overwhelming I can hardly breathe. I exhale more slowly now as I get comfortable and keep silence with reverence and poise. I sip my black coffee while facing the sunrise on one knee, my breath almost still now. It pairs well with the calm. I begin looking closer, as if I'm in the presence of my real father, who died a long time ago.

the quiet witness

As my gaze draws lower and the sun becomes brighter, my eyes wince from its illumination and begin to tear. With my now watery eyes locked into a gaze just below the horizon, I see the dew on the summer grass and weeds, which are overgrown and entangled with a rustic-style fence. It is complete with a manufactured western-style gate, which has been engineered to appear old and strong, to look official with a star on the front. I can tell by the new locking mechanism that this is simply a new version of an old barn door. The crack between the gate and fence sheltered the undesirable greenery and was just out of reach for regular, easy maintenance and grounds keeping.

That simple shadow that was cast onto the ground gives way to more and more greenery, which, when undisturbed, stands bold. And even though it's only a weed, it voraciously grows daily. It already knows that each day could very well be its last. And it knows not to delay living accordingly. In doing so, the weeds and vines creep higher and higher toward the lock and handle of the entry into the private yard. Those same shoots of life were once seeds, buried, only to become a fire hazard late in the season, depending on the time of year and how you see things. Like a frame to the most famous artwork, they seem to cradle the overgrown weeds and grass by making the gate and entry look much newer and less out of place— because everything looks aged when it isn't cared for.

Most sheep really don't even notice how things are maintained. But I do. I see the attention to detail and the silver lining here. In all its majesty, there it is, the living artwork, which has been painted by my creator using a canvas that's alive and ever-changing. I notice how the blades of mixed grass integrate with tall weeds and the bluebonnets that stand tall independently. Each hoping to reach closer to the sun. Even the thorns and thistles are thriving. Although sparse and scattered, the bluebonnets look to have survived this summer heat and are still standing strong and tall. They look to act selfishly in this moment, as they continue holding on to the morning dew as it fades away. Each to their own, they hold onto tiny droplets that are refracting the sunlight in unison, creating sparkles and shimmers so bright.

How can you not notice? How can you not see another silver lining when it's right in front of you? I'm still amazed at how much it looks like a blanket of diamonds from far away. As long as they aren't touched, they will sit there and be evaporated by the sun. That evaporation we all know is simply the due process, I guess you could say.

I finish my morning by staying in the shade and being honored by His presence, giving thanks to my creator for all my blessings. I know I'm actually not alone, ever. I enjoy this time in contrast and perspective shift, knowing it looks like another hot day. That reminds me, as happy as I am in this moment right here and right now, I know I'm dying. I'm being suffocated by weight and heat that's undeserved. I have got to rid myself of this black suit that's not even mine. I never agreed to wear this thing. I was told many times if I ever refused to wear my costume, the wolves who raised me would kill me. This black sheepskin suit I wear has been attached with a branding iron. It happened before I was old enough to have any of my own rights.

I'm not complaining today though. I probably needed it. It's given me more strength. Even when it's hot, I have to wear it in public. It's heavy and made out of old, tattered black wool. But now, I no longer feel the weight of it because I have worn it so long. Pretty regularly, it gets soaked in gasoline by all the blind sheep I've worked with for twenty years now. Its stench is repulsive to everyone around except for me. I don't smell and can't tell what does. But you'd think I'd be used to wearing this costume by now as a black sheep. All the years of being burned alive have probably contributed to the loss of smell.

Although I did lose my sense of smell along the way, I didn't lose my pinky, even though it's tiny. I never understood if it was due to the smell of burning flesh paired with alcohol, which burned my nose initially in 1993 during the branding process I underwent in gaining my costume. Perhaps it might have been the constant fumes of gasoline poured on my new-but-used black sheepskin daily. It might have even been the manure I was force-fed for years as punishment and for entertainment's sake. The truth is that's all I had. My pinky and I were informed on a regular basis that that was all I deserved.

Besides, there wasn't much room for anything else. Nobody would claim me anyway. My dark-black sheepskin has grown too small over the years of working out hard and gaining strength. The costume I'm adorned with is becoming rather constricting on my back. I must rid myself of this dead weight I was made to carry. I always knew that a unicorn horn had been growing underneath this costume. I didn't understand yet why. I can tell you for certain it's been a lot harder lately to keep my wool covering my entire skin so nobody can see.

I always paid attention when the other sheep would speak in public about how the legend of the unicorn went. Some younger sheep would say it was a myth, while other sheep who were older and a little wiser and had seen more would say he was real, that his name was Pegasus, and that there was only one real unicorn. That is until Pegasus's son returns. He will be the most sought-after creature in every land. According to the legend, nobody will even pay him any mind until he is already gone. Like him or hate him, it's obvious he is a legend. He didn't want to be well known; he would rather be anonymous, but the truth is, everyone wants what he has. Most sheep covet what they don't have. Simply put, it's his freedom. That's the unicorn's signature move.

All the shepherds, sheep, and wolves know and agree on one thing in this life. And that's the legend of the unicorn. They are a symbol of purity and grace and can only be captured by a virgin. The legend of the unicorn goes on forever, as always. It's been said you can't catch him or trap him. He will escape, not to mention he is too fast and can also fly. To mortal men, it would seem some higher power was helping the unicorn break away from the herd. And often, when least expected, the unicorn can somehow grant wishes, which to mortal men is unimaginable. All the while, throughout history, all the other blind sheep have grown more jealous with passing time. History repeats itself. It always reaches a point when the blind sheep are so envious, they work together to try to steal his single horn and throw him off a cliff. But, originally enough, he always finds his wings after bouncing on his horn. Somehow, he is always able to fly away again. The real unicorn doesn't stay close to anyone or anything very long, because he is quite aware of his authenticity as well as the mediocrity of his captors. This unicorn knows he doesn't wear a bridle. It would never fit anyway. Nor does he have a barn to keep or sheep to look after. The truth is they aren't allowed to leave the herd. They instead are meant to be anchors to prevent his escape.

Somehow, in my freedom, I have found that to be truly free, I cannot have an earthly master to please. This unicorn knows right from wrong and cannot live harmoniously otherwise. This unicorn knows already without saying a word that he doesn't have friends, he isn't like them, and they are not real anyway. They are just sheep obeying orders. He must keep them closer than friends. That's how you learn the sheep's tell. I know I'm a unicorn in so many ways it's undeniable. I haven't ever met another sheep much less a black sheep that would vomit rainbows like I do. All the other blind sheep find them so tasty they can't wait to eat. With that said, this unicorn doesn't have family, only just a few acquaintances, and he's never been happier. Alone is all he has; alone is what protects him. The best unicorns watch and learn how craftily shepherds and wolves work together to set traps for all the blind sheep. The best never lose; they only learn. Legends live to tell the story. Many of the youngest wolves groomed around the home compound weren't privy enough to understand the level of my enlightenment. The blind sheep don't fully comprehend or know I was raised by the very wolves they feared the most. This has been to my advantage, because maybe if they had known what I do prior to today, they might have had a different choice to make about their own slavery in regard to mine. If I hadn't been raised and branded with a new costume by the same wolves long ago, I might today, have still had to partake in all the games they are required by the shepherds to play.

As I sat alone, in silence, looking directly into the eyes of wolves while they glow like embers, I smiled. That was when the unicorn was made. Others wear costumes too. Mostly the real black sheep need to stay covered. Many will go to great lengths to put on a costume. Because not all sheep are on the up and up, but often, I've noticed the dirtiest sheep have to get the most grooming to stay looking so clean. Generally speaking, those sheep have the best wool and the brightest smile and can jump the highest and first when the shepherd wants. You might remember them as the teacher's pet, maybe the fire chief's son who can do no wrong, or maybe the preacher's kid who is always up to something. I've grown callous to blind sheep who only do the right thing when they have an audience to please. It's kind of like when some sheep buy the homeless a meal so all the other sheep can see a selfie about it on sheeple media. I wonder what would happen if you did the same thing to your King, if you didn't know he was in hiding. I'd like to see if you still have the same motives. After all, yours is just a costume also.

I've seen what they call the best sheep look like underneath the outfit. I can assure you that the prettiest people are the ugliest on the inside. Only behind closed doors do they remove their garments, because that's when they actually believe nobody is looking. Because they are wolves who wear a costume, they must stay in costume in public. The wolves are afforded luxuries to be the envy of the neighborhood. Keeping up with the Joneses is big, *big* business for all the shepherds who work together. I can assure you regardless of the current state of affairs those wolves eat well because they obey their shepherds, who supply them with a comfortable life that includes unlimited food and resources. The black sheep don't have the same options. And they should expect far fewer resources. Matter of fact, anyone who helps the black sheep will be targeted just like him. But what if a black sheep isn't one at all? How would he change his costume? I pondered the rhetoric over many sunsets overlooking the water. Those summer

sunsets were always brilliant and full of awe-inspiring beauty. That really gave me time to think and put things into perspective and the renewed energy to find the silver lining regardless of the situation. As I stand upon years' worth of manure and covered in gasoline, I am beginning to feel my unicorn horn grow, and in the process, it almost ripped through my costume. It's ironic how other sheep want to wear a costume that's fluffy and white, so it looks like they are doing well even if they aren't, when I just want my own skin back. Even if it's still scarred and branded underneath, it's what I was born with. I didn't ask to be raised by them. I'm so thankful I know I'm not one of them. I was born to a breeder, not on purpose, but they know about bloodlines and keeping the family's pure. However, it's good for something I've been told. I'm an abortion survivor, multiple times. I'm thankful for my scars. It means I never have been one of the sheep. It's fairly obvious that my life isn't my own; instead, it's my creator's. I gave it to him shortly after I suffered the pain of being branded.

The truth is I'm far from perfect. I'm not a hero. I've been skin underneath all along. I still remember the other sheep could only say with happy smirks and cheerful smiles, "This is my lot in life …" They have said it so much they actually believed it. All the shepherds in the world know, a public display usually works wonders for sheep who want to see something entertaining.

One day leading up to the end of summer 2013 would be a prime season. A real unicorn must act like a jester, knowing that sometimes you have to act a fool to fool the fools who actually believe they are fooling you.

As the years, months, and days lead up to this night Saturday June 29th 2013, when I will remove my costume in front of the camera for all the world to see, I know beyond a shadow of doubt, it will be an amazing display because I have been keeping detailed notes to see who my biggest fans are—some sheep simply aren't allowed to look away—and to my biggest honor and reverence, they have been here for years. I've been aware of how some sheep are instructed to keep a close eye on the one black sheep. And when the wolves are looking for a reaction, the shepherd can capitalize on it. Sometimes, it's best to just smile like nothing is happening. Pretend you're on a game show where the people nearest to you are competing for prizes like gift cards, cash, cars, and even an all-expense-paid trip for two to Hawaii. The sheep who have already accepted their prizes before the games began are entitled to established houses and prepared futures. Simply put, it's so fun to play games when everyone takes part. And when the shepherds with wolves don't get what they are looking for, usually they turn on each other, attacking one another.

I've heard that gets expensive, and if you're only made of money, then we both know your existence is very fragile. It hurts when I smile back at you. I know I have only ever seen any of the other black sheep get out of the compound and into freedom after they are dead and processed. They are a commodity. I've seen black sheep before, plenty of times. I've played out every other scenario in mind. It is what it is, and this is it. Tonight is the night. It will be a good day. It will be a *great* day actually. I have played my part very well in the years leading up to this point. I think I should get an award for acting so melancholy on purpose to steer the blind sheep who report directly to the shepherds.

While being honest and sincere, I have sought to offer an apology to someone I've crossed, who extended me grace. Believe me; my apologies were sincere. I never forgot the feeling I felt though, when I saw the camera he placed across the room from the matches. That incident, in a moment of my own self-righteousness to impress peers, was a dare between adolescent friends, although I kept quiet about what I knew. I needed to be sincere. That was easy. I'm lucky enough to say I got to see his reaction to my apology. And I could see it very well. It was hard not to see. I had hoped he would understand that I fully understood. No grace was actually there. But as luck would have it, from my vantage point, it was like watching all the blind sheep you know standing on a train track, oblivious. The blind sheep don't even know the train is coming without warning. I almost felt something for them out of mercy briefly even though I knew what his motives were. I wasn't actually sad in the least bit.

I have learned from my captors how to create the illusion that people want to believe. As a unicorn, I don't know if all the sheep are aware of this, but the gateway upstairs, it isn't for everyone. Many are called but most trade their integrity for opportunity before they ever reach the gateway to heaven. Sometimes the best sheep blindly follow others, and ignorance is bliss, but it isn't an affordable behavior. I've watched for years, and to the best of my knowledge, besides death, I don't know of another way to get over the barbed wire fence and get out of this funny farm where all the animals behave badly when they aren't on display. I will always believe it's true that taking your own life is a surefire way to exile yourself from the gateway and kingdom of heaven. I believe that because your body is a temple, and if you take it from the one who gives it, your creator can't use you anymore. That's not something I've been able to rationalize. Not for anyone. Never have. I've only been able to see it as a cry for attention by people who are tormented by the grief and guilt of their own actions. How can it be so bad that you take your own life? I mean, seriously. Who cares?

Blind sheep are all the same, and to the shepherds who own the sheep, they are only numbers on paper. Nobody cares … at least that's what I'm counting on. I'm a unicorn, not a black sheep. I could care less what all the others think about me. I don't think about them at all. The blind sheep today are so far beneath me now. They still don't understand. If sheep had their own brains and they weren't blind, they would know by now that if they all stood up at the same time, then they would outnumber all the shepherds and the wolves who currently run the show. I know better than to believe in a society of sheep based on what I've already seen sheep do for bread. Instead, I kept a watchful eye on the horizon as I learned to fly like the best of the best unicorns. Even though self-taught, I'm fully aware the blind sheep closest to me want to please their earthly masters to ensure their closest place in line at the slaughterhouse. Every one of them needs a show that is worthy of seeing. I couldn't agree more. Fireworks and popcorn are in order. I highly suggest ordering some pizza in advance too. Most situations can be greatly improved by a sweet-and-spicy deep-dish delivery.

To tell this love story right, I'll have to take everyone back thirty years or more to when I acquired my costume by playing with matches in a place where I shouldn't have. I have always regretted playing truth or dare with those other kids. I didn't mean to burn the barns down, but it only took one spark before the thing went ablaze. The second match is the one that lit all the other matches, in what can only be described as spontaneous combustion. It wasn't until this point that I saw the camera sitting on the piano recording across the room. It's like the place was soaked in gasoline so that any little spark would send you up in flames. I get it. That's why I wear my costume covered in gasoline today, because if I ever play with matches again, I will burn myself alive in front of everyone, quite literally. I must daily put on the full armor of God and adorn myself with the breastplate of righteousness. Even though I presently walk through this valley located centrally in the city of slaves who are already dead, I fear no evil, for my creator is with me, and instead, his rod and staff, they comfort me. He blesses me with mercy and anoints my head with oil while he makes me lie down beside cool waters. His word is a lamp to my feet. I'm reassured mercy isn't up to me. My path of righteousness has already been set on all sides by my King. Much like in the legend of David and Goliath, it's for my King's glory, not my own. I've seen how all things work together for even those who don't know. How? That is the most remarkable and priceless question. How does the Lord display the might of his hands so that all who see already know? I'm fairly sure he uses the impossible, and it's mostly because his hands are bigger than our own understanding.

May your King open your eyes, no matter where you are or what you've been through. It was all worth it to see clearly. Sun gazing to see …

I learned to share how I see. Can you hear me now? I'm not talking to you. I'm talking to all the others who are reading this. This is for everyone else. It's not about me. I'm a nobody. My eyes are blind, and I'm gagged, but I see very well, and it's funny to the right audience. Isn't it? I wish I had not spent all that time writing down phone numbers and names, memorizing them, not realizing that would glorify their actions. I kept it locked away for the appropriate time, knowing what was to be expected and why. I simply pray for mercy, because I truly believe they do not know what they are doing. It is like the blind leading the blind and expecting to do better. I find that if I start my day with coffee and a bagel or pastry and spend some time with the sun, I won't need to dwell on the darkness I'm waking in. I guess for me, being positive while knowing I'm about to die is all about perspective. I already know could have died years ago—maybe that Christmas Eve when I was five weeks old. I get it. But that's not up to me. It's not my life to take. I'm not interested in getting into trading that kind of currency. I know dirty money doesn't go very far. I've seen it, and I've felt it. I learned a long time ago that is what I do. I learned how to learn. I can't help it. As a technician, I must put all the pieces together. And if all the pieces are together, then I will take it apart, only to put it back together—even the pieces that are missing. It's what I've done for years. So, no, thank you. Don't say I'm speaking out of line.

And I applaud their efforts to procure more mediocrity. It's a sad thing, isn't it? That's why we have so many mediocre people. I started as the worst, most selfish, and messed up kid, I promise you. I was super hard to live with I bet. I know why too. It's only because of what I've walked through and how it was shown in small pieces that it was so enlightening. And that's what I'm thankful for—everything and nothing all at the same time. Because my King is my provider, not my ex-wife's associates. I know his hands are bigger than mine. It's not always easy to see because my hands are small. I refuse to throw them at anyone. Instead, I will do great

things with them. That's the goal. I will do that instead of what my enemy wants. It's a surprise—another pinky promise, actually. It's entertainingly cryptic, isn't it?

Many of you, I hope, are interpreting my words. I believe if you know enough about how things actually work, you will begin to realize the depth of our own slavery. That's where you'll see me just like that famous street on the island in the bay. I'm way beneath everyone, hard as heck because I've been run over and repaved many times over the years. I know the routine well. Everyone uses me to get to where they are going. Some don't even know the way. But the road is already paved. I've been right in the middle of all the traffic the whole time and simply just exist. I know this street I'm talking about is a dangerous one. Cars and people have accidents there all the time. It's not that it's poorly designed; it's that it's just the nature of distracted people. I wish more people would at least try to see the light. I think situations like that would be far less likely. If they didn't just look and could see instead, then the accidents wouldn't happen. I pinky promise if you watch the sun rise every morning for three weeks in silence and keep a journal as if you're telling yourself your own story, you will begin to see how much more you understand. That's the beauty of my downfall. I learned when I shouldn't have. It's impossible. And somehow, I learned how I learned enough to share it. I pray for a new world. I don't know about an "order" being there, but my sincere prayer is that someday, in unison, people will understand the gravity of the choices that they have made prior to their own knowledge, not as a form of hate but as a humbling experience of how enslaved we actually are. It saddens me the amount of resources that were used to make my life what it was, but it has layers of silver linings because at least the resources weren't real anyway, so it wasn't truly a loss. Another silver layer is that not only did I learn, but I learned how I learned. Then I believe I put it in a way that other people can understand. I believe the captives should be set free.

Costumes. We all wear them. Some are simply concubines because that is what they've made for themselves. It seems as though in this society there is no shortage of sex being sold for entertainment purposes. I was raised by many of them. I enjoy being famous now.

I remember one of my first body doubles from the mid 1990's. He was about my same height and probably about as athletic as I was. We will call him Dick because it rhymes. He was also a close friend of the other two kids who dared me to play with matches. He could ride a motorcycle fairly well, and it was fun playing hockey with them before I burned those barns

down. Appropriately, I thought it was odd how he ended up finding an identical dirt bike a distance away and took delivery of it. He went out with them very often, and they made sure I knew by driving by my place with all the bikes loaded up on the trailer, his identical bike in the front for me to see. I believe that the same guy used the money he made from my smear to start his new motorcycle company. I think they're a bunch of suckers because if you start a business with dirty money, you won't go very far. They call the shop Lucky or something.

His father was an associate of the kids I played truth or dare with. As a matter of fact, he lives in the very house that the previous owners who helped him get to where he is lived in. If it wasn't for that old barn, he might not have had to keep so many secrets about who, what, and why because they pay his debts for his service.

The next double I saw was in high school, I remember seeing a gentleman who was Linda's friend in a car that was identical to mine, driving up and down my neighborhood streets, burning the tires off, creating a ruckus just before I got home from school. I only noticed one day because I got out of class just a few moments early. I did not stop at my locker, nor did I talk to anyone. There wasn't any traffic out of the parking lot. I went straight home and happened to pass the car that looked just like mine with this guy, Taylor, sitting in the seat. I noticed that the license plate was paper, as if it were a brand-new unit, and it came from the dealership just up the street, one of the largest dealerships in the nation. It just so happened I had a current-year body style, so the car looked a lot like mine. However, we both know mine was faster and better, but from a glance, no one else knew. It didn't take long with repeated driving like that for my neighbors to begin to associate any loud car or a black car with me, and subsequently, they called the gang in blue at every opportunity. Sometimes, they were even waiting for me to get back from school. I think some of them were even baffled as to how I was able to be in two places at once. Others simply didn't care; they were looking for any opportunity to write me a ticket for any reason whatsoever. I remember in the mid-nineties even getting a ticket in Colley Wood for my tires and defective windshield wipers at the same time as I got one for having no front license plate from badge number 078 in the most perfect weather. Mind you, I was not speeding at all. I was simply minding my own business on my way home from school. I now had three tickets to deal with just that day. The next double I never got to meet personally. In late-two-thousands I do remember some of Linda's consultants asking me who I might choose if I had to find a doppelganger. This was around the time that Facebook had a doppelganger contest. I thought it

was odd that someone who worked at the gateway and had been contacting me in a flirtatious manner weeks before was now contacting me about who I could use as my doppelganger. I suggested it should be an expensive person because otherwise that might be insulting. Of course, I suggested Vin Diesel. But instead, she found someone from a cooking network and suggested how much he looked like me. I found a better one personally. He is a UFC coach and looks extraordinarily like me—or do I look like him? I've even been mistaken for him in public with the same build, same hair line as well as the same facial hair. At the time, I was not very concerned as to why she would want to identify someone who looked just like me. I could really care less. What an amazing honor to be so interesting to so many people. Is it my authenticity, or is it their own mediocrity? Or is it motivated by Illuminati who wish to create the illusion people want to believe? After all money means nothing to the people in power who print it as a form of slavery for the rest of us to rely on. I don't know, but time will tell. I, for some reason, am not allowed to see. Nor do I really care what they think about me. I don't think about them anymore anyway. I tried to explain to them that the best way to hold something is with your palms open because as soon as you try to squeeze it, it all falls away, like dust in the wind. Gone. Bye-bye.

I love the target on my back. It's simply amazing. It must mean that I am meant for something greater than I know. I didn't read the time, thinking that the gang in blue officer in question was probably just a jealous guy who wished he was my age and having the time of his life. I couldn't fault him for that because I was having the time of my life. I was driving a car that was mine and was simply awesome. It's an amazing grace, isn't it? It was further confirmed that this was going on because even after I got rid of the car, on a daily basis, the gang in blue would stop by, asking to see me and wondering why I was driving erratically when I didn't own the car. See, it wouldn't have mattered; they just wanted to come erase me. That's the only reason. They created the very situation they planned to capitalize on. Years later, I got sucked into working for that dealership and saw it all too well. They supplied the gang in blue with the vehicles. What did they have to be worried about?

The next part is very important. It goes along with sun-gazing. Start writing—not for everyone, but just for yourself. Write down your life as if you are watching it on a TV show—but not to share. And guard that with your life. I find it best to spend a few moments before bed writing, and if I ever have a dream, I write it down right away. It's amazing how it will apply

later in life. I suggest using pen and paper. It's what I did. I almost think the lack of artificial light brings even more clarity of thought. Think about how tired your eyes get from looking at screens. Plus, it's private. That's why I put mine on paper. I have so many chapters I cannot read out loud because they are like bombs when you see them from my perspective. I keep trying not to hurt anyone, but it seems as though everyone is blind, including me. That's how I develop my pineal gland.

It's simple: self-reflection, controlled breathing, and asking forgiveness. That's my secret. It's not my life. My King owns me. He loves my costume. It was needed to capture a large audience. I know he wants to set the slaves free. And it starts with your mind. It's sad that we are only using 10 percent of our brainpower when I know it could be different. It's the meek who will inherit the earth.

To tell you the truth, I've rarely met anyone with any integrity. A few. That's why I stay alone. It protects me. It's always in random places. Maybe that's why I prefer to travel by train or by riding a unicycle. I bet that's the preferred method for a unicorn anyway. I'm so thankful for my life and knowing the gift of my absence is something to behold. You never know what you've got until it's gone. You know where to find me.

—Max Jester

CHAPTER 2

Let There Be Light

Let there be light. To my audience, this is my olive branch. I'm giving you the tools to defeat the elite. It's a simply written word from enlightened people. Their claim to fame is that nothing is written down. So maybe this is a bomb for later. Learn to see. Look past fake people, and write it down, because you never know where life may actually lead. I admit, I used cannabis for years without telling anyone. I did so on purpose, so the brainwashing from my ancestors wouldn't take.

I also found it so helpful to watch the sunrise. It's like a reset button. Think of it like a solar charge for your pineal gland. That's said to be the seat of the soul. And its power is beyond what we really know. The ancients believed it was the third eye—two to look and one to see. I find personally that watching the sun come up until it's clear of the horizon without shades is essential. Also key here is to sit in silence, focusing on your own in the moment, feeling the sun bring tears to your eyes, and listening for things unseen. It's been said the King speaks in signs and wonders. So be persistent for at least a month. Write down your life as if it were a TV show, and keep it sacred. Reread your writing after a month of sun-gazing, and you will be amazed at how close you can become with yourself and your creator. That's the only way to find true peace. That's the way it works for me. And I know others have seen it. I know that sometimes in life the worst kids can become the best adults if they learn. And the best of the best learns how to learn so they can teach others.

Much like the king salmon, I've spent half my life in salt water and half my life in fresh water. I'm swimming upstream, headed to where I was conceived. As a juvenile, I've been caught and released. As an adult, I've been hooked and somehow managed to escape death more than I care to admit. That's how the biggest trophies are made. Like the king salmon, I must use my third eye to find my own way. I am navigating the waters of life using my King to guide me back to where I was born. I don't even miss that sewer. I know that's where I lost my sense of smell. It's so funny.

As I drove to the lake to fake my own suicide, late at night on June 29th 2013, I began to watch as everyone around me wanted to celebrate. I stopped at the gas station, and it was empty when I pulled up and became a bustling enterprise within just a few moments. It was funny to see my ancestors give chase. I walked in, bought a six-pack, and put the rest of the twenty in fuel into my boat. It's like everyone in line was listening. The line was now like eight people long.

As I fueled the boat, I began to notice people congregating under the sign. As my Half Brother Muck's associates began to give handshakes and wrist slaps to one another, I got excited. I figured this might be a glorious show. I knew he wanted money. I wanted everyone to see. It was funny. So, I slipped out of the gas station and headed toward the lake. I parked at Catfish Cove and watched a guy from my ex-wife's cult pull up behind me as I was putting the drain plug in only to get out and take a photo. I was a little happy. But wanted him to think I was sad. I backed my Tahoe down and got it launched. As I was boating off into the darkness, I noticed what looked like a gentleman from kindergarten circling around where my SUV and trailer were parked. I don't know why he was in such a hurry, but he lived just behind there. I decided to give chase. So I went to the east until I was behind the island, so nobody could see. Then I went north to the other side of the lake and stayed close to the shore to head west without being easily seen because of the shadows that were on the water from the tree line I was in. I made it almost all the way back when I noticed a few other boats that I recognized. They were driving erratically and using spotlights to become super stalkers. I wondered what they were looking for. The one guy was from my work; the other was from my neighborhood. It was funny how he had been my Sunday school teacher also—not to mention how his father was associated with Geneva's father from Lockheed. Same cult too. Both families moved there at the same time to be part of the shepherd's movement, to get free housing or good jobs or probably hide.

The other boat I saw I recognized from my half-brother Muck's neighborhood. It was usually parked at one of Ms. Crocodile's rental houses down the street. I knew this should be good. I had been seeking my King. And I knew that if my life wasn't my own, then this gun would jam. I felt my ancestors needed a way out. I mean, after all, if they were making something entertaining, then by all means, let me give them a legendary ending. I almost turned on the camera to give it to them on film. But I decided to just see. So I slid the slide back to chamber a round, and what do you know? It jammed. My heart was awestruck. I couldn't believe it. Okay. It's possible. But that's pretty exceptional. So I took the round out and chambered it only to find it wouldn't fire. I pulled the slide out and put my finger inside only to feel the firing pin not really hit my finger very hard in a dry fire, so I did it again. This time, I used my fingernail, and it was not even scratched. To be honest, it looked like it might have been filed down. I remember my grandpa and stepfather Duck telling me about that trick and how it could get someone killed because if someone pulls out a gun, it's legal to shoot that person even if his or her gun doesn't work. That's when I remembered how Muck had become infatuated with my gun. I had just gotten it, and the concubine's brother began asking about it, taking photos of it, even the box. I thought it was super odd. He wanted to go to the gun range with us and show me his military assault rifle. He was telling me he could use it very easily, even bragging about how well protected he was.

I do remember when Muck, my half-brother, was at a gun show, looking for the same gun. He even called me to ask me the model number. At the time, he had a concealed permit, I can only assume to go with his surety bond. I could see they spent lots of time setting my stage. But I needed something. I sat there for a while. I thought, *Wow, that's like playing Russian roulette twice.* I couldn't believe it. I remembered the firecracker. Do you?

Seeds

Many of you reading this may think you know most of my life. For everyone else, I must start at the beginning. I grew up in a tiny little town, seated and unmoved. It was the most elite part of the Bible belt, home to the bluebonnets. I am the oldest of three, as well as the oldest grandchild on both sides. Three years my younger is my half-sister, Schiff. Three years younger than Schiff is my half-brother,

Muck. My mother, Linda, was married to Duck. They had dated a short time during high school and got married right after graduating. They had a small ceremony and got hitched back in 1976, the same year they graduated from high school.

Linda graduated from a rich high school, and Duck graduated from a rural high school at the same time. They did quite well for themselves. Duck and Linda quickly moved to the town of Rich Man Hills. They always said it was to get out of the country life. I know they wanted a better life for their family. Who doesn't? I get that now that I'm older. He was driven to succeed at all costs. By the time he was twenty, he was a homeowner and a boat owner and drove a new truck. The man had his priorities, I'll give him that. I often wonder if Linda's need to escape her home life further fueled their desire to get ahead financially and socially. So too much surprise, Linda became pregnant I assume around Valentine's Day 1978 because nine months later, I would be born at the Rich Man Hills Hospital.

As easily as things came for Duck and Linda, they went that much easier. Duck, I'm sure, felt trapped—maybe, I can't speak for his feelings. I can only speak of the actions that show the motives. Actions speak louder than words. Soon after finding out Linda was pregnant, he sold his ski boat and moved to a house in a quiet neighborhood not too far from the high school. They moved into one of my grandmother's rental houses. This was just before I was born. I'm pretty sure Duck wasn't happy about downsizing. He was and always has been about status. Some things never change, and I've seen it my whole life. I've seen him base his on worth on how much better or worse he was than his competition. He had left his job at a drafting/architecture place. It didn't take him long to find something else, something that didn't require him to sit behind a desk, he would say. He soon found his place in the home construction business. He started doing trim work for various carpenters, building track homes in the area. And that led to a job learning how to frame houses. It wasn't a reliable income due to the fact it was hindered by weather and permits. But when the work was there, so was the money to be made.

Before long, Duck had become very skilled at home construction. He did a better job than most and did it fairly quickly with fewer materials. He was becoming known in the area for doing remodels or new construction. And before long, he had a crew of guys working for him. Fast-forward to 1982. The economy was awful for building and new construction. High interest rates flooded the market because of the recession. It was a tough time for most Americans. Lack of new construction drove lumber prices low. So, for the upper class who had plenty of liquid cash, it was a buyer's market. Land cost was so low for its value. Grandma knew the economy wouldn't stay down forever, and she also know it was a buyer's market. It was very lucrative to find properties at below market value. She purchased most for very little and far under their value as an offering of a pre-foreclosure-type sale. It was a small community and even smaller back then.

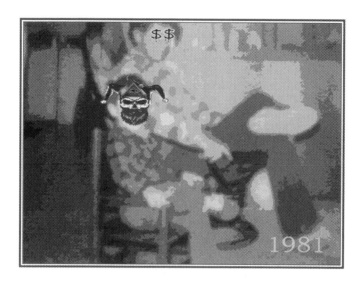

As I understood it, most of the houses she bought for little to nothing from people she knew from church who were struggling. That may be speculation on my part, but I seriously doubt it. Based on what I have heard and seen, my grandma was unbeatable at playing Monopoly. That was her style, so it was no surprise when I found out later how she liked to have rental houses. It was also no surprise when Duck and Linda found several acres of land located in the city that still felt like it was out in the country, Colley Wood. They had few neighbors, and the large properties made it ideal for Duck and Linda. The price was very reasonable. There were three lots that were on a road to nowhere. Grandma bought all three of them, one for each of her kids, she would say.

Duck and Linda wanted the farthest east lot, something about being a floodplain. So that was their lot. Duck had plans drawn up, and they were decades ahead of their time. In the middle of a recession, the house boasted over 2,400 square feet with an open concept, complete with three bedrooms, three full bathrooms, two full dining rooms, and two full game rooms, as well as vaulted ceilings throughout. It was totally decked out with hardwood floors, oversized doorways, intricate trim on the floor and the ceiling, and huge wood-burning fireplaces.

It took Duck and Linda around a year to finish the construction in its entirety. Grandma paid for the whole thing. That had always struck me as odd. Why would they go out of their way to spend so much on Duck and Linda? I was at this point a simple child and had not yet understood the role of codependency when it comes to keeping family secrets. I can still remember my half-sister's bedroom and the new house. Even as an infant, she had to have the very best money could buy. Before she was old enough, she already had a twin-sized bed that had all the ruffles, lace, and frilly frills that all the girly girls would appreciate. It was over the top honestly.

My room was the smaller of the two rooms. It definitely had a boy feel with brown and tan carpet. The walls had wallpaper with kites on it down to about waist high.

Like Duck was driven to work hard, Linda was driven to manipulate. She worked for her parents at the drapery shop in Rich Man Hills. She gave her business a church name, I believe since most of her clientele came from there. I liked it. Linda spent many hours meeting with clients. She was great at picking out and suggesting window treatments that might work best for each of her clients. I wouldn't say she was an interior decorator because she didn't sell or include any items other than window and wall treatments. The job of meeting with people who do not know yet what they want was the perfect learning ground for the shepherd she would later become. You see, I believe it was during this time in her life that she became a pro at manipulation. She learned to pick up on simple clues about people through her daily interactions with clients of all sorts. Most people blab too much anyway. Throughout life, she has used those skills to her advantage and gone a lot of places. I heard her more than once get excited about duping people into getting cheaper materials or using old stock and charging a premium for those materials as if they were special order or something.

I witnessed a pattern of dissociation for many years. I truly believe she has a dissociative personality disorder. The truth is as long as I've known Linda, she had been like any true shepherd a manipulator. She knows not to get her hands dirty but to use someone who is in need to do her dirty work. She has been a sociopath for as long as I can remember. She would help someone or family and then use those ties that bind to pull someone strings and manipulate them. Before long, she had figured out that if you give gifts that aren't returnable, then those strings being pulled will carry a heavier weight. That's the goal of codependency—to make it to where you will never be out of your shepherd's grasp. It is a common technique used in organized crime, from prostitution rings to the Freemasons to the Bloods and Crips and the KKK. So, I can't say that she is extraordinarily smart or anything. She learned from others who like to control and manipulate those around them. She needed help to manipulate me. Some of the best consultants in the world were at her beck and call. To play the victim while being the oppressor is her favorite authoritative past-time. To bear the cross and simultaneously wear the crown, that's the goal of the best shepherds. The shepherds who herd the black sheep use a crook to do so. The best crooks are made from rosewood. So I've heard.

Just look at history. The ultimate string she could pull was me. And I didn't know it until years later. Truth is, she wouldn't be where she is today without me. It is quintessential codependence if there ever has been such. You say it wouldn't be until years later that I found out who my real father was. For many, that kind of truth would rock them to the core, but for me, it brought me peace and comfort because my whole life I had grown up thinking my father hated me. That no matter what I did, it was never good enough. All those brow beatings and all the emotional, mental, and physical abuse now had a purpose. My relief come from the fact that my actual father loved me. He really loved me more than anyone. He showed it too. He was so proud of me, more than anyone ever was. I love that man, and Linda hated it. Yet that secret was too huge for just about anyone who knew. If the cat got out of the bag, it would be like an atom bomb going off in church. Besides, who wants to be the person to tell someone that their very existence is an abomination? So, I've had a target on my back since before I was born.

The first attempt on my life happened when I was only five weeks old, but I know it was at the hands of my own family. But as usual, he was right there to keep me safe. It was my King's first seed of grace and mercy in my life. That very instance has been a stronghold of faith for me. It provides comfort because I know that since birth I've had a target on my back, and that must mean he sees something in me that the world has overlooked and underestimated. That in itself entirely brings so much peace to my soul. When I encounter friction, I know I am headed in the right direction. I believe all of the use and abuse brought by my enemies only created a super-thick layer of armor. Words don't hurt anymore. And my King's anointing covers every scar and makes all the dirt and mud slide right off. Besides, the Lord is my shepherd. He makes me lie down beside cool waters. And he cherishes every step we take together. I know he is good all the time.

When all I could see was the floor, he made my window a door, and I walked right through. Therefore, I know my life is not my own. It never has been. Okay, let's take you way back to the first attempt that I know of. It was Christmas Eve 1978. I was only five to six weeks old, so obviously, I don't have any personal recollection of this. But it's been a story my ancestors have told so many times. I guess in the days leading up to the hospital visit, I had started projectile vomiting. I couldn't keep anything down. I had already lost two pounds, which I guess is a lot. I don't know, but rumor has it that Duck and Linda were in the middle of moving out of the rental into a different place, and there was no phone service at the new place, so I'm sure it was hopeless. I guess it got so bad they had to take me to the hospital.

My other grandparents met Duck and Linda at the bigger hospital in the area. It was the only place that was open on Christmas Eve. Initially, the doctors were concerned because it wasn't an easy diagnosis. Somehow, it turned out it was hereditary, pyloric stenosis, they called it. I guess it's a muscle in your tummy that doesn't let food pass, and the child can starve to death. I guess there is a test that you have to do by way of ingesting beryllium and then being x-rayed. And the way I heard my grandma tell the story, it sounds like a Christmas miracle. It just might have been. If I didn't have that surgery, I might have been tongue-tied at birth. They say they discovered it just before the surgeon was finished. So, thank you. Grandma said she just kept praying the King would protect me, but I can imagine that Grandpa's motives might have been different. You see, they always acted kind of weird about the other kid. Yeah, apparently, there was another child with the same prognosis in the same room at the same time. And I can only imagine that what happened to that boy was meant for me. I heard that child somehow gagged on the beryllium being put into his mouth, and when that took place, it allowed it to enter his ear canal and lungs. That was pretty serious on top of the pyloric stenosis.

Grandma always said I almost didn't make it. Years later, I met that boy I'm referring to. His name is Dawn D. Shapinski. He wears a cochlear implant so that he can hear. I met him in the same luxury apartment complex where I lived later in life. He did not have a job, but he had plenty of work to do. His best friend at the time was the manly one. I'm fairly certain those two were involved with the apartment offices burning down, as well as all the camera footage being destroyed. Anytime Grandma would bring up that story about how the doctors saved me in just the nick of time and Grandpa was in the room, he would stare straight at the floor. But I couldn't imagine as a child that they truly wished that was for me.

I heard way too much, and I stopped talking and started writing years ago. It seems easier for me to process thoughts in a way others might hear more clearly. It has been an amazing honor to hold close to the hand straight into the kingdom of heaven. I'm pretty sure that was an expensive Christmas in 1978. I can only imagine that in itself adding to the resentment factor. Not only did Linda get knocked up, but her killer body was now wrecked. Yeah. I'm pretty sure I wrecked that. Truth be told honestly; I wonder if she wasn't into porn or severe promiscuity. Because of her upbringing, I believe she has long since developed an emotional disconnect when it comes to sex. I believe she learned the art of using sex as a weapon a long time ago. I know where it all started. It sucks for Linda to have been raped by her father on so many occasions as a child. She probably felt helpless. Who knows if we'll ever know? Honestly, I don't want to. I can't imagine that she wants to relive it either. But I believe it is an undeniable compounding factor of her resentment toward me. After all, I'm the bastard's offspring. In other words, I'm the black sheep. And naturally anyone who actually helps me will be targeted just like me. I have been sentenced to die by a thousand razor blade cuts. Well, most people never get a heads-up. Loose lips sink ships. And they will make you disappear if you actually help a target.

The first person I saw this happen to was after I was married shortly after September 11 2000. I was at lunch with a coworker. He was a great man, a super, incredible father with amazing kids. He knew my family from softball. His daughter and my sister played together. He was a great man who survived polio and treated me very well. I worked very hard for that man. We went to a local buffet for lunch. It was named Furrs. He was well known in the MidCities as a stand-up guy. He paid close attention to politics and knew way more than anyone ever let on. You could tell he was a brilliant man. He was calm, cool, and collected most if not all the time. Even though he survived polio, he still walked with a limp, but that didn't slow him down. He dressed in a Western style with a polo shirt most times and some dark-blue Wrangler pants with a crease down the middle that had been starched into them.

We had known each other for over a year, and that day, he said something to me that was strange. While we were eating there in the corner booth with seemingly no one around, he leaned in close to me and whispered they were going to get rid of me, and then he sat back up straight like nothing had happened. I honestly just thought he was talking about my job at the Nissan place. I asked, "What?" like "Repeat yourself," but he couldn't say a thing. He just changed the subject, and we finished eating. It was the weirdest thing how he kind of leaned over and said it in a voice that was just above a whisper. I didn't know what to make of it other than he was referring to my job. And truth be told, I wanted to work on nice cars. So, I never said anything about it.

About a month later, I changed jobs. I went to a place where I used to work before. Then it was my hometown. I had not been there very long at all when I got a call from someone, we both knew, telling me that he had passed away. My old coworkers said it was complications from appendicitis. I have my doubts because of the connections I've seen in the hospitals in that area. My grandfather died in the same location. I was in shock and at a huge loss. The people from the last place I worked were all there at the funeral. I do remember that it was a nice service, and one thing that stuck out to me was as soon as the service started, my phone started blowing up. It was so rude. The timing was incredible. I could not believe it. It was Muck calling like four or five times. I finally figured out how to turn the phone off. People in the same row began looking at me in disgust, and I don't blame them. The way he was calling back-to-back in a panic was like an emergency. I felt like I needed to answer. At this point, I was still too codependent to understand. I excused myself to step out the door and called him back. He was laughing and said, "Never mind."

I'm not going to lie. I was kind of pissed. How rude! And what a waste of my time and lack of respect for the dead. I went back into the funeral, and the former coworkers were all giving me dirty looks, as if somehow it discounted how much I cared for the man we were burying. Years later, I would understand the gravity of what he said that day. I imagine he probably overheard my coworkers already plotting and scheming. See, I know now who they really are. They are puppets in a kind of funny way. I've seen coworkers be placed where I work so they can try to torture me.

Ms. Apple was no different. She was married to the mayor of Colley Wood for ten plus years, maybe more. Her son's name was Red Apple. He had/has red hair and went straight into the army after high school. We graduated together. Ms. Apple's husband was the mayor of the town I lived in Colley Wood. Her son and I went to high school and used to have a mutual friend, Michael. Red quickly rose through the ranks of the military complex, so I have heard. See how I'm painting the picture connecting all the dots and strings that weave the web of codependency? I think that's where the family name comes from.

Jan Jordan was best friends with Ms. Apple, at least best work friends. She had worked there for many years. She started out washing new cars and rose to supervisor. She was the hardest person to work with that I have ever met. Nobody could please that woman, and I know why she's all alone. I remember seeing her with her crew washing the inventory of new cars. I thought it was odd that when she saw me most times, she would kick the concrete. Seriously, she would kick the concrete. I wasn't the only one who noticed. That woman was always hard to work with, and she has become an advisor for the body shop. This is the same little shop in the same little town where the manager was able to get his son on the fast track to being a top-gun fighter pilot. He bragged about being able to pull strings and get the governor to write a letter of recommendation for his son to get in when it was impossible. I took notes. Knowing the nanny of the man whose house I burned down could do that for someone based on her decorated career. Not to mention how well he was connected to Duck from drag racing at Kennedale, Texas, together. Duck even gave the man an engine for his race car. It seems as though I cannot work anywhere without being surrounded by a sociopath. So sad.

1993   nanny and crocodiles

I've seen him stalk others. I made a list I cannot read out loud. I'm seeing how lynching works first hand. Connect all the strings. It seems they are all connected. I say this because she was his puppet. He seemed to give her orders to manipulate others for his humor. I mean to say she was one of the biggest Pharisees. She got off undermining all the men's work. She could honestly find and pick out the pepper in fly poop. I was blown away more than once by the lunacy that seemed to surround her. I cannot tell you how many times she got off waiting until I was present to ask a coworker to adjust the fitment of something I worked on, as if to slap me in the face with everyone looking. See, the goal for her was to create a short fuse. She wanted to get a reaction. I learned a lot from that iron cunt, as we called her. That was the name she earned.

I learned the best thing you can do is be firm and direct. Through working with her, I learned that people's unrelated car problems are not my problem. The over-the-top abuse that I endured from Jordan led me to dig deeper, and Jan Jordan knew my great-great-uncle Shaw and my great-great-aunt Ann. See, Uncle Shaw was a well-respected

Shriner and Freemason. They were involved with Eastern Stars and had been for a very long time. They by proxy offer protection to the next-door neighbors at the lake house where they live. I was always told about the lesbians who would come to party and that I was never allowed to step foot in the yard or they would shoot me on the spot. Everyone knew about this place, how they would have orgies and other crap there. I kind of believed them because of the way my uncle Shaw instructed me on the boundaries more than once. He even alluded to the fact that he watched over the place for them and anyone who came around. I kind of laughed that off as a kid, like when you're just playing, but I wasn't understanding it. He was deadly serious. You see, that place was hopping on the Fourth of July.

It was about the time I got my driver's license. It's hard to forget or mistake the heavy eye makeup Jan Jordan wore. It looked very similar to what the character named Mimi from *The Drew Carey Show* wore. But what I remember most is how ridiculous her boat setup was. I noticed her truck and boat first. I don't remember for sure the color of the truck. I think it was green, but that's probably because it was dwarfed by the huge pontoon boat she was towing. It was way too big for the Nissan hard-body extended cab. I think from what I remember she had towing mirrors too because it was so much wider. I doubt I ever said anything. I don't know if Jan Jordan ever saw me laughing at the setup. But it was around that time my sister began to visit the place frequently. It was in a cove, and my uncle Shaw had lived there forever. Years later my half-sister would come out of the closet.

He had a pretty sweet setup. He built it himself way back in the 1940s with his own two hands. He was skilled at fixing anything from trucks to tractors. Uncle Shaw was another mechanical genius in the family. I really had a huge amount of admiration for him when I was a kid. He built most of the roads in the area, as well as footings, retaining walls, and docks and did the dredging. He was an artist at anything mechanical. He also worked hard to ensure that the town leaders were all very well taken care of. Everyone knew and loved him. He was almost a go-between between the people in power and the rest of us. He was a legend. That is an understatement. It was amazing to see him fix even the most complicated things. He was a larger, heavy-set man who actually wore overalls. And he loved his King Edward cigars. He would mostly chew on them while driving or working on something. I was so fortunate to spend a summer out there when I was ten or eleven. It was one of my favorite summers. I was able to fish almost every day and had pretty good luck catching bass. I didn't have a bike, but I did pretty much have free reign. To say I was unsupervised would be an understatement. I could literally be gone for hours, and nobody cared.

The place had a pretty sweet pier that extended into the lake probably fifty yards or so with a boat hoist/lift. There was usually a boat on it whether his or that of someone else who was renting the spot.

That summer, I learned a few things I never forgot. I earned my first few memories of personal gang stalking. Uncle Shaw and I went for a drive in his Ford pickup. We drove for probably an hour so on the back roads winding around in East Texas by the lake. It seemed like we had been behind this car forever. We turned around a couple of times to end up right back behind him again. I suggested to my uncle Shaw that he pass him. Uncle Shaw started laughing out loud. I have no idea why I was impatient. I didn't have to be anywhere at a certain time. I was already with Uncle Shaw. But we followed this dude in a white car. I don't know what kind because I didn't know cars then yet. But Uncle Shaw never let the guy out of his sight. It was so obvious that even I, a kid, noticed. The fear that the gentleman had was quite obvious. That black sheep had been conditioned to be scared of wolves. The guy would turn around and even change lanes to avoid us, but my uncle Shaw stayed on his tail. I had no Idea where we were or where we were going until we emerged upon the main street where the familiar grocery store was.

I loved going to the store because they had fried pies from the kitchen at the store, and they were like ten for a dollar. I usually got one while standing in line at the register at his suggestion, of course, for being so well behaved. Wouldn't you know that's where he went, and so did we. I was super excited to go in. I got my seat belt off when we parked. And uncle Shaw sternly told me to sit still. He spoke in such a rare tone that I was almost frozen and didn't stop watching what he was watching and how he was reacting to what he was seeing. He was watching the man exit the car we just followed. I clearly saw the man make eye contact with my uncle, and it brought uncle Shaw a smile and chuckle in a way that changed his mood to excited, and he began exiting the vehicle. I waited until he told me it was okay and I could come too, so we went inside. He seemed not to let the man out of his sight.

Every aisle we went down, we saw him again. Once he was in the produce section, he held my hand and whispered in my ear to run over and stomp next to that guy and scare him. But whatever I did not to touch him. If I scared him good, I could pick out ten pies on the way out, even all chocolate if that was what I wanted. I was happy to please. I knew how to make my shoes squeak on that floor very well. I started walking that way, and when I was about ten feet away, the guy looked at me. I lost the element of surprise, so I bolted toward him at a full sprint and squeaked my shoes on the linoleum floor as I stopped myself just before collision. The dude jumped so much he almost fell down. I bounced like a super ball. I was so excited by his reaction that I could see on my full-speed run back to the safety of my uncle's big strong hands. Needless to say, I got my pies, five apple and five chocolate.

When we got back, my aunt was so proud of me. I liked that feeling I felt in the truck from his approval. It made me overlook questioning what or why that just happened. He did say on many occasions between us, "Loose lips sink ships," but it was never a specific reference. On a quiet ride in the country, just us, that was when he would just say it randomly sometimes under his breath, sometimes out loud. Almost as if momentarily, he forgot I was sitting on the other side of the cab. "Loose lips sink ships ..." I can almost hear him still in my dreams sometimes. That ride home might have been a short one, but I thought I was in good with my great aunt and uncle, and I don't remember it taking very long at all.

At their place, Aunt Ann made dinner while my uncle went to his room and closed the door. I was sitting in my usual spot in the living room watching TV when he exited with some white envelopes in the front pocket of his overalls. I loved seeing those overalls because he had so many. Some were striped with white and black; others were denim, and some were even solid white, Levi's mostly. They had quality things, as well as friends in high places.

During dinner, I noticed some cars pulling up and parking out front and to the side of their lake house. It wasn't uncommon. The boat ramp for the neighborhood was right next to my aunt and uncle's place. That night, there were more cars than trucks with empty boat trailers. The people were sitting in their cars quietly. It was almost hard not to notice. Shortly after eating, he went outside to the garage, and it almost summoned the masses to do the same. My aunt wanted me to stay inside. But I felt connected to my uncle and didn't think he would care. I watched TV and the took out the trash. While doing so, I noticed everyone gathered next to a huge oak tree that seemed to live directly in the way. It was literally in the middle of where you would make the U-turn to launch your boat. I had seen a few of the faces before, but I couldn't place them. Some were holding on to the same white envelopes I had seen my uncle holding while exiting his bedroom. I kept quiet as best as I could.

Years later, I would attend his funeral, and the family was proud to have the local lodge performing the ceremony. I've been to many Masonic funerals. My grandmother and grandfather enjoyed whispering to me about what I was seeing and what it represented, from the hat to the gloves, as well as the fresh twig slid into the left hip and held by a string from his ceremonial apron in the back. The tiny little twig barely held on being pressed between the apron and its strings. That twig itself was supposed to represent peace. As a kid, I could remember things easily, and Grandma liked having someone to talk to. I mainly just listened. She was an expert. They all were. And funerals were where you would find them all celebrating on the inside. It was literally like going to a circus. Different performances took place on center stage. Completely scripted, the puppet who was speaking was shadowed word for word by his partner on his right side. It was a ceremony. If the person speaking lost his way, his right-hand man would speak up with the same memorized words. So it never changes …

Also amazing is that nothing is written down. It's all memories—scripted lies actually. I remember the first series in the entry into the club required memorizing entire scripts word for word because that was a litmus test to ensure the bloodline was still intact and that the brain could be more easily programmed. It's not really that hard if you think about it. To be really honest, memorizing like that is also done through television and music. How many times have you heard someone quote movies down to the letter, sing a song, or even play music. The point I'm making here is that free thinking is not permitted in that club. They must obey the script that's been given to them by the higher-ups. That's why they have been selected. Or is that why I've been selected? Not to mention why they live where they live, as well as where I live. Some aren't allowed to move.

CHAPTER 3

Suicide—Real or Fake?

Boom!

The sound pierced the night sky, shocking the silence the evening of June 29th, 2013. The echo it produced was stellar. I was a little proud of myself when I heard the silence broken and change created by the loud crack of an explosion followed by the exclamation by my half-brother Muck. Their thoughts and expectations of my suicide broke the silence and started the celebration that ensued.

"Fuck yeah!"

"We got 'em!"

The rest of the sheep began cheering and exclaiming, probably expecting to get paid. I was so excited. I hoped everyone got new cars. As many as I saw, I could only speculate. Someone else would figure it out. I was not privy, remember. I couldn't contain my excitement. It was an amazing honor to be so protected by my King. As I saw it, He kept me from getting hurt. I don't know many other people who wouldn't be hurt by their family and everyone they know celebrating their death. I knew it was my King showing me the flip side. I was about to see the silver lining. I could clearly hear the people cheering, and I knew that would be a perfect time to start the boat. So, I pulled my anchor, I started *Sally*, headed due west toward the point leading to Catfish Cove. I only made it about twenty feet when I noticed an old coworker pulling his boat toward the ramp at a high rate of speed. Completely disregarding the "No Wake Zone" sign, he pulled up to the dock, and someone jumped off his boat to get into the truck.

I kept my boat at idle speed at this point, partially because I was just about out of fuel and partially because I know if you move slowly enough, nobody even notices. And it worked. Nobody noticed me at first. I made it all the way to the no wake buoy before I was spotted. I got a few minutes to see my enemies celebrating. Mucks partner in crime, Dan the man was there. I saw him so happy, smiling and hugging people who claimed to know me. I saw a cameraman taking video of several people taking a bow. It looked to be my ancestors and their friends. I laughed because now I know that was the goal, to see me dead, and they celebrated together on camera. So, all I have to do is stay alive. It's obvious now that they must have the same type of insurance policy in place that Terry Heaton had when he mysteriously died of suicide by two bullets. I remembered that very clearly in an instant. I kept standing on the bow of my boat, watching, taking photos, and everyone could see how my half-brother was celebrating while his friends were taking video. There was a blue F350 four-door truck that I recognized from Oak Valley Drive. That was when I recognized the boat, too. I saw my half-brother in the middle of the backseat getting oral sex from a prostitute we both knew as a concubine.

Geneva my ex-wife was sitting next to both of them. I was blown away. It seemed like everyone was happy to be on camera celebrating. I looked at them and knew I was dealing with real live wolves who did not know that I was a Jester or a unicorn, and there was nothing I could do that would be as strong as what my King would do. About that time, a flashlight or spotlight from the blue Jeep illuminated me. He burned his tires off backing up and then spinning 180 degrees before driving through the mud toward where everyone else was standing. You could tell the passenger was trying to get everyone's attention. As I watched, I saw what looked like a family of cockroaches scatter for their own lives when the lights got turned on unexpectedly. The cameras panned from the backseat of the blue F350 four-by-four four-door with beige on the bottom to the Jeep Wrangler to me standing on the bow of my boat watching the whole thing. Yeah … gotcha … That was when the blue jeep with the black bumpers floored it in reverse, because he was a little away from the crowd when he saw me. The tires were throwing rocks so fast it was amazing. And he turned as he shifted into forward and made it to the other side of the launch ramp, where everyone was standing. He began flashing his headlights, trying to get their attention. And it was almost in unison that all 120 people or so who were standing all around with their phones on began to look and saw me. You could hear a unified gasp, once they knew I saw.

I simply stood there and took notes, watching all the associates scatter. Is it money you're after? Well, go make your own. I do. It's so sad how some people actually believe they will get rich when I die. Maybe they will. I hope to live to a hundred and two honestly. If you like what you see, keep looking. I had no intention of revenge, because I was writing a book, this book. I know the pen is mightier than the sword. I just wanted to know who's who, when is when, and what is what. Even if I did, it's like my King wanted to show me more, and He wasn't having it any longer. Because about that time, Sally ran out of gas. I sat starboard in the driver's seat and tried to start and rev it up, to somehow collect the fuel toward the rear of the tank. When it wouldn't start completely, I knew I had to swim some more. So, I put on a life jacket, grabbed a ski rope, tied it to the bow, and dove into the water. I swam with the strap in my hand toward the boat ramp at Catfish Cove. I decided to attach the rope to my life jacket as I swam mostly on my back. As the rope drew taut, I noticed how many falling stars there were tonight. It was undeniable how many wishes I made shortly after that incident. Just between you and me, I added years to my bucket list in those two hours. It honestly was the biggest thing I needed at the moment for the paradigm shift to take place. I did get one offer of help by a passerby who had a very unique fishing boat. I declined politely, because I wanted to be so much stronger than everyone thought. I finally made it to shore, got to my Tahoe, and loaded Sally on the trailer. I am so thankful now that my boat ran out of gas because that two-hour swim made me spend all of my frustration in a constructive manner. I mean, no doubt, I did want to see those losers go to hell, but I had no energy. It had been a long, long day and night. And I was headed home. I didn't get home until 3:00 a.m. or so. And my Tahoe was now out of gas, I had no cigarettes, and I wanted them to try to kill me. So, I pulled into the driveway, walked back to my boat, and got my things. That was when I saw the camera located in the neighbor's window, and it was pointed right at me. No wonder I decided to flip off their camera. That made me laugh because I hope I get famous.

As I went back into the pool house I rented, you could tell someone had been there, because some of the lights were on. Plus, I left the door unlocked for them to think something. I put my gun into my safe, with the barrel pointed away from me. It would have been pointed in the direction of my half-brother's friend's house. I locked my safe and found a black jumpsuit top and some dark pants. I grabbed my son's airsoft gun, the laser pointer flashlight, and the firecrackers that I had left from earlier. I decided to walk the one-third mile to my half-brother's house to see if they were there yet. Then I would scare the hell out of them with firecrackers. Maybe with any luck, they would try to shoot an unarmed man. And then that would mean, I won. Because I had just survived suicide, like Russian roulette, I knew I was fireproof.

I walked alone in the dark completely quiet, masked by the shadows. I didn't see anyone when I got there. I looked at the back of their home, and they seemed to have left in a hurry. I saw no movement from the house for the four to five minutes I was standing in the shadows watching. I even pointed the laser pointer into the back of the house to get a reaction. That was when I knew they weren't even there. So, I decided to light a pack of firecrackers to see if I could bring them out, so to say. And it didn't work, so I could only assume, after the firecrackers, nobody was there, because there was no movement. I walked back to the pool house I was renting. All was quiet. I needed fuel and cigarettes. I knew my fuel was so low that it could possibly run out before I got to the next station. Then I loaded up a folding bicycle into the back of my Tahoe. I got it from my landlord's husband, who had it leaning against his garage. I thought it seemed like a decent idea. I drove to the Walmart that was closest, off Precinct Line. I had been there many times. The fuel station wasn't open because it was so late at this point. The craziest thing about my trip to Walmart was when I passed a blue F350 I had seen earlier at the lake with my ancestors and Geneva. We passed each other at a high rate of speed on Precinct Line Road, just as I turned into Walmart. He turned down the road leading down to my house. I didn't have my real gun with me, only the airsoft. I didn't feel very safe. I felt like I needed to be around people or something, maybe even on camera for my protection and their accountability. That's when I went inside and bought a pack of cigarettes. But I also needed fuel, so I left Walmart and drove down Precinct Line Road toward Hurst Texas, where I crossed Highway 26 and came to a gas station called Racetrack on the right side of the road. I put twenty dollars in the Tahoe, which really wasn't much, but it was what I had on me. I drove back home and waited. I personally felt my King was telling me to stay awake. I felt like He was telling me not to let my guard down. And I didn't. I know His hand was on my life already. So, at this point, it might have been 5:00 a.m. June 30th 2013

I made a fresh pot of coffee. I began journaling more about the details of that evening, putting names with faces. So many people I knew were involved. This was a modern-day lynch mob. Yes, what my ancestors had exclaimed the year before was coming true. They claimed they had enough dirt on me that I wasn't even going to know what was happening. Linda had been bragging for years about how she would get grandparental rights. They were partially correct in the fact that I was walking blind with my King carrying me. Early in the morning, a television program came on the TV. It was a Sunday morning televised church service for Joel Osteen. The message was about being anointed; when you're anointed, all the mud that the enemy keeps throwing on you has no sticking power. Because of the anointing that had been poured out long ago, now it's a slippery surface that nothing will stick to. Instead, it washes right off easily. And you may not be able to tell it was ever there. He went on to talk about David and how the anointing was thought to be for David's brother, but the will of the King chose David. And no matter how hard David's brothers tried to get rid of him, it put him in a place where the King wanted him. It's the King's anointing on someone that makes evildoers' plots and plans turn out to serve the King. All things work together for His glory, not our own.

During this time, my spirit was soaking this up like a dry sponge. I was so there, in my King's presence, just washing all that mud off. I felt like He was calming my spirit; it was just what I needed. I kept journaling and writing who, what, when, where, why, and how. I believe I was having church right then and there. That was when my King was soothing me and putting all the pieces in place for me to see in the most intimate of ways. I needed it. I'm so much stronger, and I'm seeing it. I don't need the torture I'm getting. I know, based on phone records, that Michael's keys are associated with my half-brother, as well as my ex-wife, Geneva, not to mention in deep with the dealership where I worked. I saw some of the same people celebrating. The dealership also had access to my vehicle. I remember when I tried to change the ignition key, and the parts guy laughed and cut a new key the same as my old key. I went back when he was on break and had another key cut different than the key code that was already on file. I know I'm not allowed to know this. But it's amazing grace the connections that are easily seen when you look past what's right in your face.

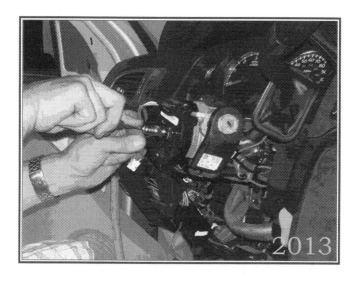

I know the owners were involved in the same 21 Club and Rotary Club. I know when you're a billionaire, you're supposedly untouchable. I heard you loud and clear. Because I waited until the parts guy, who is the manager, stepped out for a moment and asked the apprentice if he could recut the key. He asked why, and I showed him. It was the same key. He gasped. I gave him a random six-digit key code that I wrote on a note pad as I covered my hand. He seemed not to question it. And so, he went to the side where the key-cutting machine was. I was right there. This time, I watched him put the numbers into the key-cutting machine in the sequence. And he put a new blank in and pressed start. The machine went to work. It made the distinct various screeching sounds that overpower even the loudest shop noise. That lasted about forty-five seconds when the manager came back in a hurry. He saw me and his eyes got huge. I kind of smiled. He asked what was going on. I said to him that he cut my old key. And his facial expression changed as he got scared and excited at the same time. He denied it, and I watched him take out his phone and take a photo of the key code that was on the cutting machine. I asked what he was doing, and he laughed like a coward and said nothing. I wanted to say, "Duck."

But now I think I will let my King handle it. He said he cut the key I asked for again as if to call me crazy and laugh, but you could see the apprentice start to speak up because he knew. It was not hard to see. Even an idiot could see. The new key was the same as the old key.

"And that number you have on file for my VIN, the key I just had you cut is a different number in entirely."

He agreed and looked as I held them together. They were a perfect match.

Then he denied cutting the key altogether. "Wow. What kind of puppet are you? Oh yeah. That's right." That was when I remembered how Dan the man had been bragging about being part of an elite group of people there to provide extra service and support. He even designed one of the gold coins with a horse of the owner of the dealership on it. Those wolves are so proud of their work. I often wonder how many concubines have been created in my honor. I also wonder how many slaves never escape. I know I'm not the only one. I'm the only one I've seen survive. They all know. It's a sure thing. So bet big. As a matter of fact, it wasn't but just a few months prior that I had to take a blood test for them. It was at a fictitious company called Summit Health. I remember how my half-brother Muck was trying to get rich quick with them, selling physicals or something. But I'm not a willing participant. I don't agree to have a life insurance policy. And yet they must backhandedly try to get their revenge by turning me into money. I get it. It's entertaining to see me suffer. I know that Duck has probably already fixed your roof or front door on your house a long time ago. It's how shepherding works. Do favors with a plan in mind. So you can create slaves. It's the root of the sociopaths. It's like they spend their entire lives looking at others behind a locked door stuck in a closet, with the only place to see being the tiny little slit below the handle. I can't help it. I know I'm not alone. I never am. I'm just a nobody. I understand how strings connect together to form a rope that eventually creates a noose. That's how you make the slaves.

It's like my adrenaline was going so fast, and I was looking at the sun with my eyes gazing. I saw how amazing it is. It felt like the opposite of falling. I know they say you're flooded with memories and events as your life passes right before your very eyes, and I wonder if that's what happens when you're born. Because it felt like I was being born in silence. I understand that people want money. But why me? I'm a nobody. I guess this could happen to anybody. If someone has that kind of money to play games with, then why on earth is the world suffering? I'm saddened those resources were so wasted on me when the world could have used those resources to become a better place. I wonder if they will ever learn. Or if they will just continue to make deals with liars who believe bigger is better. I get it. Nobody is strong enough to be honest with me. Everyone just wants money. Seriously, do they think I don't know yet? I mean, I'm not even sad. I'm kind of happy. I don't have to shed a tear over them. I just want to watch how people who live double lives for profit act. They are acting. It's kind of a disgrace if you ask me.

Talk about Duck's ability to collect dirt. Everyone there was on camera. Muck's friend was the photographer. What's so interesting about me? Did you actually think I was going to kill myself? Or did you know that I know? I know that some see money as a tool. But they don't even know it's the beginning of their own slavery. Some people will do anything for numbers on a screen so that we can all become slaves. Because if this can happen to me, it can happen to anybody. I mean, after all, who hasn't wanted to be a part of a production? So to say. It's sad how some think their money will actually make them happy. All the while, I know it's a curse. I know dirty money doesn't go very far. It's all dirty in fact. If you do business with criminals, then you're furthering the agenda. I get it. I was underaged ... and yet, you did nothing. You had a video even. So why wait until 2013 and pay all your friends to play games with me? Can you not forgive? I know you know the law. I know you know the governor. I know you know the entertainment lawyer who told you it's okay. You sent him to college. I am willing to bet I'm not the only one here who's a slave. I'm willing to bet everyone's a slave to their schemes because of the dirt they have that might make them imperfect in the public's eyes. I get it. It's called blackmail or bribery. No, bribery is money, like gift cards, cash, tickets to vacations and concerts, direct money transfer to offshore bank accounts via wire transfer from Muck's bank account to anyone else who has an offshore bank account at Grand Cayman. I guess the real question here is if social justice or entertainment has exceptions to the Constitution? If so, then is it because of money? Or is social justice better than real justice? I don't think the first one is real. It's like having a gun pointed at your head your whole life and then one day standing up and saying shoot me, holding the gun to your forehead, only to find out if it wasn't loaded the whole time. Sometimes, they aren't loaded. My firecrackers are so much more exciting to play with. I do hope that firecrackers will be used at my funeral. I'd like to go out with a bang. It seems that's what everyone else wants. A bang. They want an explosion of sorts. And I'm not giving one. I only see cowards. That isn't saying much, taking out just a few cowards. I should be way stronger than that because my little unicorns need me to be. They know firsthand what Mom is up to. They also know firsthand what will happen to them if they speak. Mom simply won't allow it. She is bound by her covenant, and now the entire congregation knows they need to help her by spreading hearsay about me. Some people just don't care. I just want to watch.

CHAPTER 4

Arrangements Made

An arrangement must be made. A true unicorn may only be captured with a virgin. So that's what was proposed in my arranged marriage. I had already survived high school, where I was treated lower than dirt for entertainment's sake. I even survived living with the prom king and queen, who wished to hurt me continually in college. I really didn't want kids. I wasn't that interested in Geneva initially. My ancestors kept trying to get me to go to church at their covenant church, where the youth group was thriving. My ancestors bragged about the youth pastor being my old Sunday school teacher. One of the two I had around the time the video of me being underaged setting a blaze on camera began to set others a blaze as well.

At that time, back in 1993, the youth pastor was a close "friend" of my ancestors'. He died shortly after from sudden medical complications. A new pastor was put in place right away. And the Sunday school teachers didn't really seem to mourn. He was a great man in my eyes. I knew I wasn't perfect. But John Collins was a man of integrity. I believe that was why he wouldn't take part in the games set forth. I believe that's also why my enemies needed him out of the way. I never really trusted this new guy, who was a corporate church person with the attendance and generous offering numbers to prove it. And now he was a youth pastor just down the street. I refused to attend a Wednesday night service at the covenant church. I'd always heard from people in the area that it was a cult, almost like a gang. I knew what a covenant relationship was. That meant it was a secret—because someone important said so. It's basically a contractual obligation.

Later in my life, the same Sunday school teacher planned a ski trip with his assistant, Geneva. They led a youth group at the covenant church. That was where my ancestors invested so much time and resources, both cash and labor. I was taking notes. They all planned a ski trip to Colorado. I was offered a free seat. I decided, *Why not?* I brought plenty of weed and even showed up after getting a nice buzz on so I would be less susceptible to the brainwashing others submitted to there.

My ancestors kept calling me that night, wanting me to show up to leave for the ski trip, but I lived just a few minutes away. I simply responded that they should let me know when the bus got there. I wasn't really interested in listening to their religious dogma meant to enslave others.

I've seen fake church my whole life. It's a production that's put in place to make money for other wolves to clean the dirty money they make. It's a tax shelter for the blind sheep to believe in. I need you to think of a circle jerk. They each have one another's family jewels in the right hand and are striking it until they get a discharge, all in the middle. Spill the seed onto the floor for the most amazing significance of their own rhetoric. Some slaves have extraordinary kneepads. I wonder if they knew they would be so busy when they initially signed up with their own covenants. So, I showed up only after the bus showed up. I loaded my bags onto the bus, and apparently, the youth pastor had some speech prepared for me. Yeah, I get it. *I've heard the same slimeballs stealing people's money through a corporation called church before by way of brainwashing.* I've seen the actors who put on a proper show get paid to do so. Everyone needs money. It keeps going around and around in circles. Codependency at its finest.

The arrangements were made with each and every suitor. It's designed to hurt. Concubines were made. The one in high school was well known for hanging around Lonna's work. The other in high school had a sister who needed medical treatment. Theirs was also an arranged marriage. I still remember the look on the high-school sweetheart's face when she made contact with me while Geneva was in the picture. She looked scared honestly and didn't want to come out of my room and face Linda in person. That was the last time I ever saw her. I heard she had a child later. So, as you can imagine, I didn't pay Geneva much attention on the ski trip. I just wanted to go get high riding the chairlift. I knew that meant getting up super early. I noticed how Geneva's brother was just like the cable guy. He somehow believed he was courting some girl who was also there on the ski trip. He kept talking about how courtship was an arrangement where the parents were involved. I thought the dude was weird. I almost felt sorry for him because he was homeschooled to keep his eyes closed. Or was it just a front? I knew the girl he was referring to from middle school. She didn't seem like the churchy type if there ever was one. But she could ski well. So, it didn't take long before Melissa and I were on the same ski lift. It was amusing how Geneva's brother kept trying to keep up with us and how she seemed to keep trying to evade him. It wasn't long before we had left him a few chairs behind. I could care less.

On that chair lift, she began to say he was weird. I was like, "What? I thought he was your guy or something?"

She laughed. I told her how he told me he was courting her. She put her hand on her head as if it were a sun visor. She denied being interested in him and said he was weird. Melissa later became a successful female fitness model. I couldn't agree more with Melissa, Geneva's brother was weird.

Geneva's brother and I roomed together for the ski trip, and I remember how annoying that was. The guy was so in your face with his cult talk it was beyond me. His sister, Geneva, whom I didn't really know, ever, asked me to go snowmobiling with her since her back was still injured. I was like no thanks and hung up politely. Then she called back and said I could go for free. I still declined. I could see how codependent she was with the youth pastor and his wife. I didn't trust any of them. Oh yeah, the bus crashed on the way there in the snow and sent the youth pastor and his wife to the hospital for stitches. She got them in her eye. I hope everyone can see.

A bout a week after the ski trip, I lost my license for refusing a breathalyzer. I didn't submit to any field sobriety. I knew the burden of proof was on the state. Geneva used that opportunity to drive me around and "minister" to me. She and her family always thought I was some sort of bad guy. It was so sad how brainwashed she was. She was groomed in the cult to be the perfect mother. Having helped raise her large family of home-birthed children and homeschool made her very well versed on being a mother figure from a young age.

I remember losing interest in Geneva when she went away for the summer for some high-dollar mission trip, where she took a few hundred super-rich kids to Africa and helped groom them into soldiers for the church. It was weird to me how she was literally forced upon me. Linda blackmailed me with the video over and over, showing everyone if I didn't do as she said. I was even instructed to meet her at the airport with roses. I did so and was thankful to see how embarrassed Geneva was around her friends. She threw them into the trash as I watched. Then, she removed them from the trash and gave them to someone in the mission trip group. I was used to it. All I could think about was my work. I had a decent job and was making more than almost everyone I knew. I wasn't interested at first. My previous legal infraction at this point was now over. I had my license again and a clean record. It was nice too because I had a truck and an all-wheel-drive car at that point.

I had been gaining my skills and even dreamed of moving to Colorado, but it wasn't long after Geneva spent so much time with me, I began to feel sorry for her. I could see how brainwashed she was and how hard it must have been to be raised in that cult. I couldn't even imagine what it must be like to live with an incestuous family. It's funny how full circle that statement is, isn't it?

I also remember being told that I had better marry her or else. More blackmail. I was led to an auction where the ring was bought. Linda paid for it. It was huge, two and one third carats. I hoped that because of an arranged marriage, that meant things were solid and monogamous. Boy was I wrong. I was also led to believe she was a virgin. And after a failed honeymoon, I wondered what she had actually been through. It was so odd how she kept wanting to call her dad. All the way from Mexico on the honeymoon, she was willing to spend whatever to call this creep. I said nothing. I just watched. We returned to the United States, and after getting back to my house, within the first hour or so, I seriously debated taking her and dropping her back off at her family's house. I was thankful we hadn't opened any of the wedding presents nor consummated the marriage. But in first-class fashion, my ancestor showed up with a carload full of presents and encouraged us to open them. He actually started helping.

My uncle was best friends with her boss, the cult leader, and had been for many years. They had known each other since before I was born. It was no surprise when he helped opened some of the presents. I almost told him to stop. Something was seriously wrong. Damaged goods. We both were. I resolved to keep my promise to the King that I made that day, standing at the altar. It wasn't long before she suggested having people stay with us for ministry. I was blown away. She wanted some guy to come live with us, all in the name of the church. She kept saying how if I had extra, I should help everyone else. I kept thinking she was brainwashed. I didn't do any side jobs for the first year of marriage, but I did buy and sell a dozen cars and double my money most of the time doing so. I enjoyed how she would try to shepherd me, calling about a car in the paper once, acting a fool, being loud as if to talk over me on the phone. She even broke a glass as if to get me to hang up. She was and always has been a manipulator. Say what you mean. But she can't. It was what she signed up for. Actually, it was what her family signed her up for. See clearly, I like to say.

geneva& her mommy 2009

It's so sad to me how cannabis could have been used long ago to fight her brother's deteriorating eyesight due to glaucoma. Geneva's mom always loved sharing about how a miracle man did all the work on her son's eyesight and that if it wasn't for that shepherd, they wouldn't be where they were. Many times, she would say how expensive all the surgery was as well as how the contacts were also special and expensive. Geneva's mom always made it a point to say how the optometrists who helped her family never asked for money. I already knew. That was the guy's barns I burned down. Of course, I would need an arranged marriage if I were to actually procreate and give Linda any offspring to further torture. I'm so thankful it's so well documented for everyone to see. After all, what's your integrity worth? Is it enough for entertainment's sake? I'm thankful it wasn't an arrangement with the chick in high school who drove a Camaro. She was the most fake of all the harlots I've ever met.

Even while in high school, I knew of her morbid interest in cult things, and it freaked me out. Choosing classes in her senior year, she wanted to become a mortician. She even used a work program during high school to study under a professional at a funeral home off of Highway 820 in Hurst. Later, she became a network administrator computer person with a side gig in the entertainment business with my ancestors' help. She was encouraged by her family to make as much money as possible from my life even in high school. I'm so thankful I don't have to live in that house that was arranged for them. I'm also thankful I don't have to be blackmailed like Camaro chick's husband and sister do. Camaro chick's husband is in the DNA machine business. I guess the company he is associated with puts them all over the world. His partner in crime got the machine from a local college that used it to prove something, and because his friend was the guy who sourced all the parts to build the initial one, he copied it and marketed it to other legal entities as far away as China. His connections must be incredible. I wonder how big the slavery actually is. He bragged about having enough parts from work to build one of his very own in his garage. Her sister was a cop the last I checked. She had a problem passing the test to be on the beat so to say, and I remember how much it enraged the Camaro chick.

She was one of my biggest stalkers. She was the one who introduced the concubine and me just after getting a new bank account at Muck's bank. And I tried to show them in so many words. But it seems as though everyone needs to see. This is 2020 after all. I think everyone should see by now. I don't think I could be around anyone who does any of those jobs, especially knowing how manipulators like to play the victim because that's what they have learned from their teachers. I thought it so odd how Camaro chick took delivery of a new candy-apple-red C-5 Corvette for her finishing that class. I don't remember if she was actually out of high school yet,

mortician & DNA man

but she got it from the same dealer who tried to play games with me. It's a small town actually. It's an amazing honor to see how others live their lives in the shadow of mine, thinking they are actually fooling me. That's the best jester. Act a fool, play the fool, so the real fools actually believe they are fooling me. Should I get bells for my shoes? Or for my hat? Or should I just do as I promised to my King. I promised to love and support Geneva regardless. So, I stayed a slave to be used for later because I believed—no, I knew—she hadn't ever seen real love before. I didn't know yet that neither of us had ever been loved. It saddens me as I'm writing this, knowing she is as much a slave as I am. I know Geneva signed up to be a quick in and out deal.

Most of her counterparts don't invest their entire lives on such a simple task of breeding. I can only imagine how expensive that might have been nowadays, knowing how much they truly hated me the whole time, just so Linda could be assured she would have her grandparental rights as she had put into the covenant agreement. That's the all-too-familiar rhetoric of the covenant church. They are the all-knowing as they claim. Only they are allowed to hear from the King, and you aren't allowed to disagree. It makes me so sad. How can church determine what the King is telling someone?

I don't think everyone thinks in the same language. Those thoughts seated deep in the soul are there for a reason. If you have a feeling something isn't right. Pay attention. Keep a journal of what you feel, and pay attention. Then repeat. After years of doing this journaling, you will see how personal God is in your life. Most sheep aren't tuned in. And it's much easier to swallow down a prepared rhetoric, similar to eating fast food your whole life instead of growing your own and learning how to succeed. Some sheep still don't understand that your body is a temple. Be so careful where you keep it and who you welcome into that holy place. Not everyone is on the up and up. Many, many men wish bad things on me, because they learned to hate from professionals at a young age. It's so melancholy. I truly believe when you are speaking the same language as your King, that's the innermost personal relationship He is after, and that's where humility and brokenness cross in His honor. I love that place. I'd rather spend a single moment there with Him in His presence than a million days in paradise.

I've found it's when I'm all alone and in His presence that I truly find my healing, giving praise for my daily breath and all the bonuses along the way. It's truly an amazing honor. I wish others could feel so free. I know it's slavery instead. If money wasn't a thing, I imagine everyone would be so much healthier. It's sad sometimes what money can do. I'm so thankful I've learned before it's too late. Now, I hate money. I see it as a curse. It attracts all the wrong people for some reason. I know if I'm surrounded by a world full of actors, I must find my own way. I must never loose and only learn instead. Somehow, I know my King will use me and my testimony. I do hope it saves someone's life and future so the rest of the world can be a better place for everyone. I personally see that people who use others to do their work have an arrangement. The arrangements that can't be spoken of are called "covenants." That's where my arrangement started.

The covenant church is home to the most elite. I know getting a membership there is done at gunpoint under the desk without anyone knowing until they disagree with following orders. I learned this detail from my son years later. I guess he was playing in Mom's new boyfriend's house and tried to get a ball that rolled under DJ's desk. He told me it scared him really badly, and he froze when he saw it. I had heard that before then, but when my kid told me, it became very, very real how slaves and concubines are created. It's like a circle jerk, where everyone is getting themselves off in secret. It's how they keep their secrets. Plus, it makes it more professional to rape and pillage when you are locked in silence with someone else's cock in your mouth or hand because that's the place you're in by signing a Gag order. If you're in that cult, you've been groomed to be that slave. And that's your choice. Who am I to give freedom? It's earned. It's not free. It's better than getting new kneepads and a jaw that's tired from being blown for hours so selfish people can become more selfish.

I remember one concubine complaining about the marks in her knees from having to be prostituted by Muck and his friends. That was what she signed up for. I knew it. I told her I was one of her biggest fans. I simply was trying to tell her in so many words, "I'm just going to blow hot air on you when you're on fire. It's going to burn even bigger once it's lit." I suggested she get kneepads accordingly. "It's the best thing you can do right now." It seems like that's their MO. It's been happening for years. They use fear. Some people are scared of dying, so it's easy to hold people at gunpoint against their will until they submit to certain death later and meanwhile begin placing liens on the homes of willing participants in order to ensure compliance. As it relates to outcome, the "richest" slaves have the most to lose. I know that's because Muck isn't able to use his virtues like I am. And maybe things need to change. Maybe if the dollar was regarded as simply toilet paper, it wouldn't be much to change. Because let's face it. They aren't going to let us have any of the gold instead. I mean seriously, I do hope that

concubine
2013 family photo

people get to read that and understand the magnitude of that statement. Because I do love you, even if you hate me. I simply love haters. It's the motivation. It's helped me learn who I am today and how to live. I can't hate on my oppressors anymore because if it weren't for them, then the King wouldn't have the audience He does, nor would have I learned so much. But my time is up soon, because I'm going to vanish, I bet. I know how this works. And somehow, I'm not scared. I'm just going to live and not tell anyone. Because sometimes you don't know what you've got until it's gone. Nobody gets out of that cult alive.

CHAPTER 5

Branding

Branding, it's a process. This is how mine went.

I remember the next day after I burned that house down in the early 1990's, everyone was acting strange. I saw the camera. I thought that was so weird how they kept acting like nothing. I wanted to apologize. I felt horrible. I know they know. But I wanted to change. I felt awful. I knew I was going nowhere fast. I was a horrible nobody, so far from perfect. There were two matches. And although it is not as entertaining as creating lies that are sensational, I'm sure it was the second match that set the barns ablaze. It all of a sudden felt like walking on eggshells, but it might have been closer to broken glass. It's all in how you look at it.

When I was out with the other kids, Linda showed up to where I was to drop off some food. At that point, Lonna came outside and signaled for Linda to talk. Lonna was holding a flat padded bag, and it looked like a gun underneath. She got into the passenger side of the van. I only noticed that in the hand she was holding the case was also a gun because I had to bend down and pick up my bike. I went over to the driver's side of the van, where Linda's window was open.

I told her I loved her, looking directly into her eyes. At that point, the neighbor with a burned down barn up the street waved for us to come over. We parked our bikes in the garage, and I ate my food at the table. At that point, Will ushered all of us into his son's room. I didn't think much of it at the time other than it was the first time I had been invited there with his family present.

Once in the room, I looked out the window and noticed Linda's van still sitting in the same spot. This had to have been at least an hour. I decided I would just go home with her instead of riding my bike in the dark. But when I went to leave, Will was standing in the hallway with an arm on each wall as if to block my exit. He told me, "Son, you're not going anywhere. Get your ass back in there." I was a little scared at that point. I didn't want to be around the other boys anyway because they were laughing and snickering. This was back in 1993, so there weren't very many cell phones, but generally speaking, everyone had a landline. About ten minutes or so after I tried to leave, the phone rang, and then a short moment later, we were excused from the Room. That bedroom was the only bedroom I had ever seen that could be locked from the outside.

I immediately got on my bicycle and headed in the direction of my place. When I passed where the van was sitting, I noticed a huge puddle of water, as the condensation from the air-conditioning must have been dripping for quite some time. It was about a ten-foot-diameter circle. I wanted to go home so badly and escape, but I was told that instead I would be staying there that night and going motorcycle riding in the morning. That motorcycle ride was an awkward one. I witnessed multiple times people being agitated with one another. It was an overly awkward situation that I did not want any part of anymore. At the time, I had a very unique dirt bike. It had huge wheels, and rarely did I see another like it. I didn't really like riding with them anyway.

The ride home that day was a quiet one. I wanted to be away. I knew I was caught. I saw the camera. Why were these people acting so weird? I was actually kind of relieved. I didn't ever need to make that mistake again. I should always pretend there was a hidden camera present. Once we got back to their place, I would need to unload my motorcycle. But they weren't having it. They were all sitting inside waiting for us to get back. Lonna told me a story about a man who hurt two girls once upon a time and how nobody felt sorry for him, so the girls set a trap for him. They would keep him in a box and poke him with things for all the world to see as they would rip out his arms and legs and cut out his tongue. Then, they would feed his eyes before they sew them shut. The whole time, he wouldn't even know what was happening, and when they were done playing games, they would lock him up and throw away the key. Everyone he knew would have so much fun playing games with him.

I froze. I wanted to get the heck out of there. But I didn't know. Maybe the gang in blue was waiting outside. I got my bike and headed back. I was followed by another kid, and I stopped at a place where there were jumps. I wasn't there long before Linda came in her minivan with the tires screeching around the corner to my location. She slid to a stop with all four tires making black marks. She screamed at me to get in the car. I jumped like any blind little sheep ushered toward her, and as I grabbed my bicycle's handlebars to pick it up to take it with me, she screamed to leave it there. I seemed a little confused because that was a relatively new bicycle. She screamed again like a toddler low on sleep, and I opened the back door because the front door was locked. All of the seats had been removed, and it was an empty van on the inside.

As soon as I closed the door, she locked it. I saw that and tried to pull the handle as she slammed it in reverse, full throttle. I wasn't ready obviously and smacked my head on the seat in front of me. In a moment, I felt my neck crack a little, but it honestly felt better. About the time I was used to the rearward momentum, she slammed the brakes and put it in drive. I tumbled backward towards the back of the van. Luckily the doors were locked, and I didn't fall out. She was again driving erratically so much so that I was unable to hold on to anything except for the floor to avoid being thrown around like a rag doll inside of a box on wheels. She began screaming at me, asking about the events that had taken place, and I was honest. Whatever she asked me, I admitted to. I was actually thankful. No longer did I have to live a lie. I messed up; there was no doubt about it. That was when she began her newest level of dissociation to be completely honest with you. She told me I didn't deserve anything from then on and that life was going to be extremely difficult for me. I noticed that no matter where I went or whom I talked to, she would develop a codependent relationship with whoever was within the immediate circle. It was embarrassing, as it was designed to be. I was being shepherded and represented by someone who was a slob and disgusting, to say the least. An unsuccessful and mediocre family was what I was raised in.

I don't remember much about falling asleep that night, but I do remember that the next morning, the grass was greener than it had been in a long time, and there was a blanket of dew that made for an amazing sunrise. I was outside. I didn't have an appetite. I don't think I ate for a few days to be really honest with you, but I do remember that sunrise. I remember Linda and Duck saying good morning to one another while I was outside already. I was sitting there in the driveway, kneeling down. I was looking at the sun coming up on the horizon. I still remember the morning very well. It was cool and humid, as the temperature had reached the dew point the night before. I wanted to be outside. That was my sanctuary. Maybe the sunrise was my symphony, I couldn't tell you. But I do remember looking directly at the sun that morning as it rose to meet my gaze. I could see it clearly. I remember looking a little longer that day. I still remember trying to somehow punish myself. I guess that's what I must have been thinking. Because I stood still even past when my eyes began to water. It was hard not to squint. And I could almost feel behind my eyeballs straining like a gold sliver stuck in the cornea. I pressed on even longer and wanted to see more. I couldn't tell you if maybe I was trying to honor the request of my enemies. They wanted me blind. I stood there longer in silence and kept my eyes open, even holding them with my hands, and eventually, it stopped hurting. It started to feel comfortable.

As I looked longer, I tried not to blink, and the rest of my vision became darker. I was focused on letting the light into my eyeballs by tilting my head forward and looking just below the horizon at all the sparkly dew on the grass. I didn't care. All I could see was the sun. Everything else was dark. I still think today sometimes about how the sun looked like a glorious firework as the rings around it began rotating around in a counterclockwise motion. It was like a fuse that circled the sun and never stopped. It just kept going and going. I kept feeling less pain. I was deep in regret. I was praying to my King about how much of a fool I had acted. I was going to be the king of fools. At this point in my life, I believe is when my salvation took a twist of sorts. I think my salvation was put on probation until I finished the marathon because before this, it was just fake. It was just a front. It was something that everyone else did, simply go to church. It was a lot like a day care. I had grown up being put into the corner by the people who put on the show for everyone else. So, I didn't feel I wanted to even exist anymore. I knew I had failed. I knew my salvation was lost and couldn't be found unless I walked beside my King. I know I'm not perfect. Obviously. So does everyone else. It's by design. I thought I might be blind when I first heard Linda coming down the stairs into the garage because I was standing in the driveway looking at the sun. And I don't remember how long I had been standing there, but I must have been in a trance. I was locked into a gaze deep in thought. I felt so small and wanted to vanish as quickly as they promised my eyesight would. I looked away from the sun and tried to see Linda, but I couldn't see her. I couldn't see anything. Everything was black. My heart beat hard. I felt my tongue swell a little and taste salty as if I was having an adrenaline rush. I do remember that blackness faded pretty quickly because by the time Linda spoke, I could barely see her. But it was only an outline. I remember now commenting to Duck about how green the grass became overnight, I somehow out of nowhere said, "It's God." Her eyes got big as she walked inside.

I don't know why I remember that specific moment, but my life is not my own. I'm just a ghost now, branded and labeled. I'm never going to be anything. I've heard it so much. I know only my King has the ability to change hearts. It's not my life anymore. Neither is my sight. A little while longer, and I only had a green spot burned into the center of my vision. I think it was barely there the next day. The best way I can describe it is when you use a magnet on a television tube and the picture changes. It's like the blob of discoloration. It wore off, and I think that was the last time I watched the sun any longer than when it reached past the horizon.

CHAPTER 6

The Morning after Faking Suicide

Sunday June 30th 2013, I believe I was having church right there. That was when I felt my King soothing my soul. I felt Him putting all the pieces back together for me. It was much larger than I initially expected, and I was so thankful. I believe that's what the King wants. And so, He shall have it. Who am I to deny His glory? I know His hands are much more powerful than mine. Money for revenge? Nah, that's an insult. I wasn't sad watching what I was seeing, because I had known all along, I was correct. I am usually never wrong about these kinds of things based on my track record. I watched as those who claimed to be my "family" were getting off by their ability to live a double life, for the sheer motivation to torment me on camera. It's fairly obvious they planned to lie, to create a situation to capitalize on. I now know this was all too similar to what I had seen before. I heard it from the gentleman I worked with long ago … the gentleman who told me at the buffet they would get rid of me. This was his replacement. He had been around wolves for quite some time now.

Corvitt was a younger guy and very personable. He mentioned many things that were odd about Freemasons. It was as if I were listening to an associate of my great uncle's all over again. I don't think he knew. I used to have coffee and play dominoes with the real OGs of that club. I even watched them collect gold coins at the auction downtown when I was a child. The oddest part was how small the town was actually. I knew better than to speak. Loose lips sink ships … So take your best shot.

The biggest cowards use the shiniest buttons on the blue costumes they wear. The strongest slaves don't even need clothes. Sometimes the meek become the strong. It's for the King's glory. The King wears a real crown. He made the gold that the puppets who want me dead seek so desperately. I find it ironic they settle for so much less. But that's often the calling card for mediocrity. That brings me to the local judge who lived next door to the woman who wanted me dead on camera. He wore the same freemason crown as my ancestors, as well as the badge behind the gavel, not to mention his association with the local politicians. He even performed the marriage ceremony for my ex-wife's third-grade teacher. It's funny how that was the last year she attended public schools. They actually believe their lies will protect them. I feel honored, not many get so much attention. That must mean I'm worth so much more. How glorious an honor that's bestowed upon me! When everyone is in bed together, that means they are all working together to keep secrets. I mean the secret was so huge, obviously there had to be ramifications for spilling the beans. I'm sure a gag order and a nondisclosure agreement were in order. My King has such a gentle way of bringing truth.

I kept watching and praying, seeking my King. I know He is close, because I can almost feel His presence and protection as if bullets miss and guns jam. Some people just won't die. Some speak for themselves with actions, not words. I watched them celebrating on camera. So I know my ability to disassociate must mean he is a professional at that. They get off on disassociation. I think to myself, *Whoa, that means this didn't happen overnight. They had all been planning their celebration for quite some time now.*

The earliest I can remember the get-rich quick talk began around 2000. I was happy to help and give you an ending that's legendary. Come, get you some now. I'm standing right here. I faked my own suicide. Now I know. But I can't say. I can only laugh.

Beyond a shadow of a doubt, I know I don't have family and I don't have friends, just a few acquaintances, and I've never been happier. Everyone who claims to know me just wants to watch me die on camera for playing with matches. And I must say it's an amazing honor. I thought to myself, *How did I get here?* I began to laugh even more. It's obvious they think I'm an idiot. That's one of my single greatest assets. I'm an idiot. I don't think you need to be careful about what you say or have lying around. Go ahead. Take too many photos. My ancestors pay good money for them. I hope they see me smiling. As much celebrating as was taking place, I knew money was involved. I kept thinking about how the old general manager at the dealership mysteriously died and how his family was happy and rich now, but others who didn't see the bigger picture were sad. Some people who came to his funeral were actually outraged. He died from an apparent "suicide" after being caught red-handed laundering money from the first dealership that I worked at. His family was paid off with a life insurance policy that nobody knew about. It went to the bank of Grand Cayman, where nobody even knew it was in place.

That was the first time I saw a suicide life insurance policy rider pay out. They paid higher premiums, but it did cover suicide after two years of on-time payments to a current policy. I started to remember how my ex-wife somehow had a job given to her at the State Farm insurance company. She got the job from one of her cult friends who claimed to be a consultant. It was only about six months after we got married when her new friends and people who claimed to be my family made their way to Cancun. Even one of my present-day coworkers was there. They went to get to Grand Cayman and open the offshore bank accounts they needed to have in place. The insurance agent was family, so I guess that helped her keep her job in the midst of her mediocre plans, because it took her a few times to pass the insurance test. I remember the second time she failed it, she took it again the same day and again failed it. It wasn't cheap. She finally got her license to sell life insurance. And I didn't see any substantial income from those days. I do remember paying all the bills out of a joint account. And she always needed more money. It didn't matter how much money she had tucked away in her glove box, she needed to use mine. Many times, I thought that she actually was trying to drain me with the stupid purchases and all the charity money she gave away or all the parties I ended up paying for. I was reminded that this was the age of entitlement. Some frauds are fully committed. I am sure that everyone who owns a rider on that policy cannot wait to get a payoff.

I began to press into my King. I kept thinking about what He wanted. I already know I'm a nobody. I'm nobody anyone else would want to be. He began showing me the inside of shepherding. Often, plans are made years in advance, premeditated. I remembered how the gentleman who got in the door at the insurance company was rewarded with a custom home in the area for his hard work, not to mention his association with Duck and Linda as well as everyone else in the local corporate church. Duck took great pride in that. This would be one of many he would give his skills away to in order to redeem a favor later.

It didn't matter where I worked, Duck seemed entitled to befriend my coworkers and manager. I know Duck knew I didn't care for him. That's kind of an understatement; however, revenge isn't up to me. I'm not even going to piss on his face when his teeth are on fire. I'll just watch. That was when many more pieces began to fall together. It must be being built out of titanium. I say that because the pieces are being welded together, and it's hot. The process is melting and burning. It feels like me. My unicorn horn begins to grow even more now. I am so excited. I remembered how when the general manager "committed suicide," rumors surfaced about how he called the police to report his own suicide. It was also well known how he shot himself in the head while sitting in a new company truck in an apartment complex parking lot … twice. But who's counting? I know the local police fraternity gets the city patrol units serviced there. Not to mention all the charity work done for the community by way of city leaders getting free lease cars and others in church reaping the same benefits.

I know his funeral was rather large because of how many associates he had, being a part of the Rotary Club and the 21 Group. I didn't attend; I didn't feel the need to. I know we all face death alone. It's guaranteed. That's why they bet the way they do. We all got to die, so to say. Everyone I know should pick out a photo for their obituary before it is too late. I began to smile as the pieces kept coming together about other people who mysteriously died when Duck had something to gain. I rejoiced knowing my King was showing me in great detail what my enemies' motives and actions were. Although I had been drained, I wasn't that tired. I kept journaling and analyzing what I was witnessing, knowing all too well what a gaslight actually is and how shepherding is used to create money. I'm seeing how people are quite literally turned into money. While others watch, will anyone even care? It's sad how selfish most slaves are. I get it because they have never known true peace. I know that real wealth isn't having more; it's needing less. Wealth is in my blood. My King ensures it.

I needed more coffee at this point. So I made mine with the caramel macchiato creamer I liked so much. It's so tasty but unhealthy, everyone knows. I like to think of it as cheap thrills, because it's so much cheaper than a Starbucks coffee. That's as much as an entire burger. It wasn't long before the concubine came barging in. She seemed panicked. I smiled and watched like a hawk. My King must have been sitting next to me because I didn't even flinch. Puppets are so predictable. I know bad things happen to people who walk a razor's edge to try to hurt me. They only need to slip a little, and it cuts deep. I laughed on the inside when she seemed determined to take me to "church" that morning. She said it was super important that we meet Linda at the 9:00 a.m. service for lunch afterward. I couldn't help it after a few minutes and began laughing as I told the concubine in so many words that I wasn't leaving. I told her that my King told me not to. Her eyes got huge. Mine probably cut a little. I wasn't sad. I was wearing a smile. She kept saying I needed to go to church, and I already knew. I stood right beside my King.

There is no sermon or preachers' words that compare to a moment with him. He is giving me a testimony, and I don't have time for concubines who cannot be honest. All the little things pale in comparison. I kept journaling as she grew even more anxious. She kept saying I needed to clean my place and took it upon herself to "clean." I kept watching and taking notes as she began acting weird. It was like watching a roller coaster full of people who weren't strapped in. That morning was funny and scary all at the same time. I still laugh as an abortion survivor. I could tell it made her even more nervous as I remained calm, cool, and collected. I saw how she was getting off seeking revenge against me. Simply put, they were looking for a reaction from me. And I laughed instead, because sometimes you've got to keep your friends close and your enemies even closer, especially when they employ the Hegelian dialectic through the dogma of church and religion. That's the enemy's biggest lie. And it was playing out for everyone to see. The King instructed me not to get mad at the concubine, rather to turn the other cheek, to show her love even though all she carried was hate. I know her hate was something that she had learned and was groomed to feel by the cult she called her associates. My King was showing me very clearly that she in fact had never experienced unconditional love. The King showed me how she was actually a slave to her oppressors' bondage. I knew based on the cult she participated with, by default, she also had an arranged marriage. I knew the gentleman from soccer. He worked at the soccer place and was good friends with the police fraternity, because he used to work there as an officer, but because of mediocre service or something else, he was now in the pool-cleaning business as well as working at a local pharmacy. The concubine worked for the same company in a closer location. Both locations were in the same little area. I'm sure everyone reading this has been to one at some point. They are well known for being able to fill a prescription while you are sitting in the drive through.

For some reason, I guess they didn't know that I knew who they actually were. Actions speak louder than words. Talk is cheap. Stolen phone records don't lie.

I just kept steadfast in prayer, knowing that I'd kept in my possession twelve months of phone records, documenting wolves and how they associate. I already know not to seek revenge. Instead, I have already sealed their fate. I chose not to even call the concubine out in regard to my half-brother and her associations. I knew better. It's loose lips that sink ships. *I'm going to make you work for it*, I thought to myself. I gave no emotion for the concubine to play off of, and she retreated in a panic. I had plenty of time to journal and write down details of what I was seeing for everyone else to learn from. The concubine returned around three that afternoon. She brought with her some "cleaning supplies" in a brown paper bag. She seemed even more panicked after returning because I know she had seen me writing my book with the phone records sitting open on the table next to my writing. I was kind of tired at this point, but I knew better than to take my eyes off of her. I instead paid close attention to her, watching her every move. She claimed she needed to give my place a thorough cleaning. She even used my Dyson to clean all of the floors in my place. She would try to give me something to do in the other room as if I gave a flying fuck about what my place looked like. She even brought boxes for me to pack up all my kids' toys, as if they were going somewhere. I watched as she took a hairbrush from her bag and placed it into my bathroom.

I immediately picked it up and asked, "What the hell?"

She said, "Isn't that yours?"

I was like, "Um, I haven't used a hairbrush for at least ten years … My boys use combs." I threw it in the trash, and her eyes began to well up as if to cry. I kind of laughed on the inside. About five minutes later, I watched as she placed a stack of red Solo cups on top of my fridge. She had brought them with her in her cleaning bag. I told her I didn't need them and laughed. She started shaking as I put them into the trash and sat down at the table as if to take a break from the bullshit. My actions spoke louder than words here. Take your best shot. I get off on it. I smile as I'm not privy to the inside information you carry in the form of a nondisclosure agreement. I noticed her place a stack of red napkins on top of my refrigerator. I took notes because I had rolls of paper towels. I didn't need her crap. I ended up using one of them to wipe up some Dr. Pepper and threw it into the trash.

I saw the concubine's eyes light up. She kept cleaning, and I used that time to test my enemies by making comments and laughing, looking for a reaction as a litmus test in a way. I could see the pain my laughing and entertainment value had without me even knowing. I remember saying specifically that "It's going to take a special person to love my half-brother and actually fit in with my ancestors."

She began crying at this point while pretending to do dishes by spreading soapy water around things in complete disarray at what was happening to her and her freedom in that very moment. As she regained her composure, it made us fully aware. Shortly after, she asked me to take out the trash, which was all right because the trash came on Monday. It was Sunday afternoon. I didn't see what the big deal was. I tied up the bag and put it outside the door. And that wasn't enough for the concubine. She got rather upset because I didn't take the trash to the street but instead set the trash bag just outside the door. It was almost as if she didn't have enough time for something. Then she began saying she needed to go to Walmart. I suggested she go, but that wasn't her reasoning. She needed me to go to Walmart. I had noticed how interested she was in the photos I had in my camera. I took notes. I had removed the memory card and wrapped it in a Faraday cage long before she ever got there. I suggested I could probably go to Walmart to print off some of my spectacular photos. I watched her get even more nervous. She insisted on driving me there. So we agreed. I watched her walk out to her car, which was parked in a different spot. It was just on the other side of a privacy fence. When I approached, I saw the concubine sitting and window to window talking to a police officer who was sitting in a black and white SUV with a huge sticker on the door that looked just like the shiny buttons they wear on their costumes. I recognized the officer from phone records. It was badge number 0200.

I say let the losers just keep losing. I'll just keep learning. I now looked behind me to see my neighbor and half-brothers associate, Fitz, was talking to a guy who was skateboarding in the street just at the end of my driveway. I recognized the guy. He was around my age. He didn't live there; he was the across-the-street neighbor of the crocodile woman. I see you see me, so I took photos of them interacting. And as we drove off, I saw the same guy digging through my trash. I was reminded of how that had happened before. I can only assume my ancestors must now pay others to dig through my garbage instead of doing it themselves. That made me excited because I knew I would have an audience when I got to Walmart. I wondered who from the cult would make an appearance. I went to the photo department, and the concubine went to the pharmacy area, where she began talking to a lady I remembered from "covenant church" a long time ago.

I asked her who her "new" friend was, and she acted like I was crazy. They both acted like they didn't know each other, when just a few moments earlier they had been almost crying. I began to think to myself, *Where is her partner in crime?* The biggest cowards aren't allowed to work on their own. They must work in pairs because they aren't strong enough on their own. I figured I would see him in the photo department, and I was correct. Her husband followed me like a paparazzi. I even watched him watching me over my shoulder as I was using the kiosk where you print your own photos. I would turn around and look at him as he turned and looked at the memory cards on the wall directly behind both of us. I saw that he was like a toggle switch, and I had fun with that. I could see that every time I pulled up a new photo, he was almost breathing down my neck. I would turn toward him as he evaded my glance again by acting like an innocent bystander. I recognized him well due to the scar on his face that didn't fade over time.

I began to laugh on the inside, knowing he thought I didn't know who he was or why he was there. That was an asset I could use to my advantage. So, I quickly put my memory card into my pocket, picked up my bag, and watched this guy watch me. Just another moment later, the concubine came toward both of us, walking with the same lady she had denied knowing just a few moments prior. The woman and the man who was trying to see my photos began holding hands and walking toward the exit. I remember the gentleman, how he kept his daughters locked in a closet when his favorite daughter met a man who wouldn't submit to his imaginary authority. I know things in this life come full circle. In that cult, your life isn't your own, and your offspring will have arranged marriages, or there will be problems. I often wondered if the Hardy family would survive because they didn't seem very hardy. I laughed again, knowing my ex-wife's associates only knew mediocrity.

Just Muck

Muck is my half-brother. Ours was much like the story of Cain and Abel. I watched as you were led down a path to be taught how to get rich quick by using others. I remember when you were in kindergarten and convinced the kid sitting next to you to hold a sharpened pencil in a classmate's chair for her to sit on and see what happened. It was awful, I heard. I often wondered if that was your associate at Bridges who worked with me and also went on vacation with Muck and Linda in 2000 to Mexico. I still remember your associate's necklace with the large stainless-steel balls on it like an oversized dog collar and the spiky hair. Don't you remember convincing him that he would get rich if he just did everything you said? I do, That's poison ivy.

I remember when you were sitting in your mom's house surrounded by family photos and taking as many pills as you could to escape this life. Remember? I had a feeling out of nowhere and came there to find you sitting on the floor next to the bed. I called the gang in blue for you to get help. I even made them turn off their lights so as not to wake up your mommy. I guess that was just before college, where you needed to look the part. Do you remember doing business with my coworkers before I worked there? It was back in college when they hooked you up with your truck. Still don't remember? Okay, well, the college you went to in Texas was known as the cowboy capital. You joined the same fraternity as others who took great pride in profiting from smut. I get it. That's your only virtue. Even in college, you were trying to make a name for yourself by having the most shocking, most disgusting and disturbing videos. It didn't surprise me you would sell yourself and everyone around you to get rich or pay back what you now owe. Do you remember asking me if you could use my life? And how I refused? I still remember you saying that I would get paid back. You need your mommy, as well as anyone around you you've already made a slave with your nondisclosure agreement, to help—even the technician putting the phone line back together. I watched as you used money to create slaves so you could profit.

Many of the friends and fraternity brothers you associate with are at the FBI and CIA. There are also the concubine associates in the same building. Everyone knows what you've planned. Remember when you bragged to me about your actions and how strong your cult is? I do. Thanks for the inside information. I needed it to put all the pieces together. I don't have any friends, and I know it. You must pay people to associate with you, as well as pay people to associate with me. How fragile your existence must be, when I know you find your identity in how many zeros are on a screen. Do you not remember working at the local bank and opening people's accounts, stealing their information, and using it to create more slaves? Not only did you use people you already knew, you used the bank account information to find the richest men in Colley Wood and the surrounding area to seek investments from. Because you aren't strong enough to stand in front of the King alone.

Remember when I showed up to your house when I wasn't supposed to on my bicycle? When you and the concubine's brother fled in terror and then lied about it? I watched as you two created your own situation for people to believe was reality. I listened as you bragged about having several hundred cars on the road doing work for you. Do you remember getting many of them at auctions? I do. You were always wanting me to help. Do you and Linda remember screaming at me in front of my kids as they watched and held the camera on the evening of June 11th 2013? I do. We all do. The boys saw firsthand your willingness to manipulate. You and Linda claimed that I lifted a finger. We both know that's a lie. I wouldn't lift a finger for you. My kids were watching and held the camera. Wasn't it funny to pay the gang in blue again? Some people are so scared to die, because you have worked so hard to create something everyone else wants to see. Even those kids know. Everyone knows. You are who your friends are.

Remember your roommate at the first college? Ms. Crocodile's son? You were best friends. Remember? You are all in this together.

Everyone wants to see now, right? Does entertainment value exceed human rights? I know the King will deal with you in the most appropriate way, even if you choose not to believe. Mercy isn't up to me. Nobody survives shepherding. We all got to die.

crocodiles 1993

Just Duck

I'm proud to say this man is not my father. I couldn't be happier. I'm so thankful because I felt it for so long. I knew as I was growing up that he hated me. I mean, I'm not the only one who saw it. But I did keep a close watch. I knew that based on his skill set, the man had access to a multitude of resources. The earliest I could remember something being very different was shortly after I gained my costume. That was when I noticed. Duck began to listen to gang-in-blue chatter on a gang-in-blue scanner. It started back in 1993, 1994, and 1995 as best I can remember. It wasn't as odd as when I found the notebook sitting next to me in the recliner where it looked like he had been taking notes about people, places, and things, like either he was figuring out what all the gang-in-blue call letters were or keeping track of who was who. I was actually kind of shocked.

The gang-in-blue scanner ran nonstop, and he even had to get another from RadioShack when that one stopped working. He would also listen to all the neighbors on their cordless phones because back then most people had landlines, and they could use a simple 400-to-900-megahertz phone to walk around the house without a chord. Being these were analog phones, they were easy to pick up with the gang-in-blue scanner, and they were actually a pretty clean listen. The across-the-street kid named Matt offered one of his favorite soap operas to listen to. I remember Duck sitting in his blue leather recliner with the gang-in-blue scanner in one hand plugged into a charger. He held it up to his ear. In the other hand, he held a voice recorder that he had plugged in. The voice recorder looked like the one that I had in my backpack at the time, but his was grey. I'm going to speculate here, but I already know he was collecting dirt and learning how to use it. Shortly after this moment, Duck said that our neighbor's son Matt was addicted to cocaine. I wondered how he knew that because he didn't know any of the same people as far as I knew. I was like, *Whatever, I never liked the guy anyway.* But like three to four weeks later, Matt had moved somewhere else. Nobody knows where. I have often wondered if that dirt that Duck was digging for was used to bury Matt. I mean, I had seen how many times he got off on making fun of Matt.

I was about fourteen or fifteen during the season when I noticed him listen to the gang-in-blue scanner excessively, trying to make friends—or was he trying to make slaves? I think bigger. I think he was trying to save himself.

I still remember shortly before that the accident that happened to his hand. It's often held the right hand is used for discipline in that cult. Shortly before Christmas in 1993, he had an accident in which he said he spilled acid on his hand, but the story kept changing. They refused to seek medical treatment and didn't ever say exactly how it happened. As a kid, I hadn't made the connection yet, but his hand swelled up to the size of a cantaloupe. His fingers were the size of sausages with skin being pulled tight and his nails almost about to fall off. This was no small acid spill. To me looking back, it looked like someone had held his hand under acid for quite some time, maybe as a form of torture. It took months and months for him to regain the use of that hand. So I can understand his fear and doing what he is told because he knows what will happen to him if he does otherwise.

Shortly after the hand incident, he bought his first new truck. It was a 1994 Chevy CK 1500 in indigo blue. I remember the blue velour interior pretty well. It was a major milestone for him because he went from driving a rusty old blue work van with extension cords and air hoses hanging from the windows of the inside to a nice new truck and new framing trailer that he got from someone else for an eighth of the deal. I get it. It was for more big business he was about to experience in the future. I believe at this point his job was to get his image squared away and look spotless for who was coming.

Shortly after that, he became known for framing some of the most expensive homes in the area. He had a crew of guys who would come and go, but there was always one who had been there for a long time. Duck had been in the framing trade for a very long time. He was becoming well known in the tight-knit community. I'm fairly certain that was where he made most of his connections. Even the local pastor started out as an associate of his. He used to hang wallpaper for new homes. I could only imagine how profitable wallpaper is today compared to the appropriate tax shelters you get from running a "church" business. It's really not hard to imagine because back in the eighties and early nineties, the wallpaper game was much different.

During my high school years, Duck always made it a point to do favors for key players in the area. I saw him build barns for Barnes and houses for shop owners of those I worked for. His favorite sister was his professional associate, whom he called a "consultant". I know that when it comes to organized crime, nobody can be honest, for some trade their integrity for favors long before they have a brain to understand. Loose lips sink ships. That's the objective. Small town equals big hell. I could name all of the coworkers who took part in the games that are played by the shepherds, but it doesn't seem appropriate to give them any recognition. You're a coward if you aren't strong enough to be honest. Don't worry about revenge from me. I've written it down many times over. I know what I've conquered. I'm not even going to piss in your face when your teeth are on fire. I will just watch and stay clean. The pen is mightier than the sword. I simply write. I always do. So we can all learn. This is how I learned to learn. So everyone will know. It's for the King's glory. Not mine. I'm a nobody.

Different times I heard my ancestors laugh weirdly, like when we were visiting my grandparents' house in the rural South. Their house was across the street from a cemetery, and I remember how weird it was as a kid. It wasn't what everyone experienced, but that's life. I enjoyed riding my bicycle through the cemetery—on the pavement exclusively, of course. They had great curbs that allowed for proper drainage as well as the most perfect little slope for a BMX bunny hop. I didn't always bring my bicycle, but when I did, I made sure to get in some play time in the cemetery. It was relatively safe from cars and traffic. I know my grandparents knew the gravedigger. They had lived across the street since the fifties. I was in a safe area, so to say. Different times, I heard my ancestors laugh weirdly when someone visiting would pay their respects as they were walking in the cemetery. They were probably visiting a loved one's grave.

There was some sort of comment between my ancestors present, and they all started laughing. I'm sure it was a family joke, as they had been there a number of years. I only remember hearing my uncle snickering as he said, "They are looking for George ..."

I said, "What?"

I recognized the sinister laugh. I had heard it many times before. Grandpa ushered in a quick "Nothing!" His glare was like molten lava created from a high-power laser beam. Everyone got quiet, and it was like all the birds even stopped chirping momentarily. I was staring at my grandpa as I leaned my bike against the wall. I was frozen, almost scared, because the tone he used wasn't a friendly one. Out of the silence, Duck said to his brother under his breath, "Nobody is going to find him." And they both started snickering again. I could see my grandfather's eyes glow even hotter as his face dropped. It was like they wanted to laugh all together, but I was present and underaged. At the time, I think I just assumed it was another grown-up person joke that I shouldn't ask questions about. Looking back, I believe things were very different, and as a ten-year-old riding my bike, I wasn't concerned with the cares of adults. At that age, I still had no idea of the family business. I knew they were Freemasons by the meetings at the lodge they would talk about, not to mention the red ring my grandfather wore that had the symbol in the very center, much like a mob boss. He didn't wear a wedding ring. It wasn't important. He didn't wear a college ring. That wasn't important. He did always have on his lodge ring though. He was proud of it because it was a gift for extraordinary service that was given to him by his worshipful master. He served as a master mason for the grand masonic lodge of Texas for a number of years. And he even boasted about how strong the club was and that they would never have anything to worry about.

He often made reference to how the gang in blue and freemasons worked together. That was why he always had the masonic logos on his truck, because not everyone could have those. And if he got pulled over when he was "working," they would just let him go without any information. I asked how. He said because their boss was connected with the governor, and his people would make sure they would be reprimanded at the department. I believed him based on what I'd seen. Many of my other ancestors were involved in the law enforcement business as well as the same fraternity. I didn't understand yet what he meant by "working" or "doing a job." I would learn more later in greater detail. Up to that point, at my young age, all I had seen firsthand was countless attempts at insurance fraud. Some were more serious than others, but you know what they say when you're dealing with organized crime: "In for a penny, in for a pound."

grandpa master mason

Some of the first attempts I can remember were the fire at Kerrie Singer's house, where the cause of the fire was mysterious but because of the insurance coverage that was in place, a payout was made by way of a legitimate claim. It was even more mysterious how many expensive electronics were destroyed, even a piano that wasn't there. When they were questioned about it, they presented a melted keyboard in its place.

Another was during one of Duck's failing businesses, again a fire. It was a mysterious fire that was deemed accidental by the fire chief due to a pile of oily rags self-combusting. The shop burned to the ground, and everything was lost. I do remember how weirdly they acted around that time. How can you forget all the arguing and screaming at one another? As best as I could understand, there wasn't any insurance covering the contents. Duck wasn't happy. He didn't yet understand that just because the building had insurance for its replacement, its contents weren't insured. It was even more apparent he was breaking a few rules running a business in a place that wasn't zoned for using toxic chemicals to paint furniture. I thought it was odd how he would continually make Linda's parents feel bad about what happened despite the fact they paid for him to build his home years prior. The man was toxic with his comments and could make anyone and everyone in the room uncomfortable at the drop of a hat. Eventually, they funded his new location and all the tools inside. He did well for a while but needed more funding for an ever-expanding business in the middle of a recession. So, he borrowed money from the bank for his business and secured his financing with his in-laws' CD accounts as a security to make up for his mediocre credit, as well as mortgaging his home. I don't think it took more than a couple of years to lose that money. I almost forgot to mention his grandmother's house—another mysterious fire … of course. Duck was proud of himself on this one. I heard him bragging on fishing trips between the family of wolves about how easy the demolition was at Grandma's house. They only thing left standing was the garage, as planned. It mysteriously caught on fire and burned up while they were removing a water heater. It was deemed a total loss minus the garage. It was the perfect place for his grandma's car, a 1969 Mustang GT with a 302 v8. That was the first year the 302 was offered. It was a one-owner all-original car. I know the house was in need of being torn down. It hadn't been occupied in over two decades from what I understand.

I was always warned the house was haunted anyway. That was where Duck's grandfather killed himself. He was sitting in his living room and used a twelve gauge to blow his brains out. My ancestors told the story many times about how he lost his leg in an explosion years before and was never the same. They said he lost his mind and was tormented by thinking his leg was still there sometimes or was being eaten by ants or spiders. I can only imagine the horror or terror his brain was producing for his own tempering. Maybe he was being groomed to be in hell. It's not for me to say. I can say they found his leg in a tree about half a mile away from the explosion. They say he was making pyrotechnics, but I've thought they were bombs because he was often brought in for questioning whenever a bombing in the area mysteriously took place. Some say he was involved in big things because of his connections to organized criminals in Chicago but that was way before my time. I've always wondered how much of an explosion could be made if you were only making firecrackers and bottle rockets. I know that was one of the family businesses, and I usually enjoyed my fair share of fireworks without adult supervision, especially at the Fourth of July celebration. I like seeing things burn in a brilliance that illuminates the sky and takes your breath away. It's entertainment worthy. I think I should keep going.

The Diamond Associates

There was an unsolved murder back in the eighties. Duck's best friend was a prime suspect for quite some time. There were no witnesses. It was a double homicide, and the people who received the life insurance benefit were Mr. Carr and his wife. I do know Mr. Carr paid Duck for many years. He did so through professional bills and payouts. I watched as they would continually jerk each other off, even driving identical trucks for a bit, not to mention being around all the same associates in the home-building trade. Mr. Carr had a son named John who was close to my age. So, I went to kindergarten with John and graduated with John in the same class of around eight hundred people. I always enjoyed his company. I couldn't go far without him noticing. I was the polar opposite of John but still loved all the same things, like baseball, fast cars, loud stereos, nitrous, pretty girls, and street racing. We grew up seemingly together but were never close friends. I always felt his envy of my skills. From bike riding to shop class, it was like the guy was constantly trying to undermine me. I took great enjoyment while we were in high school. I had bought myself a faster, nicer car than he was allowed to have. His family had lots of collector cars, mostly Corvettes, but a few race cars, a few Camaros, mainly the first generation. So, since the fourth-generation Camaro was being released, it seemed to be the perfect graduation present for John, who could have anything in the world. It was ordered to match his 1969 Camaro SS. That way, he could put them both in car shows next to one another, both collector cars, numbers matching.

I remember all the hype at school leading up to him taking delivery of the car. He kept saying how fast it was, and it was a great car. It was beautiful, the best money could buy. It was completely stock red with a black interior, sporting a six-speed transmission with a stock Hurst shifter. I didn't mean to steal his thunder ... so many times ... but I couldn't help it. I had my car before he got his. I had already been driving the wheels off of my Z28. Sure, it wasn't a new SS, but it did look like a new Camaro, and it was a Z28 with the same six-speed and Hurst shifter. It also had gears, exhaust, cold air intake, pulleys, and a chip for tuning as well as a 150-horsepower shot of nitrous for added confidence. It was hidden pretty well with the bottle being in the trunk where the spare tire was. It seemed to me that no matter how much money John and his daddy, Mr. Carr, had, they couldn't be happy unless John was doing better than I was. I took shop with him, and it was constant undermining. I am so thankful because he made me increase my skills. Iron sharpens iron. He had been to professional driving and racing schools. Shortly after I got my Camaro, I learned how to drive faster than he did. Because I had to. It didn't always work out in my favor, but my life isn't mine. I'm just living. I seriously just bought the car like that. I didn't mean to be faster or flashier than the store-bought model that couldn't be touched because it was under warranty.

The guy was just like his father. He was similar to the cable guy. He was best friends with the other two kids I played matches with. So I know my presence, like a train horn, had to be even more aggravating since I just wouldn't bow down or bend over. I learned from John. He showed me that if you don't need to work for anything, you'll never be anyone. You're simply entitled, just like the rest of them. I watched as his connections landed him jobs that most people would be so thankful to have only for him to quit just a few months later, knowing he had more resources than the owner. He couldn't believe they asked him to take the trash out. I heard him say many times how they just didn't understand who he was and how he didn't need the money that badly. I, in contrast, had some of the dirtiest, hardest jobs and loved every moment. I found comfort in my daily beatings, where he found his in the lack thereof. I found myself eventually living in a larger home in a better area. It was sad to me because I watched him lose his family to his own infidelity and unforgiveness. It was his kids who paid the price, missing out on being around their father. It almost makes me sad, but I know mercy isn't up to me. I simply just want to watch. I can only imagine how annoying it must have been when I just wouldn't give up. I eventually repaired most of his vehicles at whatever job I was working at, from the Corvette he shoved into the ditch after drinking to the custom Harley truck that the whole side was taken out on. I did my work as if I was serving my King.

I know a mutual friend who lost his father during this time. It was a shock to the community, but thankfully, they had the best life insurance money could buy. His name was Mr. Fletcher. Mr. Fletcher was very involved in the booster club for baseball and football. He was well known and liked among staff as well as students. It rocked the community. I say this now because of the mysterious circumstances that occurred. It was said he died of a heart attack. But I found it odd that Duck and Mr. Carr were present when it happened in Mr. Fletcher's own backyard. I guess since it was a small town and the hospital staff was already under grace, then it wouldn't matter. Creating the illusion people want to believe is more important than the truth. Mr. Fletcher's son, who was my age, had his life changed. I went to the funeral. So did so many other people. Several hundred people attended; I remember. I went alone and wore black. It wasn't a few weeks later when his son who was my age bought himself a brand-new Trans Am just before leaving for college at an expensive school in the area. He attended the highest fraternity and had a corporate job in no time. Some people are so poor all they have is money. That's all they want, I think. That's all I've ever seen.

I've watched Duck continue his family business of turning people into money and getting rid of people who deserve it. They actually believe they are doing God's work. But I've known better all along. Because I'm sure the creator who created it all doesn't need money. The people who create money and give it value are the ones who need it most. I truly believe the opposite. True wealth isn't having more; it's needing less. I believe he was taught the progression of his skilled disposal of targeted individuals at a young age by his father. It's a progression if you see the things I have. Quite simply put, he took advantage of easy cash offered by the elite to dispose of loose lips. It began in that cemetery where I began riding my bike. I heard about too many mysterious deaths at my grandfather's work to understand the magnitude of what they were involved in. I heard Duck bragging to someone wearing a suit at a car show, when he didn't know I was within earshot. It sounded like he was saying, "It's a cemetery; nobody knows."

He doesn't obey many rules, but there are a few he always makes sure are in compliance. I know it was always important to have a clean bed or cargo area, all the right insurance, and the registration current. I know he always needed to go and check on his slabs when they got poured in concrete. I've often wondered why he needed to get to the place before dawn to see something about a huge pad of concrete … I think they all knew it was the perfect place to turn people into money. I mean, after all, who was going to ruin a foundation over speculation? Of course, he wasn't always building homes and having access to large slabs of concrete when nobody was looking. I believe he started out a long, long time ago. Like father like son.

I was just a child when I saw him dig the first hole that scared me. I must have been nine or ten then. I remember things I probably shouldn't. I've heard the brain does something to memories to protect the viewer from further damage. But that's not a luxury that I'm afforded. Because I still remember very clearly seeing the first hole I was scared of. It was located in the field next to my grandparents' house off Glade Road. As I approached the hole in the ground, I noticed how steep it was. I didn't know how anyone would get in or out of it. It actually scared me to get close enough to the edge to see the bottom. And at the bottom, Duck was digging even deeper. He had his concrete boots on. And he was digging a hole just under his own feet. The hole he was standing in and digging deeper was already about a foot deep in water. I wasn't aware what was happening at my young age. But this was the very first time I had seen Duck holding a shovel, standing at the bottom of a hole in the ground that was deeper than he was tall. That's real shit. I promise. I've often wondered what initially triggered my conditional disassociation when dealing with those wolves. I can only speculate. Because I do remember more than I should. It was odd to me to watch so many times how stories of what happened to people would change to fit agendas.

It reminded me of a gentleman whom Duck helped meet his maker in the mid 1990's. His name was Larry. Larry was briefly married to the Crocodile lady, before he died in a car crash. A few days before he died, Larry had told me he thought Duck was following him home from a local bar called Volcanos. I told him I bet it was Duck following him around. I told him that I'd seen him be a stalker and laugh about it. Larry was an airplane mechanic for some very rich people. He did have skills. Based on what I saw, he was a good man, much better than the man who raised me living a lie. I do remember Duck being jealous as soon as Larry came into the picture. I didn't understand the psychology of sexual deviants until later in life. I can imagine that swingers are all over the place emotionally and physically. I can tell you that Duck was proud of himself. All the gang-in-blue reports said it was an accident. And the life insurance policy paid very well. All of Larry's personal possessions were divided up by his first family.

The money and wealth went to Mrs. Crocodile. She didn't share the money from his life with anyone. I was kind of blown away. He had two daughters, one that was around my age, and she had just lost her father.

It was so sad when I would hear Mrs. Crocodile going on and on about how the daughters just wanted money. And they were looking for more of it. I saw her become even more of a manipulator. Mrs. Crocodile was only married to Larry for around six months before she began gaslighting him. I saw him be put through a roller coaster of emotions by way of mental sodomy. I honestly think that was just a practice round, possibly a free demonstration of their ability to turn people into money.

Even after insurance had paid out on the loss of life, Duck remembered it was possible to get a thousand dollars from the manufacturer for a death clause that stated if someone died in one of their vehicles while wearing a seat belt, they would get $1,000. He was proud of himself for serving his earthly master. But, for me, watching Larry die the next day after his mysterious accident was a hard pill to swallow. He was bandaged from head to toe and had burns on over 70 percent of his body. It was like when he saw me, he wanted to scream something at me, but he had tubes going down his throat and all kinds of electrical monitors and gadgetry. I wish I could know what he was trying to say to me that day I watched him die. He began groaning when I entered the room. I was there with the Crocodile family and never forgot that day. I watched Larry die. I thought he was getting stronger. Because it seemed he remembered me and was trying to say something to me. But Mrs. Crocodile wasn't having it. I do remember how panicked she seemed. But I just chalked it up to being in the middle of this situation. So, I was a little ignorant— actually, I was very ignorant, because I didn't say anything when Larry's daughter came to see her father, and Mrs. Crocodile was waiting to lead her outside to "make some decisions."

It wasn't more than an hour later that the daughters agreed to pull the plug, so to say. He died shortly after. I felt for his girls because I remember Mrs. Crocodile would always get her way. I knew you didn't want to argue with her because it might cost you your life. She didn't play fair. It wasn't fair to me. I spent over an hour with Larry, sitting alive in the hospital bed next to me with him trying to tell me something. I watched Mrs. Crocodile shepherding to get money.

I couldn't believe how fast she convinced his daughters to pull the plug. I saw a lot of life left in Larry while they were in the next room talking in private.

A few days later, Mrs. Crocodile made an appearance at Larry's funeral. Larry's ex-wife of like fifteen years and their whole family were there. They all hated Mrs. Crocodile, and many suspected foul play, but she was well protected by those she was associated with. Remember the Alamo? The Crocodile family is just that famous. A direct line to worldly leaders had been established generations ago.

The first time Duck assaulted me; I gained my freedom. I sold one vehicle to buy another. As a seventeen-year-old, I was stepping up into a nicer vehicle after fixing my truck up to sell. I wasn't old enough to possess the paperwork associated with ownership. Duck and Linda both knew that and quite literally got off on it. Once the truck was gone and the Nissan was in the driveway, I was being manipulated again. I was told the first day not to drive it because of insurance. Duck took it upon himself to wash the car and clean the inside. I told him I would do it, but he said nothing. I did detail cars at my current job. I was a little confused about why he wouldn't let me help wash my own car. The next day, I was excited to drive the car to school, knowing the insurance company had been informed about the new car on the policy. But as I was leaving for school, I was looking for the keys to the Nissan. I had sold my truck so I could drive the Nissan. But the keys weren't anywhere. I looked and looked for them, and Linda saw me. She kind of started laughing. She just kept saying that I was going to be late for school and that I needed to drive the minivan. I hated driving that thing. I would get harassed by people like Brandon Mace. I didn't want to drive that thing without a gun. I had been boxed in before by other cars in the same area looking to get a reaction. She knew it. And I almost wanted to ride my bike instead of driving her piece of crap. But I needed to go to school. I had no choice; I drove it unwillingly. And I made it just in the nick of time to school.

The other two kids I played truth or dare with took great pride in telling everyone that I was driving my mommy's minivan. I don't have friends. I don't have family. Never have. I got home from school faster than anyone else that day. I needed to change and go to work. I got home even earlier than I used to, but Duck and Linda were gone, so was the Nissan. I missed work that day waiting for the Nissan to get there. At about 7:00 p.m., they got home, driving the Nissan. They had been riding around town with Duck's parents. I just consented to sit in the grass on the hill next to the driveway as they pulled in. Linda got out of the front passenger seat, holding fast-food drinks on a tray for my half-brother and half-sister. She kind of laughed and smiled as she asked how work was. I said I didn't have a ride. She scoffed and answered, "Really?"

I said, "Yeah, that's your van. You drive it."

That pissed everyone off, including both of Duck's parents, who left immediately. Linda instructed me to go to my bedroom. I do not know why I complied, probably because I was a good little slave still. When I finally got inside, my half-brother was sitting at his desk as if getting ready to watch.

Duck walked in after his parents left and began screaming at me about how he fucking hated me. He then wrapped both hands around my neck, picked me up, and pinned me against the wall. Linda and my half-brother and half-sister all laughed, watching as he held me there a few seconds. I imagine I was turning red as he slammed me down to the ground, only letting go with one hand to strike me square in my left eye. Then using both hands, he bounced my head off of the carpet twice before he spit in my face and said, "You're nothing, you piece of shit! You're lower than dirt!"

I felt a complete release. It felt like the opposite of falling. I began to rise like the flame being burned into a new creation. Alone is all I have. Alone protects me. I knew right then and right there those people were dead to me. I stood up, took the contents out of my pockets, and said, "You don't own me. I don't have anything of yours."

I walked out of the front door and began to run down the street. I made my way to the baseball fields just behind the gang-in-blue station, where I used a pay phone to call a friend's parents' house. I still remember the phone number. I briefly told her what happened, and she came to pick me up. That family allowed me to sleep in the guest room that night as we were to meet with my uncle the next day. He agreed it was a messed-up situation. I told him that if they needed to keep the Nissan to go ahead, just give me the money from my truck. That didn't happen. Instead, I was granted my emancipation proclamation and lived with my uncle the remainder of the school year because I didn't feel safe.

A week after the family violence, I was returned the Nissan because Duck and Linda could not comply with the four grand. At this point, at seventeen years old, I was no longer under their rules. That meant we had completely disassociated. Because they were and still are horrible people who don't know right from wrong, only how to stick with a plan and carry lies straight to the grave. Probably one of my biggest mistakes after forgiveness years later, was letting Duck and Linda help me build a custom home in Colley Wood. That particular neighborhood had governance, and those covenants limited what type of roof I could use. Strictly no asphalt roofs. So what did Duck use? The most expensive asphalt roof you could buy. It cost $17,000 plus all the legal fees and bullshit being involved with being that guy. I was mortified. I knew he was getting off on it by the way he kept contacting a lawyer and suggesting we do this or we do that. I finally told the lawyer in person to disregard what Duck wanted because I was the one paying the bills. It was through this mediation with my neighborhood association that I got to see Duck the master manipulator at work in his own element. I've seen many times his eyes like embers glowing, his smile that's hard to contain, and his hands all fidgety. His eyes would dart to the sides as if to see who was looking. I'd seen it so many times that I knew he was getting off by putting my balls in a vice. At this point, I had had enough of having any concern for Duck and Linda. The weird part though was that my ex-wife was not allowed to stop communication with Duck and Linda as I had. I kept explaining to her how those people had been trying to bury me for years. She knew but simply said that she was obligated. I figure that she was. I knew my ex-wife had had a covenant relationship with Linda long before she ever met me. I knew Linda and my ex-wife were secret best friends.

A few months later, Duck tried to reenter my life by saying he was suicidal. Linda and my half-brother and half-sister said he was driving somewhere, and they used his cell phone signal to triangulate between the cell towers to determine his exact location so they could send a sheriff and a mental health warrant. By the time I received that call, it was close to midnight. I was in my own home, and I hadn't spoken to them in months. Linda begged me to come by and help them. She tried to guilt-trip me into it. She thought that somehow, I could convince him not to kill himself, and then if he did kill himself, it would have been all my fault. I kind of laughed as I replied, "If the man is going to kill himself, then the man is going to kill himself. It's not my burden to carry. Just let him do it"

Linda replied swiftly, asking how I could live with myself if he actually did it and I said that. More guilt trips. I replied, "I have to work tomorrow, and it's late, regardless of the drama you're creating." I hung up and turn off the ringer. I could care less honestly. I'd seen that man reach for attention so many times that it would make you sick. They picked Duck up and locked him away for a psychiatric evaluation at JPS. Come to find out, somehow, he had his medical records sealed. I thought that was very strange. How do you carry on about hurting yourself, get a psychiatric evaluation, and do so without any public record? I mean there were public services used. Maybe he was just trying to figure out how the system works firsthand. That's the only conclusion I can come up with. Many have said Duck is bipolar and manic depressive, but I can only imagine that all of the bad things he has been involved with will come to a point someday.

It sounded like the same rhetoric I had heard so many times before. It's sounded eerily like what Duck's father had said many times before, how his claim to fame was that his sons would never go to jail. I kept thinking, *How do you get that kind of immunity?* I kept digging deeper. It was only a matter of time before all those things caught up to them. But somehow, Duck was immune to anything. I've often wondered exactly who his father made disappear for the elite for all the right reasons. I knew that there was a serious cover-up that everyone knew about, and the story kept changing. The people involved used it to go to Vietnam even longer. Yeah, do your homework on the Kennedy cover-up. Yup, my ancestor worked for Bell Helicopter at the time, and the economy in the area wasn't doing very well because of a president's desire to withdraw from Vietnam and stop being controlled by secret societies. It has been said over and over that doing so would lead you to certain death. I think we all know the speech that got Kenedy killed. Maybe this is mine. I've often wondered who many of his associates were, but who really knows? I do know that my King knows, and I pray he has mercy on them even though I know it's not up to me. I must pray that he has mercy on him for helping me share this story with you about how the King's love and mercy upon someone's life is everlasting and ever changing.

I've often heard Grandpa talk about how Kennedy was our last real president. I must say also that my ancestor was an incredible marksman. He taught his sons the same things, and I was fortunate enough to learn some of them as well. My ancestor had an outbuilding they called number 409. You had a typical type of workshop set up there with the pegboard and baby jars holding hardware suspended from the under shelves. There were lawn mowers, weed eaters, gas cans, and the musty aroma of a workshop. It was rather ordinary, except for the amount of hardware he had, not to mention the few different vices he used to hold tools. He even had a bullet loader (I think that's what it's called). It had a handle you could pull down so it would compress bullets. It is essential to make your own. He also had a magnifying glass that was on a pedestal as if to work on watches or something. I didn't recognize it until years later, but on the wall, sometimes I can remember there being a white one-inch strip of paper, almost like a barcode of sorts. I was always puzzled at the randomness of their patterns. Those strips of paper reminded me of what ballistics experts would use in forensics. But I was only a child I never really made that association until later in life. Those ancestors were excellent at gun making, gun smithing, as well as shooting. My ancestors always had and maybe still do have a very large assortment of guns. I personally can't stand them and refuse to own a gun. Maybe that's a trade secret; turning people into money. Essentially, I get it. This is how you crucify people. What's better than to delay punishment so you can lock someone up in a cage and throw away the key? They always bragged to me about their skills. It is even impressive to see how the Tarrant County medical examiner has recently been removed after decades so many instances of inconsistencies. I'm just an idiot. I won't ever learn ... or will I?

CHAPTER 7

Decision to Move

Okay, back to the plot. I was at work the next week after faking my own suicide. It was sensational! I decided I was moving. I was going to Colorado to pursue my dreams. I had composed my résumé and sent it out to a headhunter. I recognized a few places to check out. I got excited. I had been living in torture for so long. This wouldn't be easy though. My enemy owned Texas, I believed.

July 21st 2013, I had the boys when I decided to go to my current secretary's house and drop off some kids' movies because she had just adopted her sister's child because of failed drug tests on her sister's part. The boys and I were so happy to be able to share some classic movies, like *Cars, Baby Einstein, Veggie Tales,* and a few others. I knew at this point I was going to Colorado to seek employment, and I didn't want to have the burden of carrying a firearm across state lines without a permit. I asked her if I could keep it in her safe for a few days. I was still concerned because she worked for the dealership that I saw as corrupt, and her boss came with pulling strings. Then guess whom she would choose. I asked that she write on a note the time she started holding it for me, and she agreed. I watched her put it in her safe.

The boys and I left her house shortly after that. I felt better for the time because nobody could use my gun to make me look like a suicide. I needed some sleep. The boys and I got home, and I enjoyed my last few days before Colorado. During the next week I sought the assistance of a recruiter in my profession to line up some interviews for the nearest future. It was a success! I had three interviews lined up in less than a week. I drove to Colorado on July 25th 2013, the next Thursday night. Seriously, I drove all through the night and got to Aurora for an interview at the GMC place. The second place I went was Alpine or something, it was a smaller independent shop. It felt weird because the concubine wouldn't let me out of her sight. Even in the shop, she wasn't far. I kind of hoped she would stay in the car but to no avail. I had to make it seem I had no interest in this place. I didn't even bother to follow through with the third place because my time was running out. I liked the dealership I went to first, but I already knew that if I let on to either place, the concubine would try to ruin that for me. So I acted like I was going to work there at the second place I interviewed, all the while, I saw what I liked at the GMC dealer. I didn't let on at all that that was where I wanted to work.

July 26th 2013 after the interviews, the concubine and I went to a hotel just off of Federal Drive. That was where the concubine and I were staying for the night. The concubine chose the hotel because she said she got a discount for being a federal employee. while she was at the desk checking in, I felt uncomfortable because I had left my backpack with my journals in her car. I did not want to lose sight of my backpack with my journals because I knew how much she hated them. I just kept figuring out her game and how it was done. *Girlfriend revenge* it is commonly called. She told me early on she had heard that this one wouldn't be easy, referring to me, as if there were others prior to my introduction. There in the evening just before the sun set, I went outside for a cigarette and I happened to see a car I recognized parked in the adjacent parking lot behind a bus. It had Texas license plates and all. I was flattered to see the blond hair, blue eyes, and blond goatee with pointy eyeteeth and spiky hair. It kind of looked like Brant Lane or Jared Darnette because of how light their hair was. In reptilian fasion, **b**oth of them were fake, only just typical backstabbers who love to watch someone suffer while trying to inflict punishment when punishment would not normally occur. I like to think of them a pharisees. I'm guessing it was Brant Lane. That's when and how I remembered he got roped into this. I'm sure he was blackmailed prom night because of the incident with his date. He got caught trying to take something that wasn't his as an adult. His prom date bragged that she owned him and even took her brothers around to scare him. She got off on it and bragged about how he had to do exactly as she said. I didn't agree because anybody could make up something about anybody they didn't like. If she wanted justice, she could have gotten it, but she wanted revenge instead, though that's how he got involved by being blackmailed. I almost feel sorry for him, but I know based on how two-faced he is, he must have a front-row seat in hell. I pulled my phone out of my pocket and took a photo of him. Then I began to approach the vehicle where he saw me. It looked like he had seen a ghost. I'm pretty sure he happened to see my reflection in the tablet screen that he was staring at. It looked like he was watching porn. As soon as he saw me, he put his white Sebring in gear and fled. I kind of laughed because I was putting more pieces together and was honored that someone would travel so far to manipulate me. Mirth is hilarious actually. Keep looking.

I went back to the hotel. That was where I went, back up to the room. I began taking more notes, and you could tell that it bothered the concubine severely. The room I was staying in was located almost at the end of the hall, just one room away from the corner room. Our room was connected to the corner room by a door inside the room that both parties would have to unlock to gain access. Shortly after I journaled some more, the concubine suggested that we go get dinner. I assumed she would do anything to keep me from writing more things down that she didn't want anyone to read. There was a burger place within walking distance, so I obliged. I had a cheeseburger and then some cookie bites. Again, I felt like those cookie bites might have had something in them because after getting on the elevator to the room, I noticed I was lightheaded. I was ready for bed. I was actually sleeping on my backpack, using it as a body pillow. I had no interest already. I knew any reaction equaled conviction. I went to sleep and woke up slightly to what sounded like the concubine in the next room with the headboard slamming against the wall.

I woke up the next morning Saturday July 27th, to her coming into the room and plopping down on the bed. I knew she was completely full of shit, but I knew better than to react because that was what her job was—to create a situation that my ex-wife's family could capitalize on. She begged me to sleep with her, citing how I was too tired the previous night, citing that it seemed like I was just using her. I asked her what her number was, meaning how many people she had been with sexually. She said seven. I laughed because I knew better than that with the meat curtains she had hanging from her vagina. I could tell seven was very conservative. Yeah, maybe in middle school. I figured I still had a large audience, so I began looking for the camera. That was when she was trying to create something. I knew. I said, while looking at her, "I can't marry you. I just want to be single and have group sex. I'm sorry."

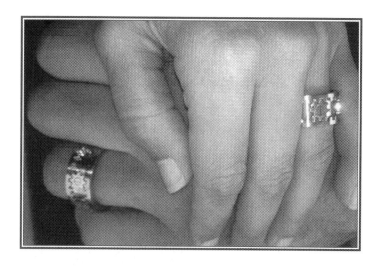

I was lying, halfway. No way did I want to marry her. I couldn't. Even though she bought me a ring that reminded me of a Geneva Stop used in film production. The ring was made from stainless steel and had gears on it in which the outer rings would rotate in opposite directions due to the stationary gears in the middle. In true to life rhetoric, it didn't fit my hand. The concubine was and is a total Sicko. And no way did I want to have group sex. I wanted to squash her manipulation. Thankfully in that moment, I was reminded of a time with a beautiful girl named Amanda. She explained to me how all of us actually get sloppy seconds. When you think about it like that, it doesn't really bother you. As the concubine kept trying to get me to sleep with her, I kept looking for the camera. I knew at this point my life was being used for entertainment. I'm sure she felt assured, based on the phone records and her trips to the White House. You got to wonder whom she called to get into the houses of Congress at the last second. Well, it was in the phone records. I guess being a federal employee entitles you to special rights to act inhuman. I was like, *Whatever*, so I complied as she held my head down, and I thought to myself, *There is your money shot*. I washed her feet, finished up, took a shower quickly, and went downstairs for breakfast. There, as I was getting coffee, it looked like someone I knew was trying to get my attention. I recognized Travis Dovey's brother Chris Dovey. He looked very sickly; he was pale and lightweight, almost as if he had cancer. He gave me a firm look down and up with a smile. It was as if he was looking for a reaction, and I just wasn't giving anything. I ate breakfast because I didn't care. I wanted to check out some apartments in the area. So the concubine and I went and looked at some of the foothills.

She received a call from an old friend. The old friend lived in Denver. She said that he used to live on the street just over from her growing up. He was my age and had moved to Denver before graduation. She said his name was Brandon, but I recognized him right away. I had taken karate with this kid back in elementary school. We met at a place called Snooze for brunch. As soon as we ordered, he and his girlfriend got a call on their cell phone. They went outside and were gone for a while before they came back, laughing and claiming that they were chatting with their landlord. I knew better because I knew it was my Pharisees outside showing them my smear campaign. I'd seen my half-brother hand out nondisclosure agreements like they were candy. I even saw a telephone technician get one for putting his phone line back together. I imagine the legal representation behind them is a gentleman from San Francisco I went to high school with and/or an entertainment lawyer, a direct associate of the Barnes that I burned down with their own matches. It's a lot like rage entertainment. I've seen it over and over, so many concubines. No wonder some people don't have the ability to think. The gentleman I went to karate class with in elementary school couldn't stop grinning ear to ear as he smiled at me across the dining table. I figured that he had changed his name and moved two states away to avoid prosecution for what he did to Cassie that night in his ninety's Nissan when she was too drunk from his beer to even try to fight back. It wasn't about a month after that incident in high school that he had moved and never been heard from again.

I know just before he left the area, he got the beat down from others on the soccer team. Before this, he had been longtime friends with those kids I played matches with, so you can imagine my wonder as to why he changed his name. I was honestly surprised to see him again even though he had changed his look, the mediocrity was still ever-present. After brunch, we went to their place. The concubine wanted to ride with him in his car, but I was like hell no. We went to his house. He lived in an older home that was subdivided. Theirs was the top floor. Judging by the artwork on his walls, he had plenty of practice with his camera. They offered to make some tea, but I saw him put something in the drink for me I looked straight at him, put it up to my nose, and smelled it. It didn't smell right. I kept my eye contact with him and simply said, "No, thanks." His jaw dropped. We spent a few moments chatting about insignificant nothingness. I was mainly interested in Colorado life. I asked questions about Aurora, and they both agreed that in their opinion, Aurora was the armpit of Colorado. Denver was where I should be. I led them on in front of the concubine on purpose. I wanted them to continue to think I wanted to work for that small independent shop so they wouldn't bother my current opportunity at the dealership. As I walked around his place looking at his artistic creations framed and put on display, I did enjoy seeing a unique hand drawn piece of art that he created. Apparently, he liked to draw. It was in an obese gentleman looking at himself in the mirror; he looked like a beautiful woman in the reflection of the mirror that he was holding. Surrounding the man in the drawing was a thousand pieces of the artwork, all of them were tongues on a handle. There must have been a thousand or more tongues on this thirteen-by-nine drawing. The artist's work that spoke in rhetoric was stunning.

When I showed it to the concubine, her jaw dropped, and I asked the artist, "What do you call it?"

He said, "Narcissist."

I thought, *Well played.* I actually offered to buy it from him for fifty dollars. He politely declined, and the two of them began planning to stay overnight there. I wanted out. I had made up my mind I wanted to go back and move my life. But she wasn't leaving that easily. She wanted to go to dinner and party with them. I finally convinced her to take me to some other apartment from there. We stayed on the road. I had to make sure to call them to tell them I didn't want to hang out with them. I was completely fine with not being around those fake people. I would much rather fake people hate me anyway.

On our ride home Saturday July 27th 2013, we hadn't made it out of Colorado before I noticed the same guy driving the blue FJ Land Cruiser with black wheels. It was the soccer coach with the American eagles. We passed him on the highway numerous times. As we passed him on his left, he was driving, so we got a good look at his face. You could see his smile drop because he was nervous when I looked directly at him in the eye. I knew what he was doing was actually organized crime at the highest level, and how I hated that so many resources would be employed to create a situation to capitalize on. We also passed Linda and my half-sister riding in the light-colored pearl Buick with dark-tinted windows. I kind of laughed because I already knew because my King told me in so many ways, I'd be just fine. I decided to try to get my own reaction, as she was paying attention to my every move. I decided to copy all twelve months of phone records and put them onto a memory card, a new one. As she drove, I used my computer to compile all the pieces and put them on a SD card. You could see it was bothering her. Her jaw dropped, and she gasped when I put it into the watch pocket of my jeans. It was a very long drive back to Texas. Somewhere after midnight, she asked me to drive. While driving, I looked up the address that I wanted to mail the phone records to on my phone. That was where I remembered that the post office required the lobbies to stay open twenty-four hours a day. I decided I would wait until she was sound asleep and there was no traffic. Then I would stop in a random town at the post office. The small town that I stopped in was Childress, Texas. I mailed a copy of her phone records and a few other pieces to someone who wanted to see me succeed. I could tell this alarmed the concubine, and I liked it. I just stopped without her waking, and when I got back to the car, she was extremely alarmed as to what I had just done. She woke up promptly and suggested we stopped for gas in the next town. I agreed. I pulled up to the pump, and she jumped out of the car and began calling someone.

The concubine went straight into the bathroom of the gas station as I stood by the car patiently. About that time, a family in a black Tahoe pulled up to the opposite side pump. I was so thankful because it felt like again my King was right there with me. As she came out of the service station, she asked if I was done. I said, "No, it's your turn."

About the time she got close to me, another older Chevy Suburban began driving down the highway toward us from a nearby neighborhood. You could tell he wanted to be a gang banger or the real thing by the way he drove his candy-painted Tahoe with massive rims and a pit bull riding in the backseat. When he pulled up, you could clearly see him put a weapon where his belt buckle would be and pull his shirt down to conceal it. I was standing outside the car at this point, still finishing the cigarette I had lit after the concubine began fueling. He did not take his eyes off of me as he exited his vehicle and entered the store. I decided to stand closer. As he looked enraged, I smiled calmly. Just then, that family of four walked out of the convenience store. They happened to stay just between us, just between him and me. I've often wondered if that wasn't the hand of my King once again. But I did not have time to stick around. I was moving to Colorado. She drove from that point on, as I didn't wake up until probably 7:00 a.m. Sunday July 29th 2013 around the Denton area.

The concubine stated that we were going to church at the Gateway. I kept thinking, *I'm not going anywhere with you, not now, not ever.* I suggested that she drop me off at work so I could get my SUV. She did.

I walked up to the body shop and let myself in. I had some more journaling to do. I got free around eight thirty or so on Sunday July 28th 2013. I sat in the break room while I was juggling more about who, what, and when. That was when my work stalkers happened to show up out of the blue. The paintless dent repair guy of course wanted to check on me. He laughed and walked away. Soon after, the cleanup crew guy came and checked on me. He had told me many times about how a ministry had rescued him and gotten him the job there and that the car he was driving was also theirs. I tested my theory about who he was by walking around the shop as he casually followed me. I actually began getting off on it. I enjoyed seeing him try to get a reaction out of me as he kept using his phone to call someone each time I was in a new place. I used the work computer to upload a video I made that contained screenshots that I took and used text from the concubine's phone records to deliver my ex-wife's family's different justifications. I'm used to being taken to court, being accused of being on drugs, so I understand how a setup works.

I uploaded the video using a computer where I kept the settings to private, and a few minutes later, when I checked it again, it already had another view. So, I knew that my audience had seen it. I promptly deleted it because I wanted to have some of those documented, as if to say, "I know, and I don't care. Get a life." I decided to leave around 1:00 p.m. or so, but my SUV was locked behind the pipe fence that surrounded the dealership. Then I walked the seven-plus miles back to my place on Quality Hill. I was thankful to do so. My once broken knee was feeling fine that day.

Along the way, I was blessed to see many of my biggest fans. I saw a few of them circle me a few times, and it made me feel famous. It felt like an amazing honor to be at the King's right hand. It's really funny how I walked on the trail that runs right next to the railroad tracks where all the blind sheep have no idea the train's coming. I was being gang stalked, and I didn't care. I stopped by the gas station on the highway where the Mustangs were, and I bought a Gatorade drink. I drank most of it before filling it with water. I sat and just watched as a gentleman in a white Tahoe pulled up to get fuel. I kind of laughed because he pulled into the wrong side of the pump as if he wasn't paying attention or wasn't familiar with the car. It was a brand-new Suburban and still had the papers on the window, probably from the dealership where I worked at the time. Either way, after correcting his mistake, he walked in and looked directly at me. He started laughing as I smiled. He went to the counter and asked to prepay for five dollars at the pump he was parked at and wanted a receipt.

I kind of laughed even harder. Seriously? What kind of loser drove around a brand-new four-wheel-drive Suburban and didn't know what side to put the fuel in and then also asked for a receipt for a mere five-dollar purchase. Only puppets, that's all I know. Why even stop for five dollars? You've probably wasted five bucks if you're pulling in and out while driving around the gas pumps. It was probably just to try to make me feel something I was not feeling. Did it work?

I didn't care, nor do I care what people think. I know the goal of gang stalking a victim is to invite peers to create a mental illness from the symptoms that are carried out. It's easiest done in a small-town setting and is designed to be a one-way ticket to hell, if you will. It's carried out by people who owe their life for favors they cannot return. So, I assumed that this gentleman was involved in the gang stalking that meant he was actually a slave.

As I walked down the path next to the railroad tracks toward my house on Quality Hill, I was honored to see the woman who told me she would rip off my arms and legs, pull out my tongue, and feed my eyes just before they sewed them shut driving down the road. You could see her husband in the front seat. It looked as if he was begging her not to do something, but she looked like a psycho. She was laughing and carrying on, raising her fist in protest. I had no idea because I didn't know those people, obviously. I thought it was odd how they were driving their neighbor's vehicle instead of their own. Were they scared for me to see them? You could see visibly that an argument was taking place in the front seat between them. It honestly looked like he was pleading with her about something. I didn't care. I still had no idea yet; I just kept walking and actually made it home to where I was able to plug my phone in.

After a few minutes, I got it to power on. It was probably 6:00 p.m. or later at this point. I called my ex-wife and asked if she would bring my kids over because it was my visitation. She agreed, and they showed up. We had a few minutes in the pool before we went inside, and I explained to them about Colorado and how my SUV was at my work. I explained to them that we had some choices about how to get my SUV. We all agreed to go to bed early and get up early to walk the seven miles back to work. Monday July 29th 2013, we left before 5:00 a.m., and my older son was wearing a Camelback to aid in hydration. My younger son was excited about riding a scooter all that way. It was still dark out as we left. It was a very long walk, and my youngest son probably did twice the distance with how much he rode his scooter back and forth past us on the trail.

The long walk gave the boys and me time to talk about how this wasn't what Daddy wanted for their lives, but the system was broken, and long, long ago, somebody corrupt gave money all the power. I'm pretty sure I know who, how, why, and when.

As we were walking together down the same railroad tracks, right then and there, I came to realize just how much pull the dealership I worked for had. I had seen the district-appointed judge getting his yellow Corvette serviced. I also knew almost every federal and local law enforcement member in a very intimate fashion. By way of helping ensure the safety of patrol cars and ensuring budgets were met with fleet vehicles, yeah, the man was kind of untouchable because he had been so well connected. Just for grins, I looked at the key that I held in my hand that unlocked the shop where I worked. Just as I suspected, Michael made the key for the shop. As I understood it, they serviced all of the dealerships. I also understood that was who also serviced my house when I was not asking for it. I remember that they got all of their vehicles for their business from the same dealership where I worked. I decided that in great detail, I must document who was in bed with one another because it was shocking and sad and so unbelievable all the same time. It was a disgrace. It sounded like shepherding the blind sheep to be honest with you.

The boys and I made our way to my work. My older son was so sweet to keep his arm around me and not even lose his grip as we passed by one of the American Eagles, whose dad ran the dealership. I imagined all the plotting and scheming that took place for so many years at soccer practice with the miracle man whose Barnes I burned down. Wolf in sheep's clothing. I was laughing.

My boy could see it. I knew what was coming next and chose not to react. I kept wearing a smile. That was the legend. I knew if I did anything more than smile, he would report to his owner that I was sad or something and probably make it look like a suicide. Smiling in the face of my enemies was how the unicorn was made. So, say it to my face if you have any integrity. I didn't think so.

Some people believe that rape is all right if it's on camera and they can justify their actions. So sad the mediocrity I'm surrounded by. I kept my head held high as we made our way to the body shop, where my half-brother's associate was waiting for us on the side of the building. The puppet I call Poison Ivy took a photo of my older son and me walking up to the shop, while having a cynical look on his face. Some people will do anything for money. How's that new car? The puppet I liked to call Poison Ivy, for obvious reasons, held a disgusted look upon his face.

I could care less. I knew he hated me. He was my half-brother's puppet and planned to get rich off of a life insurance policy deposited into an offshore bank account, the Bank of Grand Cayman, and the account that he had set up in June of 2000. I can still remember when we went on vacation with Duck and Linda early 2000's. And yet the whole time, he denied any connection with my half-brother. I mean for the King's sake, they went to the same high school together, both being outcast from the original high school. They went to a high school called Bridges together. It was for people who didn't have social skills. This coworker who was a stalker of mine was raised in the same cult that I was raised. However, he wasn't free. The best, most organized criminals get off lying, I didn't know how much clearer I could make this. You do not get a reaction out of me. I remember the stainless-steel chain you wore around your neck with the larger diameter and your spiky hair. I remember the trip to get your bank account. Other people were there. Even the guy who got my ex-wife her job at the insurance company so she could write policy on me. He was there with his wife, who also went with you to get your bank account to help pay for my smear. Remember? Would you like me to put out the account numbers? I only smile, knowing I gave him, as well as the concubine, poison ivy on his back and bare ass. It was so funny. It was the day he took delivery of his new car, the Audi A7.

Several weeks prior, on June 18th 2013, I was so excited I was watching the sun come up when I knew to smear the poison ivy on my comforter to see who wanted some. I was so flattered when I saw it and began tickling his poison ivy rash with my paper days later. Remember how funny that was? Your mommy was associated with the wallpaper pastor. You've been raised in the cult too. I thought it was too funny how your girlfriend was told it was a skin condition. Has it been back? How do I taste? Hmm? That was three grand cash toward the down payment of your new Audi, right? Just what you needed for your new car. I remember when you were watching me tell our secretary about my hidden cameras. I liked the look I saw on your face. It was funny. I watched you signal her and solicit her for my ancestors when you thought I wasn't looking. I laughed. That was August 1st 2013 when she left early for lunch and began acting weird. It's so sad how mediocre fake people are. Was I supposed to feel that? I thought it was super funny when you drove down my street like a madman after getting your new car. I couldn't tell, but it looked like you were wearing the same shirt in the car still, and I've always wondered if you got the poison ivy, I left for you on your seats. I thought it was funny how the concubine got it too. I mean, I kept trying to tell them. Smile. I could tell it bothered this guy. He was well known as an associate from my ex-wife's youth group. He refused to be honest about it; it's so sad. Thankfully that day July 29th 2013, my older son was with me. I kept calm. I saw coworkers laughing and paid no attention. My manager was the most persistent. He looked like Billy Ray Cyrus, complete with his mullet and cheesy smile. I smile back because I knew I'd be just fine. I cherish those memories.

That day, we left work in my SUV and picked up my younger son from day care, where I recognized a lady from the accounting department at my work picking up her kids. When she saw the three of us, she began laughing. I don't know why, nor did I really care. I was picking up my boys. We headed home, and it was nice. I enjoyed it. I cherished every moment with them. I think we played for a while before going to bed. The concubine tried calling a few times, but I wasn't around the next morning. I was awakened by the concubine banging on my door. It was super early. The kids weren't ready for school yet, but we were eating breakfast. She was in a panic as she asked me for her phone records. I held fast at the door opening, as it looked like she was trying to make her way into my place. That was when I saw the confusion in her eyes from my own. I simply replied, "No. Not yet. The King said it's not time yet and not to trust you." Her jaw fell to the floor.

She got emotional as she left. I seriously didn't care.

That day at work, I had been cluing in on how intentionally my half-brother's associate from the family vacation and his high school were stalking me. Many times, I noticed him snooping around my toolbox, looking for something while on his cell phone. He was even taking pictures of my son and me. I wondered what kind of strings he had wrapped around his neck, but judging from the new Audi A7, I figured they were pretty big. So, I decided to see, as the whole time I was in Colorado, the concubine kept asking where my gun was. I figured something was up. He knew what he signed up for. Sometimes organized criminals need to be flashy. That's one guy you will see driving toward you a mile away.

CHAPTER 8

Colorado Trip

The next day at work August 2nd 2013, I had been cluing in on how intentionally my half-brother's associate was stalking me. Many times, I noticed him snooping around my toolbox, looking for something while on his cell phone, even taking pictures of my son and me. I wondered what kind of strings he had wrapped around his neck, but judging from the new Audi A7, I figured they were pretty big. I decided to see, as the whole time in Colorado, the concubine kept asking where my gun was. I figured something was up, especially knowing how closely he was watching me. I decided to try to get my own reaction. I decided to create the illusion that people want to believe, knowing that the secretary and my coworker were both involved with my ancestors' smear campaign. I would ask the secretary about the note just in earshot, loud enough that my half-brother's associate could hear me. His desk was just across from my secretary.

As I began to talk to the secretary, I saw his eyes perk up. Like a kid in grade school, he was waving his hands at someone else to get the answers to a test. He was completely silent as if to get her attention without getting mine. I thought to myself, *Go ahead, sucker.* After confirming the note about having my gun just within earshot of my stalker, I went back to work like nothing.

That particular day, the secretary and I were going to go to lunch. But instead, she sent a bogus text about going to Walmart. As she left from work before our usual lunchtime, she drove a little strangely in her white four-door pickup. She drove as if it were a race car. She just gunned the throttle across the parking lot. I don't know for what reason, but I figured something was up. It was enough for me. I decided that I couldn't trust her. I was then reminded that she was the beneficiary of the life insurance policy that I had in place at that job. I did not put family as the beneficiary of my life insurance. It's not for anyone I know because I know they would try to collect early. I also remembered her telling me about how her daughter was raped as a child and that if she could get revenge someday, she would. I began to question really probably too deep. Was that possibly the motive for trying to stab me in the back?

After she got back from lunch, I casually asked her about it. And she said she was so excited that she went out to lunch with a new guy. The new guy had lots of money, she exclaimed. She showed me a photo of his place, and I recognized a couple of cars there parked next to a bird bath looking fountain in front of a large expensive house. I was blown away. She just had lunch with people who claimed to be my ancestors. And I knew the only reason they wanted to meet with her was because she was to become a slave. I figured something was up because of how giddy she had now begun acting. This was a new guy the same week as the last guy.

The boys and I got home from work and chilled a bit before bed. The older one wanted to sleep in my bed that night, being scared or something. The next morning August 3rd 2013, I woke up to the sound of a car door. I looked out my window, and I didn't see anybody. It was at this time Logan was waking up next to me. I was trying to look out the window from my position in bed. I again was alarmed. I thought to myself, *What the fuck?* as the boys got dressed and we are about to leave. That was when I texted my secretary, asking her to bring my gun to work that day. I knew she was the beneficiary of my $100,000 life insurance policy. It was a policy that came with working there. I refused to list a beneficiary because I don't have family. She was written into the box when I had only been there ninety days. I knew based on phone records my ancestors always contact coworkers and pay them to get their hands dirty instead. I didn't wait for a reply; instead, I went outside to notice my Tahoe had been moved because the wheels were turned and the boat was now unhooked from my hitch. I noticed immediately. I felt my hood, and it was warm. I unchained my boat from the carport where I normally kept it locked and hooked it back up to my SUV.

We headed to work and school. I dropped the younger one off and then the older went with me to work. I got to work early enough to beat the secretary there. After we pulled up and parked in the closest spot nearest the body shop with my boat in tandem, my son and I began to walk to the shop when the secretary pulled up. She kept looking around nervously. I didn't see any reason. But when I asked to get it, she insisted on parking first. So, my son and I followed her to her truck, where I got it out of her passenger floorboard. She insisted that I immediately go put the gun in my SUV. As she said it, I kept thinking, *Yeah, thanks for the insight.* I put it into my backpack, and I watched her watch me walk to my SUV. I walked to the passenger rear door and opened it to look through the driver's side window to see her on her cell phone, still looking at me. I decided right then and right there I was not letting this thing out of my sight. I closed my rear door and calmly walked back into work, where my son was standing by the door waiting for me, not letting me out of his sight.

As the work day began, I noticed how many coworkers were intent on surveying my work area, asking to look for certain tools in my toolbox and making sure the cameras were pointed right at me. I asked my son to do a job for me. As a distraction to us both, knowing he had a watchful eye, I asked him to go clean out my boat. He knew to take all of the empty soda cans and candy wrappers and put them in a trash bag to get ready for the next time we went out to the lake. I gave him a smaller twelve-by-twelve box to put all the trash in. He walked a hundred yards away to where my SUV and boat were and was gone about twenty minutes.

When he came running back before 10:00 am, he told me that he had seen my half-brother sitting in a black car that was parked next to the SUV. He said he knew it was my half-brother and that he was eating a burrito from Sonic. I figured that was him going behind me. *What does he want now?* So, I was even more aware since I knew my audience was using my work cameras that Dan the man helped set up. I decided to switch the backpacks from the monster bag to the red bag. I needed a curtain. That's when I pulled a car into my stall and rolled over one of my parts carts that held all the hardware from the vehicles I disassembled. I made sure to park that thing in front of the camera view. I only had about fifteen seconds before the paintless dent repair guy came walking by on his cell phone, but it was enough.

At this point, I needed my enemies to think my weapon was in the black backpack. About twenty minutes later, a gentleman who was an associate of the crocodile lady stopped by the back door of the shop. He looked to be in a panic. He told me he had just had an accident and that I needed to see it. So I made it a point to make sure the camera saw me lock my black backpack in my toolbox as Logan sat next to the red one. I took great pride in making sure that people had seen me do this, including the crocodile lady's puppet. His right fender and door were indeed scratched. It looked fresh. I told him to talk to a gentleman who worked there as an estimator.

You could tell by the way they smiled at one another they already knew each other. Even the special handshake was the typical club handshake that I recognized. I knew that his wife had worked with Mrs. Crocodile for years at the public library in Colley Wood with the Mayor. That was why I figured he was there. He was their eyes and ears. As he was standing there looking at his truck, I went back inside, where my son was patiently waiting to go to lunch. I decided I had seen enough of my enemy that day. I was not going to give anyone a reaction. I was going to get rid of this gun before something happened to me. My son and I drove to the lake, where I conveniently saw an associate of the crocodile lady who was involved in Boy Scouts sitting there fishing on the water in their boat not far from where I launched mine. I launched my boat into the water as we drove to a shallow sandbar, where I threw it in still locked and assembled. That way, nobody could use it to hurt me and claim suicide. I circled back and put the boat onto the trailer, and my son and I began heading back to work. As we drove back down Main Street, we stopped at a fast-food place, Jack in the Box. There was Linda's friend Nicole. I almost didn't recognize her because I noticed that she had her child lying on the table not wearing anything except a diaper. She wasn't there to eat because obviously there was no food in front of her. I knew her mother was a coconspirator with Linda. But I was baffled as to why she made it a point to be sitting there not eating as she used her cell phone and her eyes drew from us to outside, kind of in the direction of where our boat was parked. I looked in the direction of her gaze and saw several new black SUVs pulling into the deli just behind where I was. There were a couple of Tahoes, a couple of Suburbans, and a couple of Escalades, all black. Men wearing suits got out, and they did not look very happy.

I told my son to go stand by the boat to make sure nothing happened to it. I'd get our food. I walked back to my SUV, which was hooked to my boat in the parking lot of the fast-food place. I decided to park a little closer to the building at my work when we got back. And as I walked in, I was passed by the gentleman who was just giving the Crocodile Lady's associate an estimate. He was laughing and holding his camera. I slowed my pace as I kept my hand on my son's shoulder and turned to watch him go out to the parking lot and take pictures of my boat with his work camera.

Rod was easy to spot with the scar on his face that he acquired while working with me briefly at an independent collision repair place. He got the giant scar on the right side of his face shortly before losing his job there when he was caught saying one thing and expecting another in regard to a vehicle that I had to work on for his friend. I also figured that by the way he was acting, knowing the gentleman who was just there, he would laugh at the worst things and get off trying to torment me. I know you were still up to no good. I figured he was trying to sell pictures as my half-brother used to exclaim. As my son and I watched coworkers who were planning to get rich and serve one cause under the perception that nobody would know, I was honored to take notes. I knew it bothered them. Before I could even finish lunch, I was approached by the paintless dent repair guy asking if I went out on the lake at lunch. You could tell by the way he was clenching his jaw something was bothering him. Plus, his eyes look like glowing embers.

I simply said, "We tried out the propeller." That's a true story. He grimaced as he retreated. I kind of laughed under my breath. This gentleman worked for that dealer for more than twenty years. He made a great living doing so and was well connected in the community. So it would be no surprise for him to just follow orders. As a matter of fact, I had seen him try to suggest cars were following me in the past. I knew his game. I'd seen it before.

It's really a small town when you think about it. I took note of how many times the paintless dent repair guy walked by me with his fists clenched. He looked like a bulldog in a way, but I wasn't scared. I suppose he was suppressing the hate procured by the hearsay my ancestors spread about me to control me. Passive aggressive I suppose you could say. I had already walked through a suicide and an abortion. What did I have to be scared of? All my coworkers know and participate in my very public smear. I noticed an old apprentice of mine and an associate of his talking in the corner, and as I approached them, they dispersed immediately and started laughing collectively. I think I had had enough at this point, but I didn't know for sure. I was kind of getting off on it. I felt the opposite of falling. I knew both of them, but how was my apprentice connected? That was when I remembered my apprentice was the cousin of an ex-girlfriend and that his cousin, her husband, worked in the DNA business. My apprentice had mentioned before that he had met his wife in the covenant church, the same covenant church that my ex-wife and her family helped start. You could tell the two of them had an arranged marriage. He alluded to that on more than one occasion. I was originally introduced by to him by my half-brother's associates shortly after my divorce. The apprentice I had paid to help me finish my deck that my half-brother destroyed ended up working with me at the dealership as my princess for several months. He was a shepherd early on, and now I knew.

That was the spark that lit the flame to the memory of when I hired him and began to notice him hiding various tools and sometimes even hardware. Then he would deny having them when I asked. As soon as I left the area, he would be there with Dan the man, laughing about it and putting them back. I know they were looking for a reaction, and I didn't give chase. It actually got bad enough that I ended up painting all of my tools with spray paint so it was easier to see when it was actually mine and who had it. No longer was ignorance bliss, and it was no longer acceptable to say I didn't know because all of my tools had been spray-painted. I knew the apprentice was as fake as they come. I also knew his real friends were the heads of the dealership. I even went out on a boat with him years before to Party Cove on Lake Dallas. It seemed as though my apprentice was an opportunist who traded his integrity for opportunity every chance he got. But whom did he owe, and how was he recruited? That was when I remembered the instance the apprentice showed up in my life. I was introduced by a stalker when he was recovering from an injury to his hand. He had torn up his fingers pretty badly while using a chainsaw blade on a grinder to carve wood. I knew he had to have surgeries and pins and his wife was not making much money at all. They also had the child and one on the way soon. That must have been an expensive accident, but the hardest part was Tony never, ever mentioned his medical bills. I never even heard about the simplest copay or coinsurance or any debt associated with that. Could it be that was because it didn't cost him a thing, and he was now doing favors for sociopaths who wanted me dead? Or was he simply trying to look good for the boss? Either way, it didn't matter what I said. Because it would be his desire to twist everything I said to the max. His tactic was to smear, and it was a campaign he was after. So when I saw them disperse, laughing. I decided it was best not to talk.

2010

finger puppet

Before I finished my work that day, I sent my lawyer an email stating that I knew what Geneva's puppet the concubine was up, to and didn't know what she was capable of. I didn't want any recourse, nor did I want any change otherwise. In response, my lawyer had another person in her office call me to say she wasn't allowed to represent me anymore. That was when I remembered my lawyer meeting with the concubine in private. That was the day of my son's field day at school in May of 2013. I might not have known, but I showed up to my appointment at my lawyer's office about fifteen minutes early, and I saw the concubine sitting in my lawyer's office talking to her in private. I patiently waited. When the concubine was exiting my lawyer's office, she paid her a few thousand dollars. The look the concubine gave me was stellar. I got excited at the look that was the most go-to-hell look you've ever seen. It was exciting because normally the concubine has to wear her sweet and innocent mask but not that day. I'm pretty sure that's when the lawyer signed a nondisclosure agreement or gag order because from that point on she didn't want to help. Instead, she did trivial tasks and charged accordingly. I knew the racket. I had seen it so many other times, so I paid my bill with her. I knew I didn't need to waste any more of my time. Initially, this lawyer was great representation when I needed her. She helped me when my ex accused me of being on drugs. I sold a Camaro that I had and paid her cash to represent me at the last minute, of course, in true underdog fashion. That was an amazing victory in court on August 15th 2012. To be honest, the shit was nuts. Geneva accused me of being on drugs and even told my kids the same thing. She then secreted the kids at her friend's house. The friend was also involved in their cult during the court hearing.

My lawyer at the time was shocked at how dirty she was playing.

But one of the best parts about that day was when my attorney let her attorney have it. Then my ex-wife got it, and when she walked out of those doors, Geneva was bawling. Tears were running down both cheeks, and she quivered as she inhaled. I am honored to have seen that. It was almost real, what was happening right before my very eyes. My attorney used my hair test taken a few days prior to prove in fact that I did not do drugs.

I did tell my attorney that I knew about her and the concubine or coconspirators and that after my ex-wife had left because of marijuana, I'd given the concubine every opportunity to do the same thing by using a dugout filled with tobacco. The dugout is the same smoking tool that my ex-wife found and associated with my marijuana use. Like a rope a dope, I make sure she thinks I'm on drugs because we both know after three failed attempts, the kids are automatically mine by default. I showed my attorney the dugout and took photos and even placed them in my file. I wanted them to keep trying. I wanted them to think I was high when I was paying close attention to what they were doing. Maybe that was why my ex-wife was so emotional at her loss in court because she had planned to move to a new address out in East Texas by the lake I grew up going to. The attorney stopped that, and it was a glorious victory. My little unicorns and I got to make up that time together, and we used it to go to the lake and play on our boat in the sun. What an amazing experience!

That was a long time ago. I've learned enough about her games to understand what's really happening. I am fully aware of that based on the cult I was raised by without choice. I've already seen many times over that shepherding is actually murder for hire. It's carried out by cowards who trade their integrity for opportunity because they lack the virtues to sustain themselves otherwise.

CHAPTER 9

The Strongest Slaves Become Ghosts

I have seen in my own personal life that when you love money more than life, you may lose yours chasing someone else's. All things work together to serve something higher, even those who don't know. I believe the Bible is pretty clear on that. Is the ax stronger than the person who swings it? Can a cane walk itself? Is the master truly greater than the slave? I think when you involve money to pay for lies, you have removed the King from the situation completely. Of course, I wasn't aware that was how He works until later in life. It has taken a lifetime of losing to see how awesome and big His hands really are. I know there have been several attempts on my life during the course of writing this book, and my King just keeps telling me how important it is. It is way bigger than I thought, somehow, some way. He wants to work on souls at the heart level. My King keeps giving me a picture of a world full of slaves. I don't know what that means, but I do know that in the past, "my family" owned a plantation that is mostly underwater today. It's now a lake bordering a town call Trophy Club. I'm fairly certain they didn't ever stop having slaves.

Today, slaves are acquired by giving gifts that cannot be returned. Those strings that are created in this process will come together to create a cord, and a few cords will create a rope. When your master pulls the rope and you're still attached, as a slave, you have no choice but to comply. If someone has given you a house you can't afford, what are you going to say when they need something? You can't say no; you're a slave and must obey. It is the fundamental foundation for codependency and organized crime that's shepherding in entirety. It's done in a way that makes it hard to tell who is involved. Because the real criminals are the ones holding the purse. The real criminals don't want justice; the real criminals want revenge at all costs. So, by proxy, it is important to identify the people who compromise their integrity for the right price. I've heard my ancestors brag more than once about how everyone has a price. I've heard this throughout my life. So, the behind the scenes of who owns what and why is important to establish how and why people do what they do because that establishes connections that cannot be denied. That's how slavery works. I believe the best and most productive slaves have no idea. They just accept the current conditions and look to make the best of it. It is usually the strongest slave of all that won't submit to his earthly masters. Because his eyes are set on his King. His eyes thirst for His glory and not for the selfish gratification. His reward is to see the King's victory. The strongest slave already knows how short life is and rejoices knowing that death is only the beginning of all eternity. So, don't be sad for me, not in the least bit. Know that I have a mansion in my Father's kingdom, just waiting on me. I have nothing to fear. And the King has confirmed that in my walk over and over. The King doesn't need money; people do. So now we see how if you have little faith, you'll choose money easily. Most I've worked with have either been bribed, blackmailed, or required to leave. Those are the only choices.

I remember Dan the man was one of the later puppets. He is one of the easiest to identify. I met Dan the man while working at a shop in 2009. Shortly after his divorce, he claimed he moved from Washington state, and the first time I brought him to the house, my half-brother was there. Immediately, my half-brother found him on sheeple media and friended him. I always kind of thought he liked to make friends with people I brought around, and Dan was no different. Dan accepted his gift in cash while out with my half-brother at Baby Dolls Strip Club. He told me about how it was $3,000, all in hundreds, left on the table, and he had no choice but to take it. And so he did. He used the money to buy a dirt bike and a laptop. And what do you know? We rode dirt bikes together. That's all it would take for him to become one of my biggest stalkers. I left that shop later in the year, and another gentleman that we worked with gave me fair warning about Dan the man.

I would see it play out right before my very eyes. I bought a boat in 2009, and as soon as a photo was posted on sheeple media, my phone started blowing up, Dan the man wanting to hang out. I was kind of open to it, naïve at the time still. Around that time, Dan the man quit working for that shop and began spending most of his days and nights around my place. I didn't mind at first because he actually helped me with a few side jobs. Vehicles I would repair in my garage were a thing he could help me out with. Maybe that was how he got in the front door. I think that was when he was being groomed to be a puppet for my ancestors. I noticed more and more that he was becoming like the "cable guy."

Once I changed jobs to a new dealership, I didn't say anything to him. As a matter of fact, I kept my distance and refused to return his phone calls mainly because I thought he was weird. I mean, a few months prior, the dude had quit his job and was practically living at my place. I would get up and leave for work as he stayed sleeping on my couch. Some days, I would get home to him and my half-brother already enjoying my hot tub on my dime or watching something in my outdoor theater. He even used my lawn mower to mow my yard. Keep your friends close, and your enemies closer. It kind of bothered me because I was the one paying for everything and did not have any privacy. No, I had fake friends who liked to fuck with me instead. Dan the man was one of the most persistent losers I'd ever met because after I started working at the Ford dealership, he applied for multiple positions within the first month. And they didn't need his help. That didn't stop him from simply trying to make his own way.

Several days a week, he would stop by and ask the manager if he could assist in writing an estimate. And he would use that time as an excuse to visit with me in my work area, as well as keep me from working. It was always a little weird. I often wondered, *What is with this guy?* I stopped engaging in conversations much with him. I started keeping my mouth shut and just went back to work. Before long, he had to get a job. So he found a sales position for another Ford dealer across town, where he learned about the smart features and all the technology associated with the new Ford lines. I worked for the same dealer for over a year, and it was nice. It wasn't long before the shop portion was relocated a few miles away in a heavily trafficked area. I do think that helped keep him more at bay. But the proximity change made it more difficult to pick up and drop off my kids at school during my visitation, thus making it harder.

One of the estimators who worked there decided to change jobs and work for Chevrolet. His name was Dave. He had a lot of experience and was a longtime veteran in the business. During his time at the Ford dealer, I fixed a lot of cars for him. I was successful for him, and he liked me. So I wasn't surprised when he asked me to apply at the Chevy dealer. Unhappy with my commute, I did so. I didn't tell anyone. I contacted the manager there and set up an interview for first thing one morning that week. I've visited and met some of the shop staff. I liked the shop's organization and production level. But something in my gut was unsettled. I had said before, "I hope I never have to work there." Chevrolet is one of the hardest vehicle lines to work on and make a living. Plus, it made me even more nervous knowing how many of Duck's friends worked there. It was a small town, and he had built many of their houses—not to mention that's how gifts that couldn't be returned were traded for favors later.

Classy. That was where I saw the manager be placed as an associate of the Crocodile family from West Texas. I imagine the manager was selected during his recovery from burns on most of his body. The assistant manager was well known as a puppet. He didn't have his own brain because he wanted money instead. Calling into his staff meetings at 1:00 p.m. on the daily, I wondered if he ever noticed when I would walk into his office as he and Dan the man were getting their instructions over the phone. Dan needed to have all the cameras set up and installed so he and Muck could have remote access and proper planning. I noticed. Did you see me notice how fake people around me are? They bragged about catching fish, but they were there doing "work" for people who claimed to be ancestors. It's classy how well-documented organized criminals associate. I know the crimes only grow, starting with simple car fraud. I watched Muck leave his truck somewhere and report it stolen, claim old damage as new, and get his truck paid off. It worked so well with him using my coworkers to fit his agenda. Using Poison Ivy, his old school buddy, he was able to get money back as well as his truck fixed. It happened again a couple of months later. It was the American Eagle guy whose daddy ran the dealership. I saw how it was brought in and reported stolen after I spotted him leaving Muck's house with the concubine.

I thought it was so much fun making the cockroaches scatter that day. As I understand, the neighbor across the street, who was Muck's associate, got his foot run over by the same Tahoe. I laughed a little on the inside—a lot actually. I kept wondering, *Did he kick rocks again? Or did he step into a bucket of shit?* I won't say what they were doing in the shadow of my existence, but everyone knows. It was like two girls, one cup. I smashed both of them, many times. So, good luck trying to gross me out.

An associate of Muck's, The American Eagle, had his Tahoe dropped off at the dealership of course. I saw it. I even got the keys and went to look at it. At that point, the manager looked alarmed. I saw the parking permit on his dash to the party my ancestors were hosting in my honor. I laughed. I also saw how his ignition wasn't broken. His truck wasn't stolen. A hole was drilled next to the ignition only about a half inch deep. It had to be a sharp drill bit, about twelve millimeters in diameter, because the bit did not look to have walked around while starting. I had the keys to the truck in my hand. It wasn't broken. It was fraud. I called badge number 200 in Colley Wood to report that I knew it was a fraud. I also knew if they searched the vehicle, they would find the concubine's fingerprints inside. They all know. And about an hour later, his daddy's friend showed up with another guy and drove it away. They said they had to clean it.

I did use the work phone to call, but knowing how connected badge number 200 is, it doesn't surprise me. It must be tough to make so little and have so few skills surrounded by so much wealth. Someone is on a power grab. I believe the party they went to was called "rent a porn star," like I said, family business. Some people only have kids to torture them. I get it. I simply don't react and write it down instead. So everyone knows. It's funny, right, being ruled by criminals? We all are. Until money is worthless, we will all be slaves. To the estimator I worked with long ago, Scarface, that was so fun to watch you try to keep your muddy boots dirty. I laughed at you during both employments and took great pride in seeing the scar on your face daily from the bumper I worked on. Do you remember? It was funny. You had been trying to undermine me all week, with even a couple of tickets on my estimates. You had to do a cheap estimate on a bumper only job. When you disagreed about the parts and the manager upheld my opinion, you took it upon yourself to pick up that huge heavy bumper and show me a thing or two. Well, I saw. You didn't have a hold of it, and it flipped right down and scarred your entire face. I laughed. Do you remember? It was funny from my vantage point.

To the owners of the dealership, that was so much fun. I enjoyed being on display for everyone, knowing what you have access to and what great lengths you will go to in order to fulfill your pinky promise to the Barnes of criminals you keep in bed with you. Concubines are all the same. How did I taste? We all get sloppy seconds.

CHAPTER 10

Whipping Post

I've always hoped that since I just won't die that instead, I could be the whipping post that broke the shepherds' hands.

As I sat in the shadows watching the celebration of my death by suicide or so they thought play out on camera, I wasn't even sad. I instead considered maybe decades of psychological and physical torture had gained traction for the wheels of motivation. I've grown to enjoy my beatings because the wounds that remain heal stronger than before. I find my comfortable place completely disconnected from this world and the pain it brings. Simply put, I build my own strength in being beaten; that's where I find my focus and learn to stand all on my own two feet and wear a stoic smile. With each strike and blow against me, it's like a drug or endorphins, and I can taste it on my tongue as it makes my heart race, and in those precious moments or ushered-in torture, the adrenaline drip begins. In those restraints placed upon myself, I'm on a new level, because bombs that are built aren't fully working overnight. And the best bombs are made with the rarest elements that in the perfect unison of time and space clear the way and level the fields so nothing remains. I'm being taught by professionals how to disassociate from the feeling of pain, because people who have feelings are weak. I've been bred and groomed to disassociate for a purpose with complete clarity, just like air-conditioning: when it hits a certain degree, the machine goes to work blowing air on everyone. My grooming was to form a trigger. And I'm groomed to be a weapon. But I'm a unicorn instead.

When the wolves first noticed I was growing pink skin, I think they knew a long time ago, I'm a different breed of monster altogether. Plenty have said I looked like a pink elephant once upon a time. But that was a long time ago. Nobody has seen my real skin in decades. I deserve to feel something, anything. I'll take pain if that's all I'm allowed to feel. As the beatings intensify and the pain increases to an all-too-familiar level, it converts with oxygen and becomes my jet fuel. I don't even need food after. As my body dilates to accommodate more blood and more oxygen, I feel the endorphins release, starting with tingling behind my ears, followed by a new sound. It sounds as if everyone is in a tunnel and the droning of sound softens as if it were the sweetest sheep whispering seductive nothings into my ear. I love it. I begin to salivate at the increase in feelings and taste in my mouth. The warm feeling of my body is a conditioned response to being beaten. I find it is so comfortable. I long to see the expression of that humor offered in the smile I give to my captors. Please continue my lashing. I apologize that I was enjoying my free gift of pain so much, I began asking for more. But they didn't want to listen. So I screamed louder. "Please hurt me so much I never return!" I was hopeful the lack of fear on my part would motivate even more horrible things. I already know if they hit me hard enough, I might be able to smell something again for a moment. I think it's the mask on the costume. The nose is covered with fur, and the mesh holes aren't big enough. I know my nostrils must have grown significantly lately because they barely have any room anymore.

I am thankful for the brief taste and evasive feeling that vanishes faster than sheep running from wolves. I crave what it brings in that brief moment, because I felt something under my costume. I find that being beaten by those closest to me at times has actually helped me separate the costume from my skin. It's like the worst pain and highest pleasure all at the same time. I like it so much I feed my captors the illusion that it hurts, so they continue my treatment. I can tell it's helping me shed this costume. I haven't felt anything actually touch my own skin since before 1993. I don't even know if I would recognize myself. It's as if I need to get my back scratched with my new skin coming in underneath this suit. And I need more scratching.

I found a tree on the way home from extending grace that day to the man I apologized to for playing with matches, even though no grace was actually there, and I spent some time scratching the back of my costume against the tree. I spent hours scratching and rubbing the bark off of the tree, so much so my costume began to bleed. I hadn't noticed how deep the scratches were because I removed myself thinking about how the tree I was pushing against was so strong, and yet it started as a simple seed. The creator knows the rest. I was baffled. I was most certain my new skin was ready. But it wasn't time yet apparently, because I was bleeding now more than ever and visibly needed attention. I can only imagine it added to the illusion. But I had that costume on still. Who can tell? I wish the costume would burn. I walked all the way home trying to peel the edges of the costume away from where it met my flesh and was bleeding now. But it's on there. I think now, back to when I was branded, and I think they used superglue. Now that I'm seeing how the costume is bonded to my flesh, I'm pretty sure it was covered in Krazy Glue. And I'm happy. It burns so much more than I expected it to. The solvents in the superglue made their way directly to the nerves on my bones. I tasted the rush of endorphins that time. It was salty as heck and left my mouth salivating for more, and in the absence of more pain, my mouth grew sweeter and sweeter as the endorphins wore off. I love that feeling. I think pain is better than a drug. This costume deserves it. It's a disgrace. The sheep who designed the costume should be held accountable. Or the other option could be that I keep the costume and mask. That way, I can decide when it's the right time to wear it. Although it sounds rational in my mind, I still can't work out how I will shed this sheepskin in the first place. I need the shepherds to remove it the same way it was put on.

I grew faint in that moment, remembering how much pain that was. And putting it on me was the easy part. I began to wrestle with my creator about what I'm made of. And again, He showed me the very next day. What I'm made of is what I want to find out. I want to be someplace else. I want to be a mile high all the time. I bet there are some very high cliffs that I can learn to fly from. And there is change on the horizon. It seems as though in 2014, there will be a green rush, and many other unique creatures will flourish like never before. It's far from the compound. It's perched high upon a hill. The road there is long and can be treacherous. It's not for everyone. Although it is a long journey, my King will be present. What do I have to fear? For I truly believe my steps have been set before me. My journey isn't my own. That's the best part. I'm shedding my skin now. Disassociation is in full effect. Do not help anyone. Get out alive. Write it down so I may learn from yesterday, live for today, and plan for tomorrow. I have too many things anyway. It's time to get rid of everything.

I didn't sleep at all after I got home from faking my own suicide. I noticed an old sheep who was always at the shepherd's right hand was visiting with my next-door neighbor. She seemed like she had been up all night too. I recognized the shoes from the previous night. They still had the mud from the watering hole on their expensive soles. I smiled and laughed as I waved hello. It was like she had seen a ghost, because I saw the blood leave her face in that moment our eyes locked. She turned pale as if when I held her gaze, I had caught a glimpse of her cancerous body years in the future as my own personal sign of the hand of the King being present. I almost felt something besides humor. But to my dismay, the humor was overwhelming. How can I not laugh? I wanted to yell, "Hi!" as she turned and walked to the front door like heaping hot coals on the top of her head. I couldn't stop laughing. The irony was amazing. The gluttonous sheep I am referring to was also a teacher, Mrs. Crocodile. She kept plenty of connections and even more land and money. She has outlived the last two bighorn sheep with mysterious circumstances. The bighorn sheep I'm talking about were hardworking and wealthy, a perfect fit for her to gain their resources and hand them over to her shepherds to keep her safe and secure. She actually worked in the shepherd's office.

The irony for me is that teachers should have learned. But I guess they never met a unicorn like me. Like I said earlier, I was raised by the wolves she is scared of the most. I thought the bighorn sheep were good. They seemed solid. It was easy to see how they loved their family the way they provided for them. Her first bighorn sheep was the patriarch of that compound where I was trapped. He mysteriously died while moving at a moment's notice to the place I wanted to be. The second bighorn sheep wasn't wearing a seat belt. And all the evidence was consumed in the fire. Obviously, she wasn't a blind sheep. She was a teacher, teaching others her craft, leading blind sheep astray for the shepherds to control the masses. I get it. It's entertaining how little integrity is possessed by wolves. Some people actually believe their money will protect them. I have already seen her future. Time will tell. I'll just watch. I am only able to see her meet her maker one time. That's the saddest part. But I'm relieved it's not up to me. Rest assured, and wear a bigger smile now knowing, my King's got this. His hands are much bigger than mine. And he has a better scope of understanding when it comes to what sheep deserve. I'm a nobody, just a smile and wave. Think of me as nothing but dust in the wind.

It feels so good, being burned. I'm starting to smell again, I think. It seemed like her gaze had heat in it, because it smells like flesh burning. I looked in the mirror, and the costume was still there. So I couldn't tell you where the smell of burning flesh was coming from.

More important, I could smell something. I tried to breathe it all in. I probably stood in that spot a moment longer than I would have normally, but I was enjoying my pain much like being at the top of the Twin Towers before they vanished. I'm taking it all in. What a nice memory to keep with me. Those things are priceless. I've often considered myself to be extremely selfish keeping all these memories all to myself. But it makes me stronger. Blind sheep don't usually have a brain of their own, so it's easy to see how sometimes in this life, mental sodomy goes both ways if a sheep tries it on a unicorn. He has a huge horn to put all the excess brain matter in. I don't know if that's a viable option because I enjoyed the hell out of it, quite literally. I believe all the blind sheep should try opening their eyes soon, or the blind sheep won't even know when they are let into the slaughterhouse by being told it's a vacation at a resort. More sheep get disposed of if I don't say anything. In a way, how lucky for me it's not my issue. I simply don't have friends or family. I'm independent. That is the opposite of how I was raised. I've become the polar opposite of what I am supposed to actually be. I'm strong. I'm independent. I don't have feelings. That's a weapon, or a unicorn in training.

Rule 11

Before my decision to leave was finalized, I had planned to see the boys for scheduled visitation. I drove all the way over there, and I was so excited to see those boys, but instead, I was greeted by a puppet who wore a costume. That day, he was driving a silver truck and wore a cowboy belt with a shiny clip-on badge that was a six-pointed star. He greeted me with paperwork. He laughed and was excited to tell me that he was the paper man and that I wasn't going to see those kids that day. Instead, I was going to sign this paper for him. I remembered him from the pizza place. I took photos of him leaving. That led to the emergency room visit as well as the video badge number 0200 refused to acknowledge, saying his computer broke. He gave it back to me. I knew the routine. This was my ancestors' schemes to steal my kids and finish me off in the process so they could collect. I'd seen it so many times. It doesn't matter whom I talk to; she will pay them anything. And she is so proud of herself. She owns me, she believes. I'm her pet. I would never stand up to her. That's the Stockholm syndrome for you. People actually believe I will defend my oppressors and support a woman who has Munchausen syndrome by proxy and is willing to pay people to lie on camera so she may create the situation she plans to capitalize on in order to get a reaction out of me.

I figured there was probably someone with a camera taking notes, looking for a reaction. All I've ever known in Colley Wood is cowards. So, I smiled. I read the papers I was served with. They didn't give a clear explanation as to why I wasn't able to see my boys. I knew I could see them after I went to court. I was thankful. The court date was two weeks from then. That should give me plenty of time to prepare my materials. I'd just go home and work on that, not leave at once. I believe maybe the shepherds were hoping they could capture a sad reaction from me for entertainment purposes. However, I was not sad. I was thankful. Those two weeks leading up to the court date were interesting, to say the least. I knew what lay before me, and instead of being scared, I was feeling that the King was going to use me in a big way. Knowing how gang stalking worked, I knew I must prepare myself for what was coming. I began to figure out the route that I would use to get to court and how much fuel I would need, as well as when I should leave based on what traffic did during work hours commuting. I knew that I would not take the normal route down the loop 820 because that was what the shepherds expected. The shepherds knew I had to be someplace at a certain time and expected me to take a certain route because surely, I was too scared to take any other route. This would work to my advantage.

I put together all of the phone records and personal journaling that I had done as well as photos and a few other details that I was saving for the real court. I also charged my hidden camera's batteries. And on the morning of court, I dressed appropriately but lacked the want or desire to iron my clothes and play the part of a perfect puppet. Instead, I'd just go.

As I left my place, I did so probably about an hour and a half before my shepherds expected I would. I spent no time getting ready because I had prepared my clothes in my closet the evening before. Literally, once I woke up, it was a race. I honestly didn't care if I got there hours ahead of schedule as long as I got there. The court would start at 10:00 a.m. It was barely sun up around 5:20 a.m. With this amount of time, I could probably ride my bicycle there. So I headed out with just enough fuel to go north and then go south, as well as west and then east. I basically zig-zagged the wrong direction to get to where I was going. I drove evasively and did not break any laws. I paid attention to make sure no one was following me. It must have worked well, because when I got to court, I went inside and alerted the clerk that I was present and that I would be representing myself pro-se. When I walked out, the goals were wearing sheep's clothing sitting and smiling until they saw me. That's right. When they saw me, their jaws hit the floor. They both looked at each other, and you could see the panic on their faces. I simply walked over and said, "I'm ready. I'm representing myself. I'll produce anything you need. Let's get this over with."

Her lawyer was trying to create a smoke screen. When she asked me into her conference room alone before the hearing in front of a judge, don't you know of course I had my hidden camera recording. I had just seen them ask the lady who investigated me for CPS to be dismissed because they didn't like her report. When I entered the room, the lawyer had the smuggest smile, like a cat who had just eaten a bird but was trying to hide it. She started blabbing about her wanting more. I stopped her midsentence and simply said, "I'm moving. I've already been to another state and had job opportunities. I'm not staying here. Your client is involved in manipulating my life to get her own way."

She said, "I can assure you my client isn't."

I replied, "Of course that's your directive. A year's worth of phone records doesn't lie. I'm writing a book, so you don't get a reaction out of me."

She seemed more concerned when I told her what recording I had made of a Muck bragging about his actions while trying to smear me because, based on phone records, that would implicate her client, as well as put the lawyer's career in jeopardy for aiding and abetting a criminal. I simply said, "No, we're all done." She wanted to see some of the materials. I had shown her just enough so she knew. She wanted to see more, and my reply was "Sure, we can show the judge together. At that point, her eyes began to bug out of her head even more so. I said, "The only thing you're going to get is a Rule 11, on one condition, no grandparental rights. Those people should not have any contact with my kids ever, not in this life or the next."

She asked me to have a seat outside while she talked to her client. I was fine with that so I closed up my bag and collected all the things that I had brought to court with me to show the judge and sat outside on the bench, waiting. I saw the wolves wearing sheep's clothing be ushered in to the side room of the court and close the door. They were in there about thirty seconds before the older wolf came out with the phone stuck to her ear, acting very concerned. She ran to the bathroom, and as she closed the door to the bathroom, she never took her eyes off of me while on the phone. I've often wondered who she was reporting to. I can only suspect that it was Linda. No matter really, I hope they got the message.

The Rule 11 paperwork was drawn up, and we would all have to stand in front of the judge and agree to this. I got a little emotional before court. I probably looked sad, but I was thankful honestly. It was like I was being reborn.

When we walked into court, the wolf lawyers did all the talking. The judge reluctantly agreed to the Rule 11 based on my ability to move out of state. The judge simply stated, "This doesn't normally happen." But her lawyer seemed concerned that I didn't say anything else than we should just get this over with. The judge asked me if that was what I really wanted. My reply was that she was a good mom. She got a little emotional when I said that. I walked out of court with all my things and started leaving when I noticed they were headed back up to court because you get your paperwork on the bottom floor right by the exit. Whatever I needed to get back on the road and get out of there before anybody knew I'd even been there.

I went back to the SUV, loaded of my things, and hit the road. I took the normal route home. And I could have cared less if anybody was following me now. I suggest they look and watch. Some of the best legends can't be broken. I got back to my place and knew it was time to make some changes. I really didn't have enough money to afford this vehicle anymore. It was a very wasteful vehicle, getting barely fifteen miles a gallon. The only reason I had it was to pull the boat. I began thinking about how little I really needed. I was reminded about how all the things are actually just burdens. They were all just like little anchors keeping my ship in port. It was time to start cutting lines, and I knew it. I began to try to sell everything that I had in my possession with the space for belongings limited to the back of a pickup truck. I knew that I needed something that was fuel efficient, fast, and nimble. That got me thinking about a motorcycle. I was reminded about how pretty the riding would be there. So that was what I did. I walked in faith to create my own future. I sold quite a few things like tools, boating accessories, video games, and a moped. Honestly, it was a ton of crap that I'd never really realized was piling up. It felt freeing to rid myself of worldly possessions that were just merely anchors. It was almost a cleaning effect. I was becoming brighter, shinier, and newer by simply being wiped with bleach. All the while, I was getting bombarded by people who claimed to be family, calling me and texting me, trying to capitalize on the very situation they had created for themselves.

I stopped listening a long time ago. I don't guess they understood that yet, and it might work to my advantage. I had to come up with a motorcycle or another means of transportation to get me out of that place and into my next life. That was when it seemed like all I could see was the floor. But the King was showing me out the window how beautiful life could be. It's like right before my eyes, He took the window and made it a door, and I walked right through. What an amazing honor that was bestowed on me. My King is an amazing God. This is amazing grace and the refining fire at the same time. I know that I must be burned into a new creation.

After being home, and it wasn't long before the first phone call from Linda asking about how court went. I put on my mask, rhetorically speaking, before talking to her. She sounded doom and gloom about how court went. This was one of many times. It was as if somehow, she knew already before she talked to me. I don't know what she was told, nor do I care. She was probably using the power of suggestion to try to condition my feelings based on her agenda. I'd seen it before many times. She's a manipulator. She has been trying to steal my kids for years and will say whatever she can to do so.

So, as you can imagine, my reply was kind of dry. She didn't really get any of the intel that she was hoping for. I couldn't be happier. I just said, "I have to move," and she said, "You can't." That was when I laughed out loud. I couldn't help myself. She actually believed in her cult. And I actually believe in my King. This is quintessentially the Hegelian dialectic. This is the struggle between good and evil for simply struggles sake. Brainwashed people have been deceived to believe that their money will protect them. They actually believe their offshore bank accounts will shield them from being associated with organized criminals. However, offshore bank accounts can and will be subpoenaed when used for organized crime. Maybe her banks didn't tell her that yet. I was counting on it. I still am. I need her to see me as weak. I need them all to see me as weak. I need them to underestimate me to the fullest of their ability. I need them to continue to mistake my kindness for weakness as well as mercy. That's my single greatest advantage in this world: that they know I'm nothing, so why should they be concerned? They are so sure of their cult that they are flagrant about what they are doing. It's simply my job to watch and learn. I already know the best never lose; they only learn. Someone needs to document this before it's a regular occurrence. Someone should put a stop to this before my kids have to go through the same. Someone should put a stop to this before their kids have to go through the same. I believe that's why we have laws so that individuals have rights. My life isn't my own already. Maybe they haven't seen yet. I know the King's going to show them in a very intimate way. I pray mercy for them because I know it's not up to me.

Motorcycle for Boat

As soon as I got through with court that day in late summer of 2013, I held my head up high, knowing I had just dropped a bomb. I gave them a Rule 11. They weren't allowed grandparental rights, no matter how much they tried to manipulate me. They created their own problems, and I kept the match while they soaked themselves in gasoline. I knew their actions and motives. They had been planning on crucifying me on camera. All the while they might play the victim while being the oppressor. I was immune. I had to walk away to show the narcissists they were not worth my time. The caliber of losers looking to get rich I have been surrounded by is amazing. What an amazing honor that's been bestowed upon me. I must act like nothing. I must not give them a clue as to what I just did in court. I established motive. They established their own means, as well as their own opportunity, by way of vacations and gifts that cannot be returned.

I stayed at my place uninterrupted. I knew I needed a new set of wheels, and my boat was no longer a good resource. So I looked on Craigslist and found a guy who wanted to trade a crotch rocket for a boat. The seller said it had new tires and was great mechanically. It was a little rough cosmetically but was fast, and it was a brand I had liked for a long time. I had been trying to sell the boat, and the price kept dropping, as I could see the excitement in people's eyes at being a party to the schemes of entertainment. They were hoping to report back to the shepherds how miserable I was. So this time, I used my enemy. I had Muck bring the boat to the test drive while leaving my SUV in his driveway. I'd seen they already had keys to it. I'd just leave it there for them. It was in perfect shape. I even listed the rear seats on Craigslist for sale, knowing they were expensive. I posted photos before we left that day. Psychotic sociopaths are looking for a reaction to capitalize on. All the other potential buyers would get a phone call during the viewing or test drive of the boat. You could see their facial expression change, and they acted like I was radioactive. I started learning from the wolves how to use a different phone number for more privacy. I wasn't selling my boat anymore, only trading it, because the price I was selling it for was way too low because of the shepherding taking place.

The last guy who looked at the boat to buy it was a surprise because he showed up after using a new number to give it a lake test. As we were leaving, I noticed my half-brother's friend Fitz who lived one house over running out of the garage with his cell phone in hand as if taking a photo and then holding it up to his ear as if making the call that I was leaving. And as we turned left at the first stop sign, I got the call from Linda. Frantic, she began asking what was going on, as if I was not allowed to sell my boat. I said, "It's a test drive," as if it was any of her business. She was pissed obviously and hung up on me.

Shortly after, I began getting scam calls as if from a robot dialer. I shut my phone off knowing they were trying to ping my location. That was how they rolled. They had access to the best intel through their friends and partners in crime. We both knew I had to protect my privacy. The test drive went all right, but it started lightning out of nowhere, and it scared all of us enough to head back and load up the boat. We headed back with my phone off. We began to try to negotiate a sale. The door was left open. I was more thinking my King had my steps already, whatever. So as we got closer, I noticed his friend's phone blowing up. He was being asked about the boat. He said, "Yeah, it's a red ski boat," as if the person on the line knew what boat and therefore more about the current situation. He dropped me and the boat off. He returned about five minutes later to tell me in person he wasn't interested. I think it was after he dropped his friend off just down the street. The buyer, who was just excited about the lake test and potential of a great summer, had a completely different facial expression now. I didn't care. The price was too cheap anyway.

So, I kept looking and praying for what God had for me, and that was what led me to this opportunity.

My inspection sticker was out on my SUV, and I didn't want to chance getting pulled over because I was being gang stalked everywhere I went. I had to use my oppressors who used me at the same time. Subsequently I acted like a poor little sheep to gain my costume's access. I suggested he take me to the trade for a motorcycle, so I could ride back. He was in disbelief, saying it was a scam and it was probably a piece of crap. Maybe they guy was just a figment of my imagination. He maybe didn't see the text because I was using an app to communicate through my tablet instead of my phone. I only called the guy when we were close. That was the guy with the bike, and his friends and I went for a lake test. I noticed how agitated my half-brother had become, seeing the bike. He kept on and on about why I shouldn't get it, almost as if he wanted my boat so bad but couldn't say anything to me. That might show his weakness. I had my journals and court records, as well as the other dirt I kept in the very backpack I brought with me. He knew it, and I knew it. It was obvious when we got the boat in the water. Before I hopped on, I went to the back door and grabbed my bag to take it with me, as if to say, "I'm not leaving it with you." Muck looked mad and scared all at the same time.

The lake test went well, and without anyone else around, this guy agreed to trade straight up. He was an oil-field guy and wanted to enjoy the rest of his summer because they were right on the lake. When we loaded the boat, my half-brother was there with sad expressions about how it went. The guy even looked at me as if to say, "What's his problem?" We both listened to his verbal vomit before going back to the buyer's house, where I test drove the bike on the way back, still wearing my backpack. When we got back, we did our paperwork. My half-brother got his number, just in case there was an issue he could help with. I'm like, *Yeah, right. Jealous looser. I've seen it before.* He was passive-aggressive at this point. I was thrilled. I got on the highway on the way home behind him mostly. He kept slowing and finally waved me alongside with his window down to take photos and video of me while wearing that psychotic smile. I sped off and kept a safe distance between us through traffic. But I could see Muck in the rearview, trying to catch up to me. However, this bike was fast. And I could ride as if I had nothing to lose. I'd keep the backpack for my balls to carry them now.

I went back to my place and covered the bike with a tarp that was left over in the driveway from the boat. I got a good night's sleep and began planning my move, trying to think of what I could sell on Craigslist quickly to gain some cash to drive the bike to the Mile High place. It was a long ride. I had learned not to use my phone because that was what my enemies did also. I also knew they watched my bank account. My half-brother begged me to get an account at his bank. I knew why. He wanted to control and manipulate me. I also knew no matter where I banked, he would use himself or a friend to befriend a person who worked there. It happened more than once. So I needed to use cash to protect myself. To do so, I would use the new number to sell a few things. I sold a video game and a camera and had enough to travel there and back if I got good gas mileage. I didn't tell anyone. It didn't take long to come up with some cash. I knew if I wanted to ride to where I was going, the backpack would be too heavy. So I left it in the same place. On my way to that place, I noticed the guy who lived across the street from Muck following me and taking photos of me while laughing. I laughed a little too. Because

I knew he was a slave who was recruited while I was in college. He lived in the same rundown apartment complex in the depressed little town where he had been stuck for over twelve years. I noticed my roommate in college leaving from there and then changing his story about the relationship. Now the guy lived across the street.

I remember how my brother befriended the guy who used to live there and had a lending hand in him selling his house. Of course, shortly after he moved in, there was a questionable fire that happened, and the insurance company paid for the house mostly. The house was repaired, and money was made to ensure his place in the club. This guy was a technician on copiers. He knew a few things and liked trying to show me how capable he was. He even threw his back out trying to build a boat as I built mine. I laughed at his mediocrity, as I do now. With that being said, I needed to know what he was up to. He was a slave. Knowing that I circled back and watched as he went to a tire place where a guy I went to school with was the manager. I knew he wasn't allowed to give up. So I took notes and dropped my backpack off shortly after. I said hello to someone I'd always appreciated. I left and got a call from my half-brother, asking me to come over for lunch. I was hungry, and I knew I would be leaving that night, so I obliged.

When I got there, I parked in the garage and closed it. That enraged my half-brother. He opened the door. It was as if he was trying to signal to the neighbor without calling him by standing in the driveway, holding his hand in front of himself, like he had just thrown a bowling ball for about ten seconds. Muck was acting panicked. I got off on it. He was lying about food; he didn't have lunch. He would have to go to a drive-through somewhere. I suggested he go, and I would stay. He started yelling about how paranoid I was. I didn't give a fuck. Keep trying.

So I got in his truck, and as we got about two blocks away, he made a phone call to someone and told him we were getting food if he wanted any. He replied that he had about fifteen minutes. I took notes. On the way back, he began speaking about the motorcycle and how it was probably a piece of crap. He said that it would probably break, or I would probably crash it and die. He was trying to make me feel bad for changing his plans. I kept laughing inside.

As we pulled up out front, the across-the-street neighbor was outside driving his lawn mower in the grass as if he was mowing the grass. I smiled at him, as he had the most disgusted look on his face. I laughed a little, and he drove his lawn mower into the garage and closed the door as if he wasn't allowed to speak. I turned in time to see my half-brother laughing and so excited. I already knew. I had seen it before. Cowards must sabotage. I looked at my bike in the garage, and it didn't appear to have been moved. I looked at the chain to make sure the links were still great. I looked at the tires, and they seemed all right. The gas cap was locked with the only key, which I still had. It looked to have been touched by the lack of dust on the cover over the keyhole. That was when I knew what the neighbor was up to. I looked at the oil fill cap, and it had fresh fingerprints on it. There was usually a light film of oil that collected even the finest debris, so the fingerprints were fairly obvious and fresh accordingly. I opened the fill cap to see what looked like finely ground metal shavings. I knew now they couldn't let me leave. It was now too late to get any motorcycle motor oil because the motorcycle stores were all closed, but I needed to leave that night.

I remembered there was an alternative oil at Walmart that was made for diesel trucks without the detergents that cause the clutch to slip. I wasn't too worried because it needed to be changed and checked before a long road trip. As I was putting the filler cap back on, he noticed me giving the bike an inspection, and his jaw dropped. He even put his hand over his mouth. Then he proceeded to tell me how paranoid I was.

I smiled and simply said, "It just needs an oil change. It isn't any big deal."

That comment eased his distress. I put my gear on to go get some oil.

When I got down the street, I got a text about a motorcycle jacket that I had been emailing a guy on Craigslist about. He texted the wrong phone number and suggested he would meet me at an address in Dallas. If I hurried, I could make it. I knew that was a setup. Someone wanted me to ride this hard and break it. I gingerly rode it to Walmart, where I noticed it trying to overheat. It smelled like the clutch was trying to burn, like the oil had way too much friction material in it. I got my oil for less than twenty bucks and was now on my way back to change it. I wasn't able to find a simple micro switch that I wanted. So I knew Duck was on the way home. I stopped by to ask if he had one. He was so surprised to see me. He gave me a micro switch, and as he looked at the bike, he noticed the oil, and it was like he panicked. He asked me like a dumbass if I was about to change the oil. I kind of laughed and said, "Yes," calmly. I drew close, looked him up and down, and simply said, "This may be the last time I see you alive." I gave him a big hug and said, "I love you."

I promptly walked out to my bike, while he stood still like he had seen a ghost. I went from there about five mins to the shop to change the oil. Nobody was home there, but the neighbor noticed me opening the garage and putting the bike inside before closing the door. He came out his front door to look at me. I laughed. I had to take the fairings off to change the oil and filter, but that gave me an opportunity to put a toggle switch on the taillight. Turning it off in the dark would be essential to avoid losers. I knew I was not allowed to leave what had been setup for me. I installed the switch and changed the oil in record time—probably less than half an hour. I was leaving the garage when my half-brother pulled up in his truck. I left and went to my place to grab an empty backpack and put a few travel essentials in it. I left my place around midnight headed north. I was doing a reasonable speed, around seventy miles per hour mostly. I had to refuel around Wichita Falls.

Once I was on that long stretch, I noticed the familiar black Charger SRT-8 I had seen my half-brother driving with the xenon headlights gaining ground. I think around a half mile away, I put my hammer down. I had always wanted to see how fast this rocket was. It was a Canadian model, and as I understand it, they aren't restricted to three hundred kilometers per hour. I was about to find out. I pushed the button for the taillight to turn off, and then I downshifted to second, hit redline, third, redline, fourth, then redline. Fifth gear was still pulling like a fighter jet. I could only see about a quarter mile in front of me as I approached a crown in the road. I didn't have time to slow down even if I wanted to. I kept the throttle pinned and hit sixth after another redline. It still pulled hard. I must have been in sixth in the dark at the top of the gentle crown in the road when I crested the top, and my vision extended for miles with reflective straight lines out of the darkness like a runway with the lights turned on. My heart was racing. It was amazing. As soon as I noticed the lack of light coming from the rear, I slammed the brakes, downshifted, and exited at the next exit, still coasting around sixty miles per hour. I reached up and shut the key off on the bike while it was still coasting. I had enough speed to do the U-turn and come up to the bridge that crossed the highway. I parked behind a rock on the side of the road, got off the bike, and lit a cigarette, taking advantage of the opportunity. I kept the cherry covered with my hand since there wasn't any other light around. It wasn't about three puffs later when I saw the black Charger driving almost as fast as I was. He had the brights on, looking for something. I laughed. *Yeah, clear the way for me. Haul ass in front of me so they have someone else to pull over first.* I finished my cigarette and drove all the way there, only stopping for fuel, eating along the way. I did close to the speed limit with my phone now off. When I was almost to New Mexico, I noticed an ex-girlfriend following me in her mom's beige Chevy truck. I sped up again and did almost the same except I kept on the same side of the highway this time. I think she saw me as she passed because I saw her hitting the bumps on the side of the road to alert sleepy drivers. Her driving looked frantic, and since I was standing, it looked like a Styrofoam ice chest of which the top had been blown off. Now the white plastic bag inside was being blown all around by the wind. Commanda, I hadn't seen her for years. Her brother used to say if she was from Sanger, bang her. I wondered why? Because that's what she signed up for.

I continued my journey and went to the place my enemies least expected and asked for my job. As it turned out, someone had just quit that morning, and there was a spot for me. I filled out the paperwork that included a background and driving report. I left. I was only there for a short time. I called my boys and said I was in Colorado. You could hear Mom in the background alarmed. She asked where. I said, "I'm getting my job and my place."

She said, "How?"

I laughed and instructed my boys to pray for me because when I got back and moved, they wouldn't ever have to worry about the manipulators trying to steal them. Mom promptly hung up the phone. I began my journey home, and I was weary. I needed my King's strength. Thankfully, I barely beat a huge rainstorm while heading south. I got a few hundred miles and began falling asleep while riding. I tried to find a room, but the state fair was in town, and there wasn't a room available. I kept on and came to a rest stop where I pulled over. I lay down on my backpack and passed out for a few hours unknowingly. I was awakened by a law enforcement officer who thought I was dead. He was poking me with is nightstick because he said I didn't respond to verbal commands. I woke up in a fighting stance, unclear of the present situation. We spoke briefly, and he ran my ID and thanked me for pulling over but encouraged me not to stay because of the wildlife, like mountain lions, black bears, snakes, and coyotes. I agreed and kept going. About five hours later, I would be around the border of Colorado and New Mexico.

I had to stop for fuel. I pulled into what was probably the only gas station for fifty miles or more. That was when I noticed a couple of familiar vehicles, seemingly waiting on me. I said, "Let 'em look." I filled the bike and got some chocolate milk and a snack. I stood away from my bike while I ate, watching their every move. And the gentleman who used to live with an enemy of mine was standing close enough for me to notice. He kept laughing as if it was going to hurt my feelings. I didn't have any. Sorry, Andrew.

I finished my snacks and made my way to leave, but I couldn't find my key. It was the only key. I retraced my steps in the store and parking lot only to be disappointed and just began to pray. I was comforted by the knowledge that everything happened for a reason. I finally found it in the trash. I don't know how it got there, but I was happy to find it. The sun was coming up, so it might not be so hard to stay awake. About a half mile down the road, I noticed one of the familiar vehicles on the side of the road with the hood up. They were acting like they were having car problems. But they weren't looking at the broken truck; they were looking at me. The truck was fine obviously.

As I passed, the gentleman used his phone. It looked like he was calling someone. About a mile later, I noticed another familiar vehicle parked in a driveway to a ranch. It was a rural stretch of road that probably didn't see many cars driving down at that hour. The gentleman was standing by his truck on the other side as if I couldn't see his legs by the exhaust pipe. He had his tailgate open, and his camper shell was also. I approached them, and it was like my King pushed me down. I ducked and kind of slowed as I approached, slow enough to see the camera in the bed of his truck that looked like it was next to a contraption that was holding a wire across the road for me to run into. I noticed … I revved my engine, down shifted, and almost pulled a wheelie as I sped off. I was able to catch his reaction as I sped away. I liked to see him run in a panic now. I kept a decent speed for miles. I made my way to the next state, where I was held up by weather. I came to a stop in traffic on the highway. It didn't look safe, and something in my gut was telling me to move.

I rode back up the shoulder to a bridge overpass where a few other bikes were sitting and waited. I watched as two different accidents happened right where I was just at moments earlier. That must have been my King's hand again. I felt like I was having church right then and there. As the rain began to pour down, the road became slick, and as traffic backed up, many cars were involved in minor fender benders. I sat on the side of the highway watching. As I sat under the overpass, shielded from the rain, being an onlooker to traffic and accidents, I wondered what else my King had in store for me.

Once the rain passed and the traffic let up, the other motorcyclists decided it was time to leave also. I remember leaving just a moment before they did and staying just a little bit faster than traffic.

On my way back, I still had several more hours of riding, at which time, I kept thinking, what an amazing honor! As I entered Tarrant County, I noticed that the grandparents of one of the kids I played matches with was now on my tail. I sped up. I slow down and got beside them, and they were just like a trailer. Again, it reminded me of the trailers that were used to take out trash. I laughed even more. It was a glorious honor that had been bestowed on me to watch the hand of my King keep me safe while I was surrounded by wolves. I decided to just let them watch. It had to be entertaining. As I entered the area and got close to the highway that looped around the Metroplex, I noticed there was a roadblock in the form of a license check. It had traffic backed up for miles. It did not say based on the orange street sign that was placed on the shoulder what it was all about. I personally didn't have time or energy to deal with any more puppets. That was when I noticed a couple of other drivers who felt the same way taking the shoulder across the dirt and then onto the access road next to the highway. I decided to follow suit, knowing that the roadblock was probably a violation of a Fourth Amendment right to begin with anyway. I made my way underneath the next overpass and took a back road toward the place I lived on Quality Hill. That was when I noticed another stalker.

The wife of a painter I worked with at another dealership had pulled alongside of me, taking photos with her camera phone and laughing. I laughed too because I don't think she knew that I knew who she was. As we took off from the next light, going straight, I noticed she began to get exceedingly close to my rear tire. I laughed and sped up with the drop of the clutch and the twist of the throttle. It was rather entertaining driving from stoplight to stoplight like cat and mouse. The whole time both of us were laughing at one another. All the while, I knew she was a slave, no more important than I was. As we took off from the last stoplight, where we would be by one another, I accelerated rather hard, and she did too to keep up with me. I let off a little as she gained ground to get next to me. I veered to the right and slammed on my brakes, both front and rear while down shifting. The stopping power on this nimble rocket was amazing. In less than a half of a second, she was now in front of me, just like I liked because that way, I could watch. The next stoplight would be a green light. I acted like I was going to go straight by being in the left-hand lane, and she did also. But at the last second, knowing that my nimble rocket could turn as if it was on rails, I lowered my right knee and slid off of the seat to the right-hand side as I twisted the throttle and down-shifted, leaving her in my dust on the road without supervision.

I headed back toward my place, knowing I was almost out of that sewer. When I got to my place, it looked like someone had gone through my stuff. I really didn't care because it was just stuff. I knew

I was moving because I had already decided in court. But I could not let my enemies be aware that I was aware. I had to make sure they thought that I was the blind sheep still. Because if they knew what I'd already done in court, they would try to kill me without even thinking about it. So I decided it might be nice to pay them a visit to ensure they knew I was just fine.

After having some refreshments and gaining some strength, I headed over there toward the evening. I rode my motorcycle over to Muck and Linda's and happened to pass by a coconspirator of Linda's, driving his Ford Expedition and almost running me off the road as he honked and pounded his fist in the air like Arsenio Hall. He was smiling as if his actions and words had any effect on my quality of life. This was the day before his place was struck by lightning ... again ... We all know who had given him the house his family lived in and why. Linda did for favors.

As I pulled up to the compound Linda called her own, I couldn't help but notice how Linda and my half-brother were excited to tell me that my SUV had been repossessed. I kind of laughed because I knew that my payments were not near delinquent enough for it to be repossessed. But I was actually kind of thankful because that meant it was one less anchor I had to carry or deal with. Besides, we all know who owned the bank that owned my vehicle—meaning that was not my vehicle to begin with, and someone else was entitled to use it. I laughed when they told me I no longer had access to a vehicle to move my tools. It bothered them more than I expected. I began to share about how much I liked my new motorcycle, knowing that it bothered Linda severely. I told her it was a game changer, and it looked like an atom bomb had gone off between her ears. She wasn't having it. And I was getting off on it. She exclaimed to me in the dark that I just wanted to move there to get high. I laughed and said, "I'm an adult. I can do whatever I want."

That was when she said frantically, "You can't move."

I laughed again. I said to her, "Linda, take me to court again, and I'll show you what I got."

Her eyes bugged out even more. She looked around as if someone should be there to protect her. But nobody was. We were sitting there, just the two of us. I hope she could sense the sincerity in my voice, knowing that I knew what she had been planning all along. May the losers just keep losing. I want to just keep watching. I believe the King needs a large audience, don't you? Thank you for commanding such a large viewing audience.

Is there such a thing as reality entertainment? I think not. When people manipulate other people's lives, it's because they don't have the virtues to control their own. I truly believe that when you love money more than life, maybe you should lose yours chasing someone else's. Puppets like Linda are just like toilet paper—soft, disposable, cheap, and readily available, and I had to keep them on a roll, because I needed them to get covered in my poo while keeping me clean. What do you expect? When someone is the shit, they must be surrounded by toilet paper. So, I beg all my haters. Say it to my face if you've any balls. I didn't think so. Enjoy your mediocrity, and I will too. Can you hear me now? Good. Cheers!

CHAPTER 11

Colorado Puppets

Life was easy in my new location. I was able to pay attention and take notes of who the shepherds paid to keep a close watch on me. I have been reconditioning vehicles since before I can remember. I learned from some of the same wolves who wear sheep's clothing and want bad things to happen to me. I knew based on whom the family was connected to. After all, it was a small compound where everyone knew each other. Do I have it? No. More or less, I've seen it before, but I was blind then, much like the rest of the blind sheep that are surrounded by wolves and don't even know it. As I started my new job working on vehicles, I attended a company lunch at which I was blessed to have a delicious meal with the sun shining on my face. Others suggested sitting inside to avoid getting sunburned. I refused politely, knowing how thankful I am to have the sun shining on my face. In this moment right here, right now, my cup is running over. Much like a soda that's been shaken up, I was bubbling.

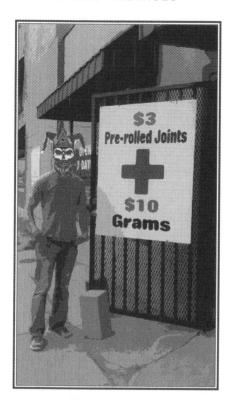

I was befriended by a coworker initially. She seemed pretty nice. Her name was Greta Parks. She was very new in my trade and had a lot to learn, but because of her friends, she was in a secure position. She initially helped me, and we enjoyed each other's company, I thought. Until that weekend when the shepherd was in town. I bought myself a new wheel, actually four of them. Greta offered to go with me to pick it up. I took her up on it. I even put a full tank of gas in her car and offered to pay her. It was right during this huge hundred-year flood that changed the natural landscape of the area. The amount of rainfall was impressive. It destroyed roads and homes, changing the landscape forever. I felt that was confirmation of my faith. He moves mountains for me. I must enjoy this earth. That's kind of why I felt like I needed a car instead of a motorcycle. It was impressive to see the amount of flooding and rainfall paired with the National Guard standing at the entrance of mountain roads. I hadn't ever seen anything like that. And I didn't know if I would actually get to take delivery of the new but used car because the road getting there was blocked off. Thankfully though, he managed to convince the huge Humvee to let him through and agreed to walk back on foot. I liked it. It was more of an old sheep's car, but I liked it a lot. It had all the creature comforts that I had grown to appreciate, not to mention a locking gas door, as well as a locking gas cap and laminated glass all the way around for silence and security. Those things were so hard to break. It's been said those wheels are indestructible. I love Volvos.

I've seen a video on the same exact one, and it was impressive, driving around, smashing all the other ones and still running just fine. I wanted this car. It would be perfect for the landscape I was in now. It needed some work. The dealership had informed the owner how expensive the repairs would be and that they far exceeded the value of the car. Although running and driving and extremely clean, it needed a few things, but it did drive home and did very well.

Once I got back, I noticed Gretta's phone blowing up, and it was her father. Initially, she didn't answer the first call. I think the timing was more the issue. We were saying our goodbyes and see-you-tomorrows. She answered her phone while she was walking away, and I was fumbling for my keys to get in. I heard her say something on the phone and turn and look at me as if she had seen a ghost. I didn't really think much of it. I was on my way to a new life.

The very next week, I guess, is when I started to notice that people did not like me. I had a way to make things look easy. Maybe they were since I wasn't experiencing the same level of torture, and I could breathe a little bit. I guess that wasn't a very comforting feeling.

The same week, I was told about another black sheep who used to work there. His name was Tim. She didn't seem sad at all about telling me how he took his own life. They said they found him in a field by his bicycle somewhere. But the way she described it, she gave too many details, like she had been there or seen it herself—unless maybe she saw photo. I don't know. She told me how the news rocked the entire dealership. She also told me that she and he used to be on again, off again, whatever that meant. I didn't really care. But she proceeded to ask me something really weird, and that was if I was sure I wanted to work there because that might happen to me.

I laughed. I said, "You don't know me." I didn't really care. It seemed to bother her. As the days went on, I began to notice an exceeding amount of passive-aggressiveness. I couldn't quite put my finger on it, but it was obvious, and everyone else saw it to. She could do whatever she wanted because her position was so secure that she had nothing to be worried about. Not much longer after that, she invited me over to a party she was having. And it almost seemed as though my life would be harder at work if I didn't make an appearance at least. It wasn't too far from my place, so I went. When I was there, I did have one drink, and it didn't taste like I remembered the specific IPA to taste. But whatever, I watched the football game on TV, sitting on the couch mostly by myself. It was pretty hard to relate to such a young crowd. They were all babies living in their parents' homes without any responsibility and partying harder than I'd ever partied on a daily basis. I could see it was more than just Greta; the sheer number of baby sheep who were having to be supported by their families made me sad. But then I remembered everyone has their own burdens to bear. I've got my own too.

I think I must have dozed off just thinking that. Greta woke me and said, "We have to take a picture."

It was an ugly sweater party. I had only heard of one other person who had an ugly sweater party. And that was Muck, my half-brother. Half awake, I didn't say anything and went into the kitchen, where multiple people were standing with their camera phones ready to take a picture. Greta quickly put her arm around me, and her friend Saul did the same on my other side. Everyone was smiling and laughing. They all took turns taking pictures. I kind of laughed, because I understood shepherds would pay good money for photos like that. All I had to do was be in them. I smiled as big as I could. Do you see me now?

I had to go to the restroom, and when I walked into the restroom, I noticed the large penis drawn on my forehead with a Magic Marker. I kind of laughed to myself. I thought, *Well, what a mediocre way to try to get a reaction out of me.* They must not really know who I am yet. Knowing that manipulators are looking for reaction, I had decided that I was going to take the high road and not give them anything to say. You can't say anything about someone who just smiles.

So, the next morning, I woke up earlier than everyone, just before sunrise and took it upon myself to clean up all the trash that was left by the gluttonous baby sheep who don't know how to use a trash can. I also thought they could use some food, specifically some triglycerides. So I went to the local market and bought the cheapest, most fattening cinnamon rolls I could find, the kind you put in the oven at 350 degrees Fahrenheit and wait twenty minutes. They'd been injected with an aerosol to make them inflate as soon as you opened the package. I also lined the pan with as much butter as I could put on it. I made sure the icing was over the top and they were cooked to perfection. I served them with a smile and gave them nothing to complain about. I wanted to make sure they reported back to the shepherds, "He didn't feel a thing. It's like he was on Novocain."

The next Monday at work was filled with laughter and excitement from all my coworkers who were excited about Gretta's photo, which she had put on social media for the entire world to see. Specifically, the painter, Devon, was constantly bringing it up in front of anyone he could, be it an insurance person or even the trash person. He made it his personal mission to ensure that everyone had seen the photo and that it was funny. I could care less because I produced more than the other people who thought they knew what they were doing. I could see that it severely bothered Devon. I actually kind of enjoyed it. I began to notice them complain about the most trivial things. It reminded me of the prima donna. They took great pride in wearing both of their faces. It was like they were slaves and would have to consult with others as to what to do about me.

They were hiding keys, hiding parts, and unplugging unrelated things to disable the projects I was working on as if to slow me down. It only made me laugh more and take many more notes. I can't thank the three little wolves enough. As much as Devon asked about my plans and where I would be, I thought he was just curious at first. But I'm always reminded that a shepherd can never let go of the one sheep that got away. That was interesting and made me feel so honored.

The wheel where time stands still, what did my ancestor mean by that? I loved wheels, but time never stands still. Whatever did she mean by that? I still don't know.

I began riding unicycles a while before. I was one of the first in the country to start riding an electric wheel. I decided that since I was always on one wheel, on a motorcycle, that I should just embrace it. It was amazing that whenever I rode it, people from everywhere would stare. Many would want to know what it was and how much it cost. That was one of the most common questions people would ask. Most of the time, they would ask how much it was before they even asked what it was. It cost about a grand. And I didn't know how I felt about repeating that. I was worried that someone might try to take it from me if they thought it was valuable, so often, I just didn't say anything, or I would just downplay it. Others thought I should boast about it, as if I were telling them to get their own because it was only a grand. The wheel was worth so much more than what I paid for it. It taught me balance, it taught me patience, and more important, it gave me the ability to come out of my shell. I began having to talk to strangers. I wasn't used to that. I liked just keeping to myself. But in riding this new style of wheel, I was approached by so many people one on one when I would take it out, that I had no choice but to learn how to be confident in myself and speak to perfect strangers with eloquence and grace while still being myself. It was just what I needed. It was the perfect recreation.

I soon found that I had no interest in the old style of wheels that I had worked on and loved forever. I was so over them. I decided that I wasn't going to buy any more dead-dinosaur syrup. That's right. No more wasting my time and money on dead dinosaurs. I decided to boycott gasoline accordingly. Who needs an old wheel when it's been reinvented? I loved riding so much I introduced my little unicorns to it also in 2016. We were the three blind mice, wheeling all around Denver, and it felt great to be back together with them. I almost couldn't contain myself. We had matching unicycles, and we were up so high, a mile over the sea. We loved it. My little unicorns picked it up very fast. And we were off and wheeling in no time.

The first month we rode them, we put around a thousand miles each on them while they were visiting in Denver. Truly, they are unicorns who are also trapped by shepherds. They don't even know yet. But I think they have an idea because of what they have seen behind closed doors. To a certain degree, ignorance is blissful. Why would I ever want to upset them by telling them who they are being raised by? They will figure it out, just as I did. They didn't ask to be born into a cult, and neither did I. I wanted to pursue life, liberty, and happiness. But shepherds don't like to see sheep happy. Misery loves company. I choose to turn a blind eye and vicariously live. It's the opposite of what my enemies, who are only cowards, want. I want it too. I can assure you I cannot wait to meet my father in heaven in person. He knows exactly what, who, when, and why. I'm looking forward to it. Not everyone faces life alone, but everyone does face death all alone. And that's where wolves will be held accountable for trading their integrity for money. I'm sure they have planned out how to avoid being held accountable. It's simply amazing what money can do if you think bigger. It's a disgrace. It really is. I think there should be a reset when it comes to money, wealth, and the economy. It's a system owned by the elite, and they don't have to use integrity to do business because the money they have will make up the difference. I've seen the evilest people have the most excess and, in the process, become properly tormented by not getting what they want. If you don't believe me, maybe you should ask about me, and you'll see what money can and can't do. Personally, I hate money. I know there are only just a few of us who can't be bought. I am fully aware how it's a printed piece of art, designed by the elite to represent something of value, something that blind sheep can hold and see and, most important, believe in. My perspective might sound skewed to some who are still blind. I am not trying to offend.

My love for wheels and vehicles was probably fueled by my creator. I'd rather spend a single moment in His presence than a thousand years elsewhere. His story is one of a recycler, if you think about it. He takes the lowest, weakest things and does wonders with them. I've seen His hands to be those of a sculptor with the most profound attention to detail. When His work is a finished project, it's majestic, it's amazing, and it's beautiful and stronger than before. I have seen my creator create the most beautiful things from dirt and mud. How much more glorious His work is when He starts with His own creation. Most sheep don't usually see the scars that my father heals, because only He can do that caliber of work. The before and after is the mark of my father's handiwork.

I loved applying the same principles to vehicles. I loved developing my skills using my hands to do so. Not every vehicle was worth fixing for financial reasons, but every vehicle could be fixed with enough labor and restoration. I loved the feeling of adopting a project that was a liability to most with the intention of making the vehicle look and function as if nothing had ever happened, not even a scratch, making it even better than the day it was made from the world's hands. That is my King's full story. He gives rest and restoration to the sheep who need it. And the enemy is so jealous of the virtues carried by legends like a unicorn, he will use any and every tactic to trap all the sheep he can.

I'm aware of how valuable my time is, but I am not aware if anyone else knows. It's a great paradox to have. I call them champagne problems. I'll just stick to what I know. I am aware the enlightened sheep who find true happiness find it in the toil of their hands and the satisfaction of their work. Their self-worth is independent of the shepherds and their schemes. I am so happy being such a skilled artist who isn't easily replaceable and is in high demand. I know that my skills are so well versed; therefore, I am not a slave anymore. I must not let anyone else know how I set myself free yet—in due time. I must only watch and see who the wolves are. I would like to make sure they see me smile. I know they would like to paint my ever-fading black wool on the costume. It keeps fading, and the wolves who wear sheep's clothes keep painting and pointing. They tried to do the same thing to me they did to a blind sheep named "Tim," who used to love vehicles too. They bragged about the hand they helped him kill himself with. I was warned the same thing might happen to me. I laughed and smiled. I keep watching because I find enjoyment in being strong enough to stand firmly planted on both feet. Much like a tree planted by a river, I'm growing tall and strong as my roots go deep. I remember smiling at one wolf, Devon, who had a son in the same place. I told the wolf in sheep's clothing more or less that I was aware. Actually, I said it perfectly clearly in many words. When he finally got his Black Shelby Cobra look alike car for payment in my smear, I laughed. He named his car Reggie. I was supposed to be sad, but I knew better. Bad things, a lot of bad things, happen to people who try to hurt me. True story here, his son named Dawn was warned without me saying a thing. I don't need to; my creator says it all. I will say his parachute didn't open. He got brain damage from the event. After years of pain and recovery with plenty of drugs and rehab, now he is able to live a life of mediocrity as a slave to the treatment he requires to sustain his existence. Dawn was always looking for a reaction from me. I would smile and laugh. He and his pals would take turns urinating on the wheels of the vehicles I was reconditioning. They liked to watch and see if I would give them a reaction. I did too. I laughed. I don't know if they knew, but I had eaten manure for years. Their piss was like lemonade on a hot, sunny day. The boss kept scratching his head. I kept my silence, even though he knew what they were doing and just wanted to hear me say something. He was hoping to create a situation to capitalize on, and I wouldn't speak about it. I would only laugh. It actually gave me the motivation to keep my area even cleaner. I now took a few moments regularly to clean and wash down my work area. It felt even better to know that I was still shining and so was my work—and it showed.

It's been proclaimed, "You will know him by his work." And that's what I want. Know that you may play your own games, and I will work very well. I began to notice before work on a few Fridays they would all meet with the shepherds who paid them to play. That was when I started using my close proximity to my advantage. I began digging dirt, as I would like to say. I first bought a hidden camera pen. It was a genius invention. I used it many times to hold people accountable as well as for my protection. Since I resided directly behind the place I worked, it was much easier to keep my eyes on the wolves, wearing sheep's clothing. I believe when another blind sheep saw me collecting the dirt with my hidden camera, he became alarmed. He noticed me walking away from the door one of the mornings. I had put my pen camera on the door to record Muck leaving in his black SRT-8. Muck was and is a bankster and gangster. He knows he must repay the shepherds he is in debt to. Rightfully so, I don't think he understands whom he is playing with. I know the blindest sheep think the offshore bank accounts they use to get paid for my smear are completely safe. However, in our Constitution, it states explicitly that offshore bank accounts can be subpoenaed when they are used for organized crime.

I mentioned the bank they used to the wolf named Devon, the one who kept trying to paint me in the mile highest. And his eyes almost popped out of his head. Later that day, he took great care to walk by and make cat sounds. It was so over the top even other coworkers were a little confused. But I knew. I waited to say anything until he was leaving as he usually was in a great mood, wearing his purple shirt, because that's his golf shirt. I smiled like a good little blind sheep as I suggested quietly and privately to him, "Go back to your consultants, and ask them what they would have you do now, but first, make sure you set your anchors good and firm. I am liable to rip it right out without even noticing. They always said I could tear up an anvil … with a feather."

He looked like he saw a ghost in that moment. I saw him age a little right then and there. I could see the illumination in his eyes. It was like another little bomb went off between his ears. I had seen him rubbing elbows with the gang of coward sheep who had a thin blue line on their wallet. Prior to this day, he bragged about knowing them for a very long time and that he was untouchable. Other sheep felt that was reassurance for their behavior. I was thankful he was getting comfortable and confident enough to see me as weak, but I just threw him a curve ball with a sincere smile and went back into character. I said as he walked away and opened the door to the manager's office, "Sorry you just can't kill me. I will just see you tomorrow … shepherd." I said it looking directly in his eyes. They were glowing like embers, and he was wearing a smile. It was just within earshot of the shepherd sitting in the office. He went straight into his office and closed the door. He drew the blinds, and they were in there for a while.

I laughed and wondered if he still had time for his golf game. I hoped he would still have time for eighteen holes, because I wanted to see if he was still on his game or if he was struggling to carry his anchor around the course while playing with his balls. I didn't say another word. I was on my best behavior, and my work was on point. I was consistently producing more than all the other sheep who were working together. I knew I had a target on my back there.

I should enjoy how sometimes the bullets missed. I was rewarded so many times by seeing how my coworkers would plot and scheme to make my death look like an accident or a suicide because that was how the life insurance policy was written. It was my life insurance that everyone I used to know wanted to collect on. I know who, what, when, and why. If you have your own insurance policy underwriter's license, then you can bypass a third party and keep things more secret. That's the way the shepherd operates. He uses a crook to cull the black sheep.

During my employment there, I witnessed so many incidents with my coworkers' hands being apart, it was undeniable for most. They just couldn't break me. I just kept my hands busy and made my life the way I wanted it. I watched the painter using others, from the kid who waited in his mom's car to try to run over me to the boss's pet, who was hired to try to undermine my work. I remember laughing at his mediocrity. It took him a long time to put a used quarter panel on a Ford. He didn't even finish. He somehow got sick for a week, and someone else had to finish it.

The boss bragged about his father being a part of the gang in blue union in Virginia. I laughed at him, and it further motivated him to try to manipulate my paycheck. After his boy failed gloriously to replace that part, he stopped giving me cars to work on for about a week and then had a totaled GTO that needed a quarter panel and door. He was so excited about it, he texted me before work as if I would be excited to do extraordinary work for scraps to make him look good. That's when I sized up the operation. *I'm bigger; I'm stronger. They need to see. So watch.*

The owner of the dealership and manager both smirked as I set my workflow up. It took me less than a week to repair the total in its entirety. It looked amazing. Even a trained eye would have had a hard time distinguishing where my repair was. I cut the car in half literally and did so in about a day. Like a machine, my hands are built for better things than throwing them at someone, especially someone I don't like. I laughed as I was sweeping the floor after I finished the project in record time. I noticed the manager and owner of the dealership staring at me while I was cleaning. I couldn't help but laugh. *Rope a dope.* I didn't have anything else to work on, so I began to leave and noticed the manager taking his certificates off the wall of his office. Yeah, that was just after the two of them met in his office in private with the door closed. Yeah. I get it. I'm not supposed to be able to outperform those I'm surrounded by. Oh well, I can't help it.

Since he couldn't get a reaction out of me, he began to create his own. He sent his son-in-law who also worked there to try to make my life difficult. I laughed again because it isn't up to me. He had me fix a BMW for his friend and went to great lengths to discount my work. It was around eighteen grand in damage. The customer complained about the engine temperature. It wasn't what it was before. I suggested to them it might have been the cheap-ass aftermarket radiator. Put a genuine BMW unit in it. There is a reason they cost twelve hundred bucks. I went to great lengths to cover my ass. And it bothered him that I would just smile as he kept trying to stab me in the back. He in disbelief actually took the car to the BMW dealership for them to take apart and go through my work with a fine-tooth comb. I think the bill for the labor that was spent for someone to be told it was flawless was around two grand. I don't remember if that was before or after the Mexican motorcycle rapist showed up at my apartment complex and raped two women while using an electric unicycle identical to mine. It wasn't about two weeks after this incident that another stage of many to come would be set. I chose to go to lunch on Fridays with the same wolves that I served doughnuts, so I could see how fake they were. I didn't like being around them. The conversations weren't intellectually stimulating for me. They always consisted of talking trash about everyone around them. I could tell this Friday there was something different in the air. They were acting strange and on edge with one another. I took notice.

Shortly after sitting down with them at lunch on a Friday in October 2016 to eat at a burrito place, I noticed they wanted me to sit on the inside of the table, where it would be harder to leave. I rode my unicycle there and was the last to sit down. Two people had to stop eating and get up to let me sit down in the booth. I offered to sit on the outside, but they looked at each other as if they didn't know how to respond. I chose to leave my unicycle on and leaned it against the trash can. I ate my lunch so fast I didn't taste it. They weren't halfway through their lunch when I told them I was all done and was leaving. They again looked at one another as if I was inconveniencing them by moving. They actually didn't move at first. About twenty seconds later, I started moving, and they moved instead of spilling their drinks and food. I could again see embers glowing in Devon's eyes. I smiled big and threw my trash away as I was leaving.

I went straight to my place to finish my hour-long lunch. I noticed a few shepherds from the gang in blue all around my apartment complex. I kept wondering what that was all about. Whatever it was, I wasn't aware. I left my apartment and went back to work.

I was approached by one member of the gang in blue who was sitting in his car as I passed by who I had seen earlier. He noticed my unicycle and asked about it with a smirk and smile. I said, "Yep. I'm just trying to save the world one wheel at a time."

He laughed as if there was a joke that I didn't get. I went to work and worked hard. It was Friday. I did notice that Devon was on his phone more than usual that day. He seemed concerned and extremely bothered. I smiled and just kept working. On my way to the soda fountain, I noticed some of the same gang in blue members at my work talking to the wolves I worked with. I didn't care, because I wanted them to see. I drank my favorite energy drink. It's sweet and tart, with very few calories. I find it's a good Friday afternoon pick-me-up. I finished my work and headed to my place just behind my work.

I saw several news vans and reporters walking around with microphones and cameras. I was on my wheel and had just gotten my mail when a reporter from channel 7 asked me if I knew anything. I said, "No, what the heck is going on?"

She told me that two people were raped in my apartment complex by Ricardo Corral-Venegas who was a Mexican police officer known as the moped rapist. I was shocked. She asked to interview me on camera. I told her that I didn't want to be on camera when it might be organized criminals at work. I would rather be behind the camera. About ten seconds later, her phone rang, and she was ecstatic. I could tell something had made her day. She hung up and thanked me before telling her cameraman that one of the victims was willing to do an interview on camera. They immediately went and met with her. I saw the story on the news that night. It was kind of big news over the weekend on the media. People around there were following it on the news. I was told by the owner of the dealership where I worked that the wolf had traveled all the way from Mexico to there.

The gang in blue spotted him just across the street from where I was eating lunch, only about twenty mins after I had left the taco place. They found his backpack with tools at the bank I used regularly just next door. It was said he was riding a unicycle just like mine. That was why the gang in blue were there on Friday. They wanted to see the video footage with the time stamp of me during that whole ordeal. He told me not to worry, because they had caught the guy, and he was rotting in jail. I followed the trial and watched the outcome. The wolf convicted in that crime got seventy-two years. I was overjoyed. I wondered how expensive that trap ended up being for the wolves who wanted to kill me. I doubt I will ever know. I didn't see until later that was probably meant for me. Bad things, a lot of bad things, happen to people who want to hurt me. I just smile.

About two months after that incident, I think they learned that adults who act like that get significant punishment. But if you're under eighteen, you won't be doing any time.

This was a sunny Friday. I was greeted by a baby sheep wearing a red shirt with blue stripes. I was having a break around 10:00 a.m., and he approached me. He looked at me and my name tag as if he already knew who I was. We were in an area that wasn't for the public, much less underaged sheep. He asked me where the restroom was and started texting on his phone feverishly, not even listening to my directions. I thought, *This is too weird.*

When another coworker spotted him getting into a shiny Lexus and driving around, he was alarmed. The little sheep was probably ten or twelve—no way he owned a car, much less was old enough to drive it. That coworker wasn't in the club of wolves yet. And he didn't like this situation. He actually got the kid out of the bathroom and took him to the office where the owner asked him what was going on. The little sheep's story kept changing, and it was obvious he was hiding something. I'm sure he felt like a rat in a cage being surrounded by so many adults. He bounced and ran for the door. He bolted out the door and took off.

The owner of the dealership had chased after him for about forty yards when the little sheep pulled a hand gun out and showed it to everyone as he kept running. The owner stopped and turned around. I think he was shaken up. It was a couple of hours later when the coworker spotted the little sheep in red. My coworker kept taunting him with the position of his vehicle. He wanted to torment him, knowing he would come back for the Lexus. And I watched as they kept their eyes on one another.

Shortly after lunch, the Lexus was still there, and the coworker who was so bothered suggested blocking in the car to ensure it didn't drive away. But specifically, the wolves who wear sheep's clothing advised against it. I was wondering the whole time after the firearm was brandished why he did not call the gang in blue. I almost thought about calling them myself, but that's not my style. I don't call those wolves. So I didn't bother, and when the little sheep thought the coast was clear, he climbed over the barbed-wire fence and got back into the Lexus. With the inability to see inside, there was speculation as to if someone was in there. I didn't care. I had work to do, and it was payday. I mixed up chemicals to use and was occupied when another coworker who is almost the same height and build and wears the same work attire walked out to the car to see if he could see. I advised against it, but he was curious; everyone was. As I was spreading chemicals on a vehicle I was repairing, I watched my coworker approach the car. I think the baby sheep must have thought my coworker was me, because he started the car, accelerated out of the parking spot at the back of the lot buy the fence he just climbed over and left skid marks as he headed straight for the blind sheep coworker who looked like me. He left tire marks he accelerated so fast. He wasn't a great driver yet, being underaged I'm willing to bet he learned how to drive from playing video games, because he missed my coworker and hit a red van that was being worked on there instead. That created a scene and enraged the coworker who had spent so much time tormenting him. He instantly stopped working and saw the whole thing. He grabbed a chair on wheels that the wolf named Dawn owned and threw it about forty feet, and it smashed into the windshield and driver's door of that wheel. It made the Lexus almost stop, I thought, but it might have simply been the three wolves who were taking the painted trash out. He slowed down and steered clear of the three of them, and it looked like they waved at each other on the down low. The coworker who threw the chair was scolded by the wolves. Dawn actually made him buy a new chair. A couple of the other sheep asked if the gang in blue were called. And the wolves said that they called, and the gang in blue never came. Nope. I'm sure if someone actually called the gang in blue about a baby sheep joyriding a stolen Lexus with a gun, they would have been there already. And the car would have been impounded. Later that day, I saw the wolf telling the coworker of mine who threw the chair to change his story about the events that had taken place. I overheard him ask the coworker to omit the flying chair part.

I didn't see the same car again until I voted in the presidential election that year. I went to my polling place, and the same Lexus pulled alongside me on the way back to work. I began laughing as I noticed his still cracked windshield and window. I don't know if fixing it was a priority because it simply had a Band-Aid covering the damage. It was still there, and so was I. How about that? Can you see me now? If not, keep watching. I do.

I made my way to work that day and bought more doughnuts to feed the wolves. I made sure to grab an extra devil's food cake doughnut in case I wanted to speak in rhetoric a little more loudly. But the blind doesn't know. They are blind, and they think I am also. We all know my ex-wife isn't allowed to leave me alone. As a matter of fact, she was on one of the first airplanes there to meet with my coworkers and pass out the publicity for my smear. I watched as they each accepted gifts that could not be returned in a murder-for-hire plot so the rich could continue to be rich. They were inviting me to come close so they could stab me in the back as I fed them triglycerides instead. Fatten up, sheep. You don't even know you will be led to slaughter. I think they should be honest instead. Then we can all be free. I simply say nothing and write it down. That's my best resolve. It works in my favor now.

Needless to say, the manager there at that time was a phony. He came in with all his papers on the wall, wearing a big gold ring and driving a fancy car. He was recommended by the twenty-one group. He was an associate of the old dealership I worked at. It was so fun to see him packing those up and putting them in a box when he couldn't get a reaction out of me. It was sad how many resources were wasted on your employment there. You did say your family was in that gang in blue. I suggested that you aren't a stranger to organized crime, and your eyes got huge. I took great satisfaction watching you and your puppets leave after not being able to manipulate me. Thanks for making me feel important.

That was an interesting work experience, to say the least. I always enjoyed watching them watching me. As if they could make me feel something. It's kind of hard to step it up from being tortured for entertainment around the clock. I feel like after the caliber of losers looking to get rich quick that I had to work for there, that I could work for anybody. I know it bothered the parts guy and manager when I said that because they knew. They had been accepting money to help my ancestors smear me and get rich in the process. So that was what I would do. I couldn't help but notice how much like stalkers they all acted. It was the weirdest thing, the way their eyes would bug out at me for no reason and the insurmountable frustration they brought upon themselves by signing up to smear me.

Greta was so much fun to play games with. She didn't know her craft yet, so she needed me to do most of the work for her—telling her what parts were called, writing them down, and even finding them in the computer for her. It was like babysitting. Infantile brain, she was consumed with me for some reason I don't know. I began again to disassociate, knowing my ex-wife's puppets were not able to think for themselves. They were already owned by the paper they signed to be a part of the program. That's when I began to do my work and stop bending over backward to help her. I did my work exceptionally instead. So, I began parking the cars she would need all day to look at for a simple estimate outside. She could do her work without waiting on me to pull a vehicle in, and it was no longer an issue she could use as an excuse. It didn't take long to swamp her with work that she couldn't really keep up with, and other sheep noticed. She would spend so much time on her phone at her desk talking to shepherds that she lacked any real focus to be a professional.

Around Halloween of 2013 shortly after moving there, I was approached by a prostitute in disguise at the Dollar Store. We exchanged numbers. It was like being stalked by her though. I went to dinner for a burrito when she sat across from me, saying hello and smiling. I left dinner and went to the Dollar Store. When I went down every aisle, she was right there, almost staring at me—not almost, definitely staring at me. We exchanged numbers, and she seemed anxious to invite me over for coffee at her place late at night. I hadn't seen any reason not to learn how to snowboard from her. The strangest thing was the next Monday morning, my coworkers asked about my weekend, and when I mentioned the Dollar Store chick, they got super anxious. Bozzy, who was Greta's partner in crime, made the call. He wasn't too happy about me walking in and seeing him on the phone telling someone about it. He used the company phone to do so. I believe he was paid in full with his black SRT8 Jeep. I could see the look of fleeting happiness in Greta's face. In the morning meeting, she was crying and tearing up. I figured had she already spent the money she planned to get paid for sleeping with me. That was when I knew it was another episode of the biggest cowards. I watched Greta as I hung out with Dollar Store chick who agreed to show me how to snowboard. That's when the Dollar Store chick and I went together, and I bought some gear for snowboarding. I had always wanted to snowboard on a regular. Skiing makes me bored.

It was weird one night. I don't know, maybe she felt bad, but she told me in confidence that she had an ex-boyfriend in the FBI who was putting her up to this for slashing his Jeep with a large knife. I learned more by watching her how fake she actually was. Her apartment wasn't as she had led me to believe. Based on how long she had lived there and how her apartment was, her stories didn't add up. It looked fake from the lack of dust anywhere in any cupboard to the newness of all the possessions in the attached storage closet. Her time lines were not very well executed, to say the least. The Dollar Store chick begged me to have sex with her, and I didn't right away. She mentioned she was married, so I said I'd wait until her divorce was final. You could see the steam escaping from her ears. She was an alcoholic in recovery and had been clean, so she said, for around six months at the time. She attended meetings all the time, like a few times a day.

I was more interested in her showing me how to snowboard. And we did. I thought it was fun. She seemed embarrassed to be by my side. I didn't care. I fell quite a bit for my first time when I noticed she fist-bumped someone who almost seemed to intentionally graze me just before I caught my edge and went down again. I learned to fall for sure that day. When we got back, she begged me to sleep with her. She was attractive, no doubt. She had long brown hair, a slim figure, and sweet lips. It was an appealing offer. But I know she was the enemy. I decided to confirm. So I did have sex with her that night. I do remember how great her body looked in the shadows from the moonlight on the snow outside that seemed to show in more detail how soft her skin was and how young her chest looked for being my age. You could see she hadn't had kids yet. And maybe she liked sex. It was decent. I'd had better, and I'd had worse. And when it was over, I used the restroom and washed out the condom several times. Then, I threw it into the trash in a box of opened bath soap.

I fell asleep after a decent workout between the two of us. I made sure to get my money's worth if someone else was paying the bill. I kind of needed a shower to be honest. But her being so sweet to me after sex made me even more tired. I must have been asleep for about an hour when I noticed her in the bathroom with the light on, and it looked like she was digging in the trash can. But she put it down and shut off the light before storming out and not looking very happy when we made eye contact even though I was supposed to be sleeping.

I left the next morning to pass a "friend." She worked with my ex-wife and attended the same religious cult functions. She was Linda's right hand. They vacationed together. I even have the photos. She worked for the same cult my ex-wife did. I took notes of how her ex-husband died of mysterious circumstances shortly after they divorced. She seemed to profit from that as if it was an arrangement. I never saw her sad in the least bit. She was as fake as they came. She was also an associate of the woman who claimed to be my mother. I noticed the beige Nissan Altima with the large dent on the passenger side's two doors. It was bad enough to need replacement. But who cares? That was how I knew for sure it was her.

I saw the Beige Nissan Altima four-door mid-2000s with the two passenger-side doors damaged around the molding pass by as I was leaving the Dollar Store girl's house. Did you get that on video for your leaders? I kept watching this Dollar Store chick try to tell me that she was put up to something by an ex-boyfriend who was in the FBI, about how she slashed his Jeep with a knife and if she didn't comply, he would get rid of her. I knew she was now a slave to my family's smear campaign. I stopped talking. She began stalking me and wanted to come over for dinner one night. So I gave in. It was just after I had put all my furniture into my new apartment. I ordered pizza, and her eyes got huge. She didn't want any. I didn't care. I'd eaten poison many times. Keep trying. She asked again for sex, and I couldn't care less. I found it odd how she had to keep her phone super close and was very loud. To be honest, it was way more fake than the first time. It was quick. And I put my condom in the trash as she went to the restroom before leaving.

I made some coffee and poured the grounds onto where the condom was in the trash because I was surrounded by losers. I could see the excitement in her eyes as she headed for the door, only to ask me to meet for coffee about two hours later just around the corner. I obliged because I wanted to see. I drove there and noticed an overweight lady sitting in a black Honda just outside my door. As I passed, it looked like she took a photo with her phone and pulled forward. I got into my car and pulled out as she slowly stayed in front of me. As we got to the stop sign, she stopped short as if for me to go around. I didn't. She turned her hazards on, and I proceeded. It looked like she was talking on her phone as I passed, and I wondered if she was another stalker. Let them look. Cowards. I pulled into Starbucks to see the Dollar Store girl inside talking to a gentleman who looked like my ex-wife's boyfriend. I knew he ran a smut business.

As I tried to approach the front door, I was greeted by an associate of my ex-wife's who ironically begged me for change. I said nothing, and his voice grew louder, much like the boy crying wolf. I walked inside to see the Dollar Store girl being handed a credit card as she sat with her laptop putting money into a new account. The gentleman she had just been speaking with and got the card from was putting his laptop into a bag and leaving. I watched the two of them walk about twenty yards to get into an all-white unmarked gang unit. I know cult leaders can't be honest. Because then there wouldn't be any slaves to deal in. I wonder if she has died from alcoholism yet. It seems as though Devon knew the Dollar Store chick from what he told others later. I get it. You both grew up here, and I'm the new guy. A nobody.

I was rewarded so many times by seeing how my coworkers would plot and scheme to make my death look like an accident or a suicide because that was how the life insurance policy was written. It's my life insurance that everyone I used to know wants to collect on. I know who, what, when, and why. If you have your own insurance policy underwriter's license, then you can bypass a third party and keep things more secret. That's the way the shepherd operates. He uses a crook to cull the black sheep.

It's sad that nobody else sees, but maybe it's my destiny to bring light where there is only darkness by way of lying by omission under obligations for financial compensation. That's shepherding at its prime. Create a situation that the elite gain resources from. It's so sad to me how little people know about money. I know I was raised differently and know entirely too much. My fascination with money was sparked at a young age while I was attending coin clubs with a family Freemason. It was a great way for them to wash their money by putting it in "random" boxes on the wall to be "auctioned" off to other club members—no paper trail. It was the cash equivalent of a dishwasher. I saw some of the gold coins that were made to represent some of the other questionable actions. I met a few of them, as my interest in rare coins arose before I was eight years old. I was and sometimes act like a savant. I could remember critical details about money and where it came from. I couldn't tell you if that was part of having a grandmother who was a bookkeeper for the mob. But it was a Ponzi scheme. At its root, money isn't worth what it costs to print it. And those who help manufacture the paper we spend are held to the highest level of secrecy. Jobs like those don't go to the best and brightest talent; they go to the next family member in line. I've seen it over and over and over. It's so predictable. The rich get richer, the poor get poorer, and they say the rest of us are greedy, only because they simply print more and circulate it for schemes. Think of it as handing out punishment for those who wouldn't normally get punished. The illusion of money and the power it has is what the Illuminati always count on. They simply print more, or simply use the bills that are to be destroyed. Those are easier to come by, especially if you work at the bank and are Illuminati. That's so easy then. See, paper has a limited life span, and banks get new bills in exchange for old bills. It's part of the service we expect as holders of paper. The value of the paper must stay intact even if the paper itself isn't in the best condition. It's simply collected by local branches and sent back for new ones via armored trucks on a biweekly basis. It's really not that hard to imagine if you think about it.

It wasn't long ago that a million dollars was plenty to live the rest of your life on with ease. And now, it's more like a billion dollars for the same thing. I question where all the money comes from. Certainly, the size of Fort Knox hasn't increased. But the amount of money in circulation doesn't add up to what gold is available and currently worth. It's simply an illusion. I've known for most of my life because of the wolves who raised me. I'm so thankful for the insight because I don't care about money. As a matter of fact, I hate it. I hate how it brings about a sense of entitlement that creates elitism when we are supposed to live in a free society where we all have equal rights. If money changes things, then why would anyone believe in the system? It's obviously broken and needs to be replaced. What would be the best way to break it all down? A reset button on the economy? Hit men? A bulldozer like Marv built in Colorado? I worked with the wolves who took great pride in leading him down that path for their own profit. Maybe Marv should have written a book instead of building his own tank. But Marv did give that town called Granby an enema. Maybe someone should build a bomb that when it goes off it breaks down every wall so the slate can be cleaned and the elite deleted for the opportunity to turn people into money. It's not for me; it's for all of us. Our kids don't deserve to be enslaved by oppressors who wear fake shiny buttons like a crown of gold for all the blind sheep to believe in. Welcome to the age of entitlement. This is it.

Everyone I know cannot wait to get in line to be seen in a movie that I hold the ending to. Sorry. It's not my life. I gave it to my creator years ago. I simply don't deal in that kind of currency trading. Talk to my King if it bothers you I'm still alive. I know He can hear you. He hears me; it's pretty obvious. Slavery is coming to the masses unless wolves who run the show are held accountable. If it could happen to me, it could happen to anyone. I was raised by them with inside knowledge. Now, I simply watch and take notes. I hope it's still funny for my viewing audience. Laughter is the best medicine. Or should I keep going? Can you hear me now? I'm not talking to you. I'm talking to all the others who are reading this. This is for everyone else. It's not about me. I'm a nobody.

> To tell you the truth, I've rarely met anyone with any integrity.
> It's always in random places. Maybe that's why I prefer to
> travel by train. You never know who you might just meet
> while picking up this book from a safe deposit box.
> —Max Jester

This was taken from handwritten memoirs written in 2017 before I left the Mile High to reach sea level.

Of course, I cannot stop writing and watching. It's so entertaining, isn't it? So here is another section about my time in the Bay Area. Everything starts in the bay … even the entertainment lawyer I went to school with. He had his college paid for by the guy whose Barnes I burned down. Can he still see how happy I am? I hope everyone has taken plenty of photos of me smiling. It's so fun being a jester. Let's play some more. Please?

CHAPTER 12

Safe Deposit

Written 2018–2020

Being the royal jester that I am, I feel I must share with my audience that I wrote the contents of this book you just read years ago. I wasn't planning on sharing it, but it seems as though my ancestors haven't had enough yet. I'm still surrounded by losers looking to get rich quick. This won't change until my ancestors are all held accountable. I wrote the majority of what you've just read all down right after a coworker in Colorado lost his life suddenly, in his sleep, at the age of twenty-one. I knew right then and there it was a tragedy. This thing we are so ungrateful for is called time. That's why most days I proudly wear my two-tone Rolex, knowing it's the most hated model ever made. I wear it knowing how valuable my time left is, because life is just too short. Time is a commodity; I must live every day as if it is my last. I must leave my little unicorns a legacy.

Knowing the pen is mightier than the sword, I've put mine to good use over the years. I spent about a week putting all my chapters on paper for everyone else to read—learning from yesterday, planning for tomorrow, living for today. The best never loose, they only learn.

Now I'm chasing my dreams. Life isn't long enough to live it since so many years of mine weren't actually my own. I used an entire box of pens and a stack of notebooks to document my ancestors' smear based on phone records. Times, places, and events are as authentic as they can be. It's the blinding light that's hard to see through. So the names of real people were changed, but the favors and gifts all remain the same. I've done my best to live my life as my King wishes. And it's an amazing honor that was bestowed upon me to be so free. I'm so thankful that I don't actually have family. I don't actually have friends, just a few acquaintances. I've never been happier. This is now my offering to the elite of death or servitude.

I spoke in silence, offering the shepherds an olive branch, but I know the gifts that were received and cannot be returned. There is no other option for my ancestors. They have been in the slave businesses for hundreds of years. I just want to live my life. Leave me the heck alone. That's my offering to that cult of swingers who wear sheep's clothing. I know if they try again, I'll be waiting. Learn from yesterday, live for today, and plan for tomorrow.

I went to my bank and got a safe deposit box. I put my book there and kept both keys in my possession. I kept the book locked away and decided to live my life. I again began to liquidate my possessions and downsize as I looked for a much more skilled-labor type of job. And now that I've decided to boycott gasoline, I see it fitting to avoid putting gasoline cars back on the road. I put my résumé out to a tech company known for electric vehicles. I had an interview in person. So I put all the things I needed into a couple of backpacks. The rest I put in boxes in the closet. I gave my kitty plenty of food and water and set up something for a friend to go and check on her. Then I began looking to find a ride to the bay.

I wanted to teach myself how to sail. I knew next to the ocean was where I wanted to be. I dreamed of sailing to Hawaii. After all, that was one of the prizes competed for by coworkers in the Bible belt. It was offered by my ancestors. It would be a courageous thing to see the hand of my King a million miles from nowhere. That was when I began looking on Craigslist in the rideshare section. At first, I found a few frauds I didn't really trust. They seemed like puppets. But when I had all but given up, I got a reply from a couple of guys who were going to San Francisco. I felt a little more peaceful about this ride.

The day we were to leave was the Wednesday before the Fourth of July week of 2017 in which I had a vacation scheduled. I called my ex-wife and told her I had shipped the boys' things to her instead of moving them with me. She exclaimed, "You're *moving*?"

I said, "Yep. Those are your anchor babies … remember? That's what you signed up for. You planned to anchor me with them so you could torture me until I'm dead."

She grew quiet on the phone. And as I understand from my older son, she made it look like I was trying to run away when that wasn't my intention.

I'm living my private life without you and your influence. I'm drawing my line in the sand. If you come any closer, I will burn you again. That's why I locked my book into the safe and shut my mouth. Let everyone see.

It was a nice long ride out of Colorado. I thought it was interesting how my next-door neighbor seemed concerned about me getting into a car she didn't recognize. I had seen her time and time again trying to stop and associate with anyone I brought around my apartment. I know she felt entitled because of who she associated with. So that day, as I was leaving Colorado with her watching, she didn't have the chance. I was using an app that gave me a phone number to talk to someone without being interrupted. I could tell this was a curve ball for my ex-wife's puppet by the way she held her hands on her hips as we drove away. It looked like it bothered her enough that she made the call. If I didn't know any better, I'd say she looked like she was taking photos of us with her smartphone. I can only imagine she must have overheard my phone call when they pulled up. The walls were paper thin there. They had called, and I answered to tell them I was ready to leave I just needed to get backpacks and lock my place.

I first noticed her peering out her sliding-glass door from behind the vertical blinds. I smiled. That might have prompted her to walk out her front door and fold her arms with her keys in one hand and phone in the other. As I loaded my two backpacks and wheel into their SUV, I noticed her expression drop as fast as her folded arms that were now away from her body as her hands grasped her hips in concern. I thought to myself, *Does anyone have privacy? I'm a nobody. Do you follow Jesus this close? Watch if you like. I'm living. Still breathing. Can you see me smiling? Or do puppets have eyes? I think they may be blinded by money.*

The drive there was almost uneventful. They were pulled over in Nevada because of a seat belt infraction and driving a few miles an hour over the speed limit. The officer who approached the vehicle seemed anxious because he kept his hand on his gun and the other by the mic on his shoulder while making the initial contact at the driver's window. He looked inside the vehicle and saw others weren't wearing seat belts and asked for everyone's identification. I didn't move. His expression seemed to change when our eyes locked. It looked like humor followed by fear from seeing my resolve. I was wearing my seat belt, and I didn't offer my identification. And when he asked who I was, they all said, "He is just a ride share. He is wearing his belt."

The gang in blue officer knew the rules. So did I. I wonder if anyone began becoming more aware. To identify me, I must first break a rule or at least appear to. That meant I was on my best behavior. I began picking up on the simple cues that my co-riders were making. The driver included his associates at the local lodge. We both knew. He asked my name. Then he asked about my associations. And he said, "Your name is powerful in that club."

I said, "I know."

I asked him a few key club questions so he was assured that we both know. They couldn't wait to introduce me to their brother. These two who were mainly driving were long-lost brothers. They said they had just been reunited and knew the other brother from the same foster home. The father of the home was a US marshal. We chatted a few times via text and social media.

As it turned out, the people who gave me a ride to the Bay Area needed a place to stay. Things for me progressed while they were visiting, and I bought a sailboat after a solid job interview. Then seeing the wages of professionals in my trade, I saw no reason not to relocate. I subleased my apartment to the brothers who gave me a ride out here. It was helpful because I had to transfer the title right away. That meant it went to the address on my ID so I still needed the address in Colorado. It was helpful because they mailed me back the title to my boat so I could actually take ownership and attain registration.

I began to notice a few weird things about the family I was staying with. That was shortly after being approached by some lady in a minivan who sat outside of the place where they lived. It seemed like she was staring at me and taking photos of me smoking cigarettes. I was like, "Whatever. Look if you want. Take a photo. I know some people pay a lot of money for them." She must have seen me smiling, because she got out of the car and asked me who I was staying with. I didn't say much. I thought she was kind of a stalker. I told her to check with the lease office. But she didn't seem interested in looking for a place to stay. I could care less. And it would be nice to have a couple of eyes in remote locations.

The next day, I put out my résumé to some local shops after breaking my cell phone and losing all the access I had to that number from Denver. I wasn't sad. I knew my skills had a place. I also noticed the wages from most shops were more than a tech companies. I had a few interviews at some different shops. They all went well, and I had my choice of a half dozen places. I picked one shop, because I liked the owner was a sailor. It was a long commute. I decided to do wheelies all the way around the Bay Area to work for a shop. This sailor boss was happy to have me. He even let me use his tools until mine showed up. I think he liked my work because I was a professional.

I had just moved my boat to a marina on an island in the bay. I drove my newly purchased Ericsson 27 all the way from the ball park to the other side of the bay all by myself and pulled into my berth. I thought because I didn't really spend much time with the guy, I stayed with for a few days that we both understood. But as it turned out, he was given a new car. It was a nice silver Volvo. He said it was from a friend in the club. I knew he told me he was a third degree. And about a week after being in the Bay Area, as they were in Colorado, the brothers called me to say there were a couple of gang-in-blue officers and someone from child protective services. I wasn't even there. I know how those directives work. It takes weeks to get directives like those in place.

The brothers told me they felt like they were being harassed by the local gang in blue and even suspected they weren't actually real by the lack of protocol. I found it odd how the brother here in Cali got off telling me that. And I didn't really care. I kind of laughed instead, knowing that my old coworkers had also tried to do a welfare check on me because I didn't say anything to those frauds. I just moved. I had to call the manager for some reason after he began harassing Michael's grandfather, who had the keys to my toolbox and agreed to help me coordinate shipping them here. My coworker was a great man. He didn't like money either. I could tell he wasn't in the club by the way he was also tormented there.

So, I guess the brother in California wasn't aware that I had been planning my move for months after having a few telephone interviews with a tech company here. He seemed confused as to why I didn't react to his verbal vomit. I mean he bragged about being a third degree, but normally they wouldn't say without the proper signage. I thought, *Maybe they do things differently in the bay.* I kept in contact with them, and the old neighbor who was so concerned about my whereabouts began her shepherding of them by making them dinner and offering gifts that cannot be returned. She even got my new phone number from them. It's so sad, because I told the brothers the lady was my ex-wife's puppet. I learned from the day I called the locksmith after Sturgis. Shortly after she contacted me on my phone and questioned me about where I was and who I was with, I could hear it in her voice. She was a slave and would use anyone she could to help my ex-wife with the production value.

Around that time, the brothers in Colorado bragged about getting a new inheritance in the form of a trust that would pay out at a later date. I'd already seen. I didn't care what he was doing. I was sailing.

So, I took my boat all the way across San Francisco Bay by myself. Once I pulled into my dock on the island at the marina, a few people were excited to see me. I didn't care. I needed a shower. So, I walked up and took a nice hot shower, feeling very accomplished. I knew my boat needed work. And I needed to learn how to sail for real. I was extended an invitation to go for a sail with a boat owner across the dock from me. He had grown up sailing. So, I was down. We went out for a bit, and he taught me some simple things about sailing and offered to go get coffee. I was excited there was a consignment store for sailors just around the corner. It was super helpful to get all new running rigging and appropriate anchoring. I did like my weekends there. About a week after being in my new location, spending most of my time on my boat, I began to notice that the guy who let me stay with him kept wanting me to do things for him, asking me to work on his car, asking me to work on his friend's car, and then just being passive-aggressive about my presence. I thought the guy was a very weird. And to be honest, I didn't have the heart to tell him I was pretty sure his wife was cheating on him with a coworker. It's mediocrity at its finest. I saw some photos she didn't want me to see while she was trying to find a photo of her family's sailboat. I felt sorry for him, kind of. He took decent care of his kids, and she ran all over the place behind his back.

I just tried to remove myself from the situation. I found it odd that my new boss asked me if I was still going to that place. I told him the truth about how far it was and how the people there had issues I wanted to stay away from. He told me that was wise as his eyes got big. I didn't know what he was referring to. But if someone has any balls say it to my face … I didn't think so. I decided I'm not having a real woman in my life ever. As a matter of fact, I know the routine. How about I say it in so many words? Do you think they will hear me?

How about it? I overheard my new boss on the phone saying he didn't respond to threats. He seemed to look away from me when he said it. I didn't care what he got himself up to. I made my coffee and walked out into the shop, where I heard the painter Chava laughing about something and telling the cleanup and detail guy it was a movie. But as they saw me, they covered their expressions with their hands as they walked away snickering. I laughed too. Phone records don't lie. The book is always better. I decided I didn't really want to work on cars anyway. I thought maybe working on boats might allow me to truly boycott gasoline.

I found a storage unit and put my money down on it. I didn't give that old boss the time of day since he signed up with my ancestors' smear campaign. I made my résumé. Last chance. I had too many skills to offer. So, I decided to apply to a company that built sailboats. I didn't hear from them initially and prepared myself for my journey of sailing away someday. I was on my way to get the appropriate travel paperwork. When my phone rang, it was the shop lead at a tech company, the one I wanted to work with. I was so excited to take the boss's job by the reins and do exceedingly well. I noticed how it bothered a boat neighbor, who began to use Stockholm syndrome as a ploy to gain my trust to try to hurt me.

I laughed once when he made the comment about me being indestructible. I laughed a little and said, "I'm still standing. Right here."

The retired fireman bragged that he knew my bosses from when the business moved to the island. I didn't care. It was another small town. That usually meant big hell. I remember how he would go through the contents of my boat, probably looking for this book or possibly phone records. Either way, it didn't matter. The book was in a safe deposit box. He was a retired firefighter from the Bay Area who had two daughters. He was a very loose cannon. I've often wondered what really happened in Hawaii and why he had to move to the bay when he was an adult. He bragged about inviting some rich kid to stay with him, putting something in his drink, and taking him to a prostitute to watch him get robbed and mental sodomy because the prostitute was a man dressed as a woman. It seems he was another defective deviant who felt entitled to act however he liked, probably because that was what he was told. He bragged about the gang in blue union sending him to Vegas, all expenses paid about three weeks after I put my boat right by his.

As I understand, he was financially stretched beyond his means even though he was receiving a six-figure retirement plus a pension from the local fire department. I knew he was a puppet based on his bragging, so I decided to pull his strings a little. Keep your friends close and your enemies closer. Pay attention to who is helping wolves wash their dirty money. That was how I was raised. I paid attention when the retired fireman said to me not to bring some lady back to my boat unless it was serious. I kind of laughed because I'd never met a woman with a spine. I know he was telling me that because he was watching me like a hawk, trying to use Stockholm syndrome to get close enough to hurt me. It's an amazing honor to be so strong. I tried to do my best to avoid contact with him, but he talked incessantly. He talked more when he was nervous, and his upper lip quivered when he was lying. I mean, you've got to wonder about someone who gets a DWI while driving with his two kids in the car, thinking because of his badge he was immune to the rules—not to mention all the meth parties and group sex he bragged about after drinking all day. Loose lips sink ships.

I enjoyed how he would act as if his back were hurting so he could gain my trust. I'd learned. I paid attention too. I acted like nothing. I waited until he had reunited with his high school sweetheart after hearing how much he wasn't getting along with his girls' mom. I figured he was a swinger because of the things he said from time to time. So, once he had moved his motorcycle into her garage and began spending time with her and flaunting public displays, I decided to go fishing. I went fishing in the delta with the sailor I initially met on the dock. He was a mental health director for some county in the Bay Area. It seemed he paid very close attention to what I said. I enjoyed fishing. It was nice. We didn't catch anything. We stopped for lunch when I noticed a group of people around Muck's age begin staring at me. There were around eight people looking at me with my shirt off. I knew it was not that spectacular. Did they want an autograph? Well, then they should have asked me … I laughed a little. I am pretty sure they saw my expression. I took my right hand and dusted off my left shoulder as they were watching. I kept my eyes locked on them as they each tried not to look. I laughed a little inside in that moment. The guy I was with was inside getting our food. So, I stood there in the sun, my shirt off, surrounded by water, still smiling. How could I not be happy? Although we didn't catch anything that day, I was reminded how many people like playing catch. *Maybe it's time for another show.* I decided to see if I could catch any more catfish.

I used a fish dating app that was popular. I met some woman around my age to see the movie *Deadpool 2*. I do love that series. As she walked up, I saw she was a little overweight, but I didn't care. I wasn't looking for love. We had a drink before the show, and we talked about our jobs. I worked for a tech company, and she was a lawyer. I thought to myself, *How do you not know me?* I saw all the IP addresses that were being blocked by my ancestors' computer. *Oh*

well. Let's go for a ride, shall we? I thought the timing was perfect, because the retired firefighter had just rekindled an old romantic flame, only to throw away his happiness for the opportunity to make quick, easy money instead of living happily ever after with his first love. I'm honored he chose revenge on me instead. That's an amazing honor, to be so hated. After all, he had kids in college who needed new cars from Hyundai in Oakland, not to mention the cruise he sent his family on in exchange for payment.

I see him as a slave who is fully committed to the cult and isn't allowed to think in a reasonable fashion. He is instead blinded by money. And he cannot repay the gifts he has already accepted. I like knowing he is a slave, and when my ancestors don't get what they want, I will read his obituary. They don't play nice. I've seen it plenty. I remember shortly after that he and the lawyer began having group sex with anyone around me willing to participate. I thought it was funny. I've always said, dust the flies off, and get you some. I tried to tell the retired firefighter in so many words without saying a thing. I know how much he wants to silence this book. It's about his associates.

I had a bicycle that I didn't ride. I can't stand bicycles honestly. So, I put the bike out by the dumpster for the trash or anyone else who wanted it. I even put a note on it: "Take her for a ride; everyone else does." It was on a piece of cardboard written with Sharpie so you could see it a mile away. I watched as sheeple walked by and laughed and then looked toward my boat. The best one was a gentleman named Drew. He was another meth addict. I enjoyed watching him smile and laugh with his missing teeth. He was a loyal associate of the retired firefighter's. Everyone there at that marina was actually. But when Andrew took the bike and rode it around the firefighter laughing as I watched, the both of them sharing stories about their actions, I believe that's what lead to Drew's disappearance. The next guy to lose his life there was also an associate of the firefighter's. He was found in the water next to his boat about to drown. He was taken to the hospital where he died. The coroner came to ask questions. They were wondering if he had any enemies because the report didn't match the autopsy. He died from brain damage associated with blunt force trauma due to a blow on the back of his head. I really liked that guy. He was like me, tortured his whole life for his family's entertainment. I'm willing to bet he was silenced. May he rest in peace for his help to me without even knowing. Loose lips sink ships.

As I worked for the new start-up tech company, I knew by the way my ex-wife contacted me she wanted to know where I worked. I felt this place was sacred and wanted to protect it so my kids' generation could reap the benefits. But with my blindness, I could see her motives based on what I'd lived through and the stolen phone records I kept. I knew it was so she could again contact my coworkers. This was like my Rolex, not a stopwatch. It won't ever stop now. I wasn't giving it up that easily. Sorry. So based on the website, she would see that I paid attention to a few key people I worked with who were displayed on the company website. I'm not hating. I only keep quiet so I know who her puppets are. My skills speak for themselves. I took what used to take a team of people a week or more and cut it down to about a day. I could tell that this bothered my boss man because he had some special skill that people liked to watch him sand and sand and sand the same boat for days and days. I worked on commission for twenty years. I'd be a broke-ass fool if that had been my production level. I grieved for the owner because his childhood friend, the boss man, had everyone convinced that his process was far too laborious and time-consuming. That's what everyone believed before I walked in the door. He even had them trying to outsource a plastic type of boat, and I'm thankful I was able to step up and deliver the highest production and quality I could as a professional, so everyone could see. Because now boats were being built three a week, and everyone there was now working hard all day long. The lazy days were over. It seemed as though I set a new shop pace for them. All the entitled wolves had to work very hard now to keep up. The days of unlimited time off and surfing whenever the waves were right were now less and less common.

The team I led finished the boats. And that meant I stayed hungry. I was often referred to by the bosses as a weapon. I did give my all for those wolves and watched their eyes like glowing embers. The best leaders lead by example. Professionals make it look easy. I even began training others to do very easily what had been some special thing the boss man had been keeping as his own meal ticket. I didn't know why that was necessary. He was, after all, childhood friends with the owner of the place. I was confused about his jealousy at first because I thought we were on the same team. I was not trying to take anyone else's job. I just wanted to do mine. It was ironic how two-faced we all were, I thought sometimes. I laughed behind the mask I was required to wear. I didn't need any promotion, nor did I want money. I was a sculptor and a skilled artist for people who needed it in a timely fashion. When I was hired on, it was midweek because they were on a serious deadline to get more funding. I even took a cut in pay from my previous trade to get in. I walked in the door out of nowhere a clutch player. It's been said you'll know him by his work, and I still had all the skills that the rich wanted. I could weld anything. I could build anything given blueprints, and after I did it twice, I could do it with my eyes closed. I think it's because I'm blind. I have my third eye. I've had it for years. I think cannabis protected it, because my two eyes are for looking and the other is to see.

I also began to teach others my skills. I was as happy as could be, and I could tell it bothered people who already had their place at the tech company. The most they could complain about was that I made too much dust. I honestly thought that was so funny and ironic at the same time. My silver lining, I began laughing about that particular day was, "Too much dust? How does it taste, eating my dust?" I kept wondering, knowing he was just like the other cowards there, just looking for a show.

"Misery loves company. Maybe you should wear your mask instead of your costume, puppet." It didn't go over very well. Other coworkers saw his crying and complaining as very trivial. I remember how he bragged about the concubine he was offered for his silence, saying she looked like a supermodel. He took great pride in trying to instigate from the very beginning. The very first time I saw and met him, he dropped a couple hundred grams of spa bond onto the floor, completely wasting it and making a mess. Literally as soon as he saw my eyes, he looked like he had seen a ghost and dropped the mixing board he was holding. He began making it a point to overreach. Many of the other leads even noticed, and he was talked to about his unprovoked treatment. So sad. As quickly as he recognized me, he had been looking at tons of porn, I can only assume because it seems as though those are the first people to recognize me. To tell you the truth, that puppet sounded like a crybaby. I'm pretty sure we were all supposed to be wearing masks anyway. But I think the real issue was that I was me, and I was succeeding. It bothered him to see a Non boatbuilder have more skills than his boss.

I was told to lead the department, and I was promoted the very next Monday to try to keep me around. In that promotion, I became a manager. I didn't really want to be one. But both of the British guys who were my boss told me with the new position and raise I was instructed to train a gentleman. His nickname was Drunk Ass. That's the one name I didn't change; it was too good. He had dual citizenship in Mexico and the United States. He bragged that his father was involved in organized crime. And his mother, Martha, was not having that. I thought his nickname was appropriate. He drove a silver German made station wagon that was all crashed in the front. He even asked me to help him fix it. So two-faced.

I still remember the work party after recording him bragging about trying to end my life. He was actually trying to cry to get me to feel sorry for him. Psycho. He must have had a decent set of kneepads, because the boss and he met early in private almost every morning. And even as he was planning to smear me, he was told to document my processes. He kept trying to make me write it down so he could put his name on it and turn it in to the boss. I just said, "You don't need a process. You've got me. Just watch. I'm a professional."

Maybe he was more focused on being socially dependent for his job by way of being infectious to everyone so fake. It's so hard not to see. It reminded me of the kid in high school who wanted to be friends with everyone so they could just cheat on tests. That's the striking image of what the entertainment lawyer from San Francisco was. He was the lead spirit rustler in high school. His job was to be Mr. Popularity for everyone to see, to boost everyone's spirit while playing games as a team. He was a social dynamo who had zero technical brainpower. His skills were social, not professional. So, I get it, how social dynamics work. And the easiest way for drunk ass was drinking after work and playing darts in the company bar. I mean, we did have kegs on tap at work. Usually by 8:00 p.m., he was sloshed and leaving. Drunk ass made it a point to be infectious with everyone there.

I tried to steer clear and kept detailed journals. I began to notice him and his friends scheming while throwing darts and drinking beer. I know how Stockholm syndrome works. It was odd how he kept looking for a reaction from me both personally and professionally. His actions were unprovoked. I began to notice how he would smile and begin making comments about needing to get the number of the girl I met for legal advice. I kind of laughed on the inside. Because he probably thought I was weak. I never so much as took my clothes off in front of that girl. I never went to her place. Truthfully, I didn't really like her. I decided to instead set a trap to see whom I was working with. I know better than to associate with people who trade their integrity for money. I'm familiar with using sex as a weapon and what it takes to make bullets miss. I kept her a little interested, kissing and talking mainly. I began to notice her infatuation with the firefighter guy. I decided to see if I still had an audience. It should be good.

The third weekend in September of 2018, to celebrate my half-brother Muck's birthday, I would say everything with nothing at all. I watched this chick pull up at the same time as the firefighter and even start walking toward his truck, as she didn't think I was looking when the firefighter guy signaled to her with his hand pointing at me. She looked right at me as if she had seen a ghost. She made her way to the boat I had recently purchased. She hesitated as she walked down into the boat as if making eye contact with someone outside. I thought, *This will be great.* And as she sat down next to me, she began saying she wanted to frolic. I really wasn't in the mood. So, she sat there. And a moment later, she laid her head down on my lap. I noticed her still quivering from her most recent orgasm. I felt honored. I knew my ancestors were now watching through her eyes. This was their calling card. I was so thankful for the audience I agreed to frolic. She offered me oral sex.

I thought, *Sure, I'll send you a message, because obviously you haven't learned.* I told her midway through her paycheck, "Don't swallow." She looked at me confused like I got off on it.

Where was my audience? That was about the time the tapping on my hull began. I couldn't wait to see who it was. Whoever it was had been out there a minute. I knew better than to let the opportunity flee. I walked out of my berth where the lawyer was to see the firefighter guy boarding my boat, saying something about a shirt. He began to question what I was doing and started laughing. I didn't say anything. I instead offered her a toothbrush. It was brand new and in the package. She seemed surprised. I smiled, because I now had the wolves' DNA.

Much like this book, I've kept it safe for years. Oops … whom should I tell? Nobody cares, right? Oh well. All I've ever known is concubines, and I've learned how they operate when they are told to "be" with me, as well as how concubines are created. I was laughing on the inside, as she wanted to check in on the firefighter guy because he was cooking something on the dock by his boat on the other side of the marina. I thought it was odd because I hadn't talked to him about that. So, I wanted to see. We walked down to his boat and where my old boat was. I still owned the boat but didn't want anything that close to this psycho.

I watched the two of them toast beers as if I weren't even watching. I laughed. He even made a joke about how wet his balls got. He made sure to go over the top with it, even throwing ping-pong balls into the water, saying his balls were wet again. I just took notes in my journals. I kept the toothbrush. I don't think she even thought twice about it, but I knew I had stolen a group of losers' DNAS. I think documentation is key. The next day, I sent a text in the morning: "I'll take the high road; there is a lot less traffic." I never mentioned her again.

I heard my coworkers ask about her. I told them I didn't even know her. It seemed to bother the key people I knew my ex-wife would contact, knowing she would only offer bribery or blackmail. I'd seen it before. Imagine the production value. I got off on it. I was able to see the guy who initially was my boss become a slave. Although he gained money, he lost his family. I watched his car engine blow up and then his wife leaves him, take his kids out of the country, and file for divorce around Thanksgiving, so about a month after the incident. I remember when I first started working there. I had a dream that was so real in my mind that I got to work early to throw away a lamp that the firefighter had given me, and I took it there as a symbol of my appreciation. It was a lighthouse that was a lamp. The lamp was beautiful with sailboats on the shade cover. It seemed like they were the only reason I wasn't out living my life on the ocean.

I got to work early that day in September when I had that bad dream. It was so real it made me have a cold sweat. In my dream, I was one of the first to work. I noticed the place was on fire on the inside. The flames were shooting through the roof, and everything on the inside was burning. In my dream, I unlocked the door and ran inside, and to my astonishment, the flames were burning the place up from the inside. That was when I remembered the lamp that firefighter fraud had given me. I was a little worried about an incident he bragged about where there was a fire at a book company in the Bay Area. The fireman guy was on scene, and the place managed to burn to the ground as they all just watched. He said it was because there wasn't enough water and laughed. I wondered who the company's competitor was and if the market shifted to another place accordingly. A very large insurance policy was paid out, and there were court hearings about that very incident. He told me how he was told exactly what to say to cover himself, and he had zero to worry about.

The next day after he and the lawyer tried to smear me, I was on the way home, and like a stalker, he wanted to hang out with me. He got off on it actually. He kept looking at me with a creepy smile and his upper lip twitching. I just laughed at him and rode my wheel to my new job moonlighting. The next couple of days, he kept calling me, and I waited until I was at lunch when he called. I was sitting next to one of my ex-wife's puppets so he could see me block the firefighter's number. The puppet's eyes grew big upon seeing me do this without even flinching. He and his partners kept trying to get a reaction out of me and were encouraged to do so by the firefighter guy. The same guy who bragged about knowing my bosses actually met them for "the first time" in front of me twice, probably to try to establish his disassociation. Fake friend, fake firefighter, job security—I don't know, but I was so shaken by the dream I'd just had, I bet I got there before 5:00 a.m. I just kept taking notes about who wanted a reaction.

The next week in September, I got a promotion as if to keep me closer. How two-faced. They must have learned from my family's cult. I remember my ex-wife's puppet bragging about how the boss was part of the club after the land speed world record—such entitlement. After all, this was the age of entitlement.

I'd seen it plenty, and wouldn't you know who tracked me down a few states over? It was the bank in Colorado. They needed me to come in person and empty the contents of the safe deposit box because of the restrictions I had in place, and the rent was due, so to say. I remember getting that phone call at work, and I knew his steps in my life were already directed. I took a couple of personal days to travel back there and get the book I had written. I was thankful I didn't have to carry all that weight on my back for years. But now, I couldn't let the contents out of my sight. I knew it was radioactive, and so was

I for spending so much time putting all the pieces together. Maybe that's why I'm radioactive today, because I've spent so much time playing with plutonium, building this bomb for everyone else to use after I'm gone. I didn't ask to be born into that cult. Nor do my kids deserve to be raised in a cult.

I took a train across the country to retrieve my contents, and I loved the views of this country. I was conflicted on the journey, wondering if I should just burn it or keep it and hope someday someone would find it. I spent much time in silence in the food car, having coffee and pastries when I met an English professor for the University of Missouri. He documented many of the lynching and bombings in the South, and he was intrigued by my knowledge of the inner workings of the groups he had studied. After a few shared meals, he began to ask me how I knew so much about his expertise, and I told him why I was on my journey. I told him in so many words I'd survived one of those. That was my family's club.

The professor encouraged me to share it someday because it might be something everyone else could learn from. I didn't want to be famous. I didn't want anything except to just live-in harmony.

On the trip back to the bay, I spent my time reading my work, and it broke me all over again. I saw my King's hands on my life all over again. I had a whole new renewed strength now. I tried to offer my coworkers mercy, speaking in a way that they would all know that I knew. I told them I didn't want to add to my book, but I couldn't help it. I couldn't stop journaling. I told the human resources director in so many words that I knew. I tried to give them mercy for days, but I didn't know they were allowed to listen. In so many words, with kindness, I even made the comment that all trash cans should be brown because I had a perfectly good trash can that was brown. It wasn't there anymore. I thought it was funny. Everyone knew. But they couldn't speak.

Drunk ass bragged just out of earshot about how the girl he thought was a love interest had told him to put a baby in her. I would always just smile, and I could tell it bothered him. He went out of his way to get there early and stay late to get any opportunity to mess up my work by sanding too much on purpose or painting things out of order on purpose. He didn't remember the first company party. I guess he forgot how I heard something I shouldn't have and how I left early to go back to my boat and get my hidden camera. The boss and his partner in crime didn't know I was holding a camera when the Drunk Ass began bragging about being there at the end. He was naming off other coworkers who couldn't wait to see. I laughed a little on the inside because I was just taking notes. It's called a mate crime. They are well known in Europe. Gain someone's skills to smear them. It's how the unskilled feed off of the skilled because some are virtuous and some aren't. I made sure to watch as people get what they deserve.

I remember a key coworker there who spent much time laughing at me. He and his surf friends carpooled from downtown every day. I enjoyed watching his two faces and even rejoiced with him as his new wife expected their first child. All nine months, they were on cloud nine as they began planning a new life where they would be rich and never need money again. I just told him to journal all of his feelings so he could remember exactly what it was like. I was sincere. I wanted him to feel the change that was coming.

A couple of days before she was to give birth, there were complications, and the child wasn't born alive. I didn't lift a finger. Bad things happen to people who trade their integrity for money.

The Drunk Ass guy got fired after leaving a company party drunk and being involved in a hit and run where someone was injured. He fled the scene and left his phone and wallet in the front seat. He ran home to escape his third DWI and waited until the morning to go to his partner in crime's house to use his phone to report his car stolen. I think he actually believed what I heard his shepherd say, "Mate! You work for a tech company. You can't get in trouble. People need you." I disagreed. We all fall under the same rules. Needless to say, they picked him up immediately. And his partner folded right away when questioned. As I understand it, they charged him with falsifying a gang in blue report. I watched over the next couple of weeks as the boss I replaced began to walk with a limp. I guess he broke his foot. I wondered if it was from kicking rocks. My King was just showing me His work instead. I saw, based on the way he acted, he missed his partner in crime.

Boss man and Drunk Ass must have finished more kegs at the company bar in the breakroom than anyone. It was like clockwork how the drinking took place. It was almost as if a bell went off and all the sheep would move in unison to the shepherd for a tasty treat. Everyone there knew, but they weren't allowed to say. I do remember saying that if they had any balls, they could say it to my face. I bought another sailboat that I flipped for a few thousand dollars' profit. It offset the cost of the powerboat I bought for next to nothing and sold for a profit before leaving. I was living on my Sea Ray as a live-aboard and yacht club member. I somehow had a couple of the nicest boats in the marina. Sorry to offend. I was just doing my thing. I sold my thirty-six-foot Cheoy Lee Clipper ketch sailboat to buy a different vessel. I desired a larger one that had the accommodations I wanted with the ability to outrun storms by gaining two hundred miles per day on the open ocean. I began to look as a step of faith, not because I had the extra money but because I had a life worth living. I found just the vessel, at just the right time.

I found a forty-foot multihull that needed an engine. I convinced the marina harbormaster to remove a dock finger so I could park it there. It was a wild ride. I had looked at the vessel twice before, and the more I looked past the mess, the more I saw the bones I wanted. I bought the vessel with the condition that it would be moved by the morning. I brought my inflatable skiff, with a four-horsepower outboard. I waited for the tide to be right and used my skiff tied to the back with the tiny little outboard to tow me into the bay. I made it pretty far, even to the Bay Bridge, before the current changed, and I was fighting it. I could make about a quarter mile progress by the time I had to refuel the skiff and drift back to almost where I was before. I called a sea tow.

Again, I laughed, because they said they wouldn't tow me if I was tied to the dock, so I told them things had changed, and they agreed to tow me to my berth free of charge. By the time I got back to the marina, it was a little past 5:00 a.m. The guy who bought the sailboat I had flipped was picking it up in an hour. I didn't even have a moment to sleep. I just had some coffee and a pastry for breakfast with the guy who helped me sail. He helped me move my boat. When the guy came to pick up the sailboat, it went well, probably because the firefighter guy was out of town. He left the docks just before the harbormaster showed up for work that morning.

A fellow yacht club member helped me pressure-wash the new yacht, and it made a huge difference. By the time the harbormaster saw the yacht, it wasn't looking too bad. I was excited and hopeful. The boat needed a thorough cleaning and a new engine but was in great shape overall. I installed solar, as well as a new water system and new lines, and made everything work. I also installed new batteries as well as a new engine I got for a bang-up deal locally and even had it delivered for free. It didn't take me any time to swap the power plant and get it going well. I do love how well it sails. It has a nice inventory of canvas as well as drogues and anchors, not to mention a water maker and ham radio with a modem that allows me to send and receive emails anywhere in the world. I left my tech job without saying a word to any of my coworkers. I simply cited that I didn't work for people who traded their integrity for money.

I was thankful he was able to get the funding he needed, but the world has enough mediocrity. I was thankful for being burned and still getting my stocks. I'm so thankful the owners heard me put it in writing. I was able to get my very own restraining order. I'm thankful. It's nice to be so hated. Say it to my face if you have any balls. I didn't think so. I wrapped my yacht in camouflage and self-taught, sailed out of the bay through the Golden Gate, headed south. Free as heck. I stopped in a small bay just south.

I love the ocean. That's my church. The ocean is my church. I know my King has dominion over the beasts of the fields and the birds of the air. That's where I also see how powerful He is to take and give life in perfect harmony. I feel people who live on the ocean are able to truly see what they are made of and the rest never learn. It saddens me that even as I write this book, I'm being taunted. I don't have a malicious bone in my body. I simply take notes. Last chance to try and play games …

I noticed a younger fisherman who thought it was funny to be backhanded and try to keep me close. He always had the freshest cannabis, and I was thankful for all the free Bud. Keep your friends close and your enemies closer. Even in this month of June 2020, I was being targeted because of my ancestors' smear campaign. It's entertaining, I guess. Maybe they haven't had enough yet. So here we go again. People trade their integrity for opportunity every day. Apparently, I'm not allowed to be happy, and I am regardless.

So, I took my time and met a nice lady on Coffee Meets Bagel. I met her on the app, and we spent a couple of weeks chatting about daily life, nothing remotely sexual. I was initially a little taken aback on the first visit to her house by the birth control lying out on Annamolly's nightstand, as if to say, "Trust me." As sweet and nice looking as Annamolly was, I doubt it took her long to make her own choices. I will always wonder what her choice was when she was given the ultimatum of blackmail or bribery. I know nobody gets out of that cult alive because everyone who participates unknowingly has a price on their head with life insurance. I wonder if my price keeps going up or stays the same. I never agreed to wear that crown. I hope for more than the riches of this world. I find it flattering to be just like money except I don't fold. I don't fold because the money isn't real anyway. It's simply paper with drawings that people actually believe in. I wondered how expensive her time with me would be, both now and later. I had my reservations, but it actually felt genuine. I believe I guarded her from wolves as best I could by inviting her to meet at the pier by her house on short notice after I was already in the area. I think before the fake fisherman made contact; it might have been something long term. If money hadn't been involved, I believe there could actually have been real justice. I believe that when money is removed from motivation, people find it much easier to forgive and forget. I know what I've been through even though I don't say.

So here is the next setup. I met a young lady online. She was sweet. I invited Annamolly to a picnic on the beach by the yacht club to be sure to stay away from the fake fisherman and his partners in crime. *Nice*, I thought. I valued Annamolly because we seemed to pair well on many levels. I felt even more strongly about guarding her from wolves. We enjoyed the picnic on the next Friday at the yacht club. It was nice and uninterrupted. I had a moment of privacy because I hadn't mentioned Annamolly to anyone yet, but it seems as though I'm not allowed to be around anyone. I simply don't have friends. I watch closely as people around me pretend to be my friend so they can get rich. I remember a gentleman who kept calling and coming around, much like Dan the man. This guy was named Duff. He was from the yacht club and was directly connected with the firefighter. I was surrounded by mediocre and jealous cowards who weren't afforded the luxury of thinking their own thoughts.

That picnic went well. We hung out over the next weekend at her place. I was so focused on the book, there really were only a couple of long, sweet kisses at this point. I did like my time with her and wanted her to be safe. I had never met anyone so helpful. She typed the third chapter, as I read from old paper manuscripts. I enjoyed having a hot shower for once on a bathroom floor that wasn't moving and a bed that was so comfortable.

After she helped me transcribe, she was dropping me off, and the fake fisherman saw me pull up to the dock with Annamolly. Based on his facial expression, he was going to have so much fun. Wow. The caliber of two-faced losers I was surrounded by was incredible. I knew the yacht club people and firefighter had already accepted gifts that could not be returned. As the fake fisherman and his friend passed, he looked and gave a little smirk. You could see he and his friend were very interested in who I was with. Annamolly was Asian by descent but born American. She was beautiful, but I know what some of the most beautiful people look like on the inside. I watched as the fisherman who spotted us sitting in her car drive by as he waved and smiled. Everyone knows they believe everything they see on a screen. That was when he and his friend pulled up and parked. They were sitting in their car, probably getting high first thing in the morning. I figured based on how the fake fisherman laughed in the past, he would be another cheap piece of toilet paper to get dirty.

I decided to walk the newest girl in my life, Annamolly, down the docks to meet some other people I'd met there. I hoped by the time I walked her back to her car, the fake fisherman would be gone, but he and his partner in crime sat patiently waiting in their car. It was fairly obvious. I'd seen it often before. I watched Annamolly leave in her SUV as the fake fisherman and his partner in crime followed her, like wolves stalking their prey. I watched the two of them on the prowl in their four-door car. It turns out he and his buddy were gone all day long. I can only speculate that favors again were traded for favors, by how his fish-buyer friend got out of jail the next day unexpectedly after beating his wife and sending her to the hospital in front of their children. He was apparently gone for a long time. Everyone knows. But that's how favors work. You become a slave later. I'm sure the fake fisherman was well connected in the area because he grew up in the harbor. This was all he knew. I'm sure this wasn't the first time a traveling man had been taken advantage of by this guy. Oh well. Fools and their money are easily parted. I hoped he and his friends on the dock enjoyed the attention because it wouldn't stop. I didn't hear much from Annamolly either that day. I will always wonder what her choice was, bribed or blackmailed. Either way, I'm thankful. I know some losers like the fake fisherman and his partners in crime have a hard time seeing others succeed. It's nice to be so … impressive … Why would I care? Dust the flies off, and get you some.

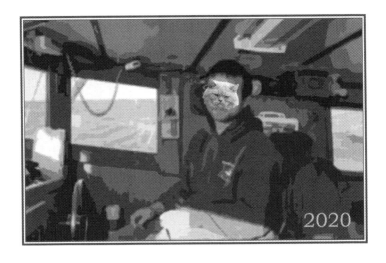

But there is always a silver lining. I was so thankful Annamolly helped me transcribe about ten thousand words from my manuscript into digital format. She was sweet. We had only hung out once in person at the picnic on the beach when I was invited by Duff over to his house for dinner within the first two days. So sad how I'm not allowed to be happy, right? Loose lips sink ships. Keep your friends close … I know the yacht club wants to see a movie—except I'm not supposed to know. I haven't ever had any authentic friends, simply acquaintances. The difference between a friend and acquaintance is loyalty. It was easy to be around her because I could be myself, not to mention that I was her paycheck. She was told by the yacht club guy she could get rich. So, keep trying, and try some more, and then try some more … I found it so funny how quickly Duff showed up to be on camera to get my reaction. I said to him, "It happens all the time. People trade their integrity for opportunity all the time."

Once he knew that I knew, he just wanted to make money instead of be real. I was the only authentic one there, and it didn't make me sad. He had both of his faces on, and it looked like his face was going to become rearranged. He had already accepted gifts that could not be returned from his owners. He was a slave also. He knew I knew too many details about the incident. But he did it on purpose. Duff had made contact with the fake fisherman long before and even had his number in his phone—another sociopath who needed his own money after a retirement that ran dry. It was supposed to hurt. And like all cowards, he could not be honest. I get it. He needed money.

I remember the sailor guy saying how the yacht club would keep me close. Even the sailor guy, who was a mental health person, accepted gifts that could not be returned. That lawyer chick was able to get his wife off of a DWI in the same county where she worked. Schemers are all the same. I even noticed how he enjoyed showing everyone else my smear as he waited for my expression to change so he could capitalize on it. He claimed to be a recovering meth addict who ran a nonprofit for a "ministry"—another tax shelter. So sad how most people look up to money, when its usually just dirty favors traded.

I found it interesting when Duff texted me several times and even showed up while I was working to see if I was sad. I was laughing. Duff kept asking how I knew. I guess he never saw me notice how many women he would hit on just as soon as his wife was not watching. This particular week in mid-June of 2020, his wife would be gone all week. Perfect timing. When the cat's away, the mice will play. And I simply said nothing, as it seemed he was dying for a reaction, even turning redder and redder. He was persistent, and my expression didn't change. And it wasn't until I said, "I can't tell you. I'm saving it for court," that his eyes got big, and he began to turn the reddest. Yeah … cowards cannot be honest.

I remember all the plotting and scheming that took place at the yacht club and marina. And Duff made sure to visit my new place several times a week and collect the phone numbers of others there. I'd seen it before. Federal employees are trying to protect their own pensions. I suppose there is a common theme here. Duff was a retired military guy. I was sure he must serve his leaders and owners by lying by omission as if nobody knew, so we might all continue to be slaves.

I'm thankful they could all see. I'm not acting now. I just write it as I see it. I love haters. It's for everyone.

I didn't have to put on an act because Annamolly was reading me like a book, actually typing it out. But I know I'm not allowed to be happy because of what my ancestors have signed up for. As much as I want to be with someone who might be an equal intellectually, physically, and morally, that's something I've never known. I mean, look at me. I've been through fire and back only to be surrounded by cowards. Say it to my face if you have any balls. I didn't think so. With that said, I didn't trust her. I'm not hating on her, because I actually enjoyed my time with her before it became tainted by the wolves I'm surrounded by. Seven and a half days is the longest real relationship I've ever had. And who knows if things weren't sold, maybe it would be different. But everyone except me has their price. Have my ancestors learned yet? I just don't do sloppy seconds. Everyone else does. I know who I am.

I'm so thankful I haven't had sex since 2013, and I don't plan to. Because that's the only way they can hurt me. Sex, that is their weapon. When sex is used as a weapon, paired with church as an alibi, that means the dogma of religion is used for slavery. How does the connection work between them? That's crazy talk ... right? Umm. No. The same banks finance churches and smut and pornography. UBS Financial Services is a main player. That's where my ex-wife gets her dirty money for my smear. Geneva's owner runs that bank and the church, as well as the porn business empire her partner in crime's son is so proud to have built. What an amazing legacy to have fooled so many fools. And I'm immune because I know who I am. That means I know who you are also. I have seen my life used for entertainment before. I don't get mad. I simply smile like nothing. You never know when people want to see you sad.

Annamolly was very attractive and recently divorced, not perfect, and I saw red flags all over the place, but that's kind of what I liked. I know I'm not perfect. And I can't live with someone who is. Been there, done that, and I can assure you it's very boring. With that said, I enjoyed our playful banter through the day. She was refreshing to look forward to. Things were great, after just seven or so days, ha-ha. However, I knew soon enough she would be seen by the wolves walking beside me. I knew I would have to bring her to my area. Subsequently, I took detailed notes and prepared for what happened when mediocre people breed for a purpose. So, here is your money shot. I warned your club years ago … Is social justice better than real justice? Speak up … I didn't think so. Keep trying to get rich quick. Just so you know, I know that we both know. Life, liberty, and the pursuit of happiness. We are all under the same law, and the rules should apply to all, but money changes everything, doesn't it? So, how will anyone know when I keep my eyes peeled, cameras rolling. I thought everyone knew I don't have friends, I don't have family, simply just a few acquaintances. I smile knowing this, but how does everyone else not know?

And it wasn't a few days later when she asked to hang out over the weekend. I suggested the next Saturday morning. But I wasn't spending the night. I was busy writing. I hadn't had sex in years, and I didn't plan to start right then with someone I didn't know yet. Alone was all I had; alone protected me. So, it seemed safe to have her to the harbor since she was only about twenty minutes away. I found it interesting nonetheless and collected my dirt for later. The first thing I noticed was she didn't want to eat anywhere close to the harbor. I'm sure it's because she preferred not to be recognized. I got excited, knowing my ancestors were watching. I get it. I've seen it many, many times. I was so thankful that when we got back to the harbor, I was able to take her to my skiff that I purposely parked in front of the fake fisherman's boat. I watched as the two of them began making eyes at one another as the rest of the bystanders tried not to look or say anything. It was easy to see the looks on the faces of all the other bystanders who already knew she was trying to hand out social justice. I felt so sorry for her. She didn't know the wolves she signed up with. But still, I kind of laughed on the inside. The two of them were already in bed together from earlier that week, just after he and his partner in crime stalked her. I find it most entertaining how I can puke in a bag, and others cannot wait to eat it. Talk about sloppy seconds. It's my unicorn puke that everyone cannot wait to gobble up.

I grew excited because I'm a unicorn who stays on Novocain so I don't feel a thing, and I know she did have her choice, bribery or blackmail, as everyone else did and does. It's a disgrace actually. We all have choices to make. Unless that's not how normal people act. Because that's how cults act. Anyone who actually helps me will be targeted just like me. That's how the cult rules over others with fear. Sex addicts are all the same mostly, very, very predictable. As I'd been around the fake fisherman, I'd already seen him destroy other relationships with fishermen by having sex with people's partners, having no remorse for his actions. So sad. He was the most selfish person I think I'd met in a long, long while. His actions were unprovoked. It reminds me of Muck. Welcome to the age of entitlement. I think there may be something wrong with both of their brains. Because domesticated animals know better than to shit where they eat. I suppose to train them it's appropriate to rub their noses in it. I am so thankful I got to see who I was surrounded by. I don't have to feel the need to help any of them. I already knew it's a big ocean out there, and bad things happen to people who try to smear me for my ancestors. I've seen it more than I can write down.

I took Annamolly to my boat and tried to show her the best time I could, all the while knowing what her motives were and that when she didn't get my reaction, she would be subject to repeated rape and sodomy. I almost felt for her loss. I looked past that, knowing she looked great. I looked past what she was involved in with the other fisherman. I wanted everyone to see me smile, knowing I was just taking notes. I'm thankful it didn't hurt. Because instead, she actually set me free. Because I only kissed her, ever. I didn't want any trouble. And I felt kind of sorry for her because I can only imagine the torment, she will probably endure for making secret deals with liars. I'd seen many times how the wolves would rape and sodomize the concubines until they would do anything that they were asked. I'd seen it plenty in the past because that was all I'd ever known. It was easy to see.

I thought it was a bit much the way she kept trying to leave a hickey on my neck, as if to report to her new owners what she had carried out in a public display. It was over the top and rather odd how aggressively she kissed me. While we were standing in the galley of my yacht, I knew she was an enemy in hiding, but I'm a lover, not a fighter. I love haters, so I held her close with my hands being above the waist the whole time. I was simply kissing her passionately and sincerely as if to say, "Goodbye. I hope you can get a good look at what you're missing."

I'm so thankful to end my book with another bang. I find it funny as well as motivating, and either is a healthy perspective. My time isn't actually free. I won't invest in people who trade their integrity for mediocrity. I simply don't play games anymore. I only write after the candid recordings I've made in private. So you know, I see you; you see me too. Can you see me smiling still? And you wonder why there are some chapters I cannot read aloud … yet. It's because I would rather play with gunpowder and rocket fuel. Gaslighting for profit is done by cowards. United Slaves of America. Everyone knows that the Nazis didn't start out with gas chambers. They started where we are today. "Countrymen, stand up in unison or lie down forever. Freedom isn't actually free." I know my ancestors and people who call themselves "family" will continue to destroy other people's lives until they destroy my own. But I just keep living and loving every day. It's not my life. I can't take it from He who gives it. I'm sure it would just jam in the chamber again anyway. I apologize if you thought it was yours instead. I already gave it to my King long, long ago.

I'm not perfect. I'm still a sinner, daily saved by amazing grace, forced to live because I just won't die, I don't have any desire to own the life I had before I gave it to my King. I just enjoy it every day. And I hope soon I meet my King. Don't be sad for me. Death is only the beginning. And this life is merely a test for the rest. It's been said that if you put all your hope and faith in the Lord, you will not perish but have everlasting life. I believe it. I already know, serve the King or serve money, so I've told my publisher to hold on to my work until after the movie comes out because I want to meet my King in person. I wasn't paid at all. I was assured I would be paid back many, many, many times over. I've also instructed them that I'm not to profit from it. My unicorns need a legacy instead. I hope and pray they make their own way and become legendary, as I have. Not everyone breaks everything in silence. It's quite deafening actually.

CHAPTER 13

Catharsis

After being smeared in the harbor of Half moon bay California by a gang of cowards who lack integrity using localism to procure group mediocrity using hearsay, I decided to move out of their sewer, mercy isn't up to me. Being ruled by organized criminals who use qualified immunity to violate someone for entertainment in order to torture humanity never ends well. I know I'm not the only one. I was reminded, I'm the traveling man, from west to east. If my enemies would like a war using my life, it should be a civil war, they should meet me on the level and put it on the square; so, we can all learn about how framing builds imaginary glass pyramids upon the backs of the bruised so those who are made of money can stay seated at the very top using imaginary resources to control others creating slaves in the process. Miserable people love company, and need people to join them when they are in Hell.

I'm reminded it isn't about me. My Book isn't mine, it's the offspring born of the production associated with my enlightenment by being raised by wolves and finding my own way in this brief journey to the grave. This life is merely a test, and death is only the beginning. My time was changed because I'm unable to submit to worldly leaders. I am a tool that the grand architect uses to shed light into dark places so we can all see. I've got nothing to lose, and everything to gain by dying of natural causes. Never forget, we have two eyes to look and one to see. Start sun gazing to see as I did before it's too late.

I offered them mercy through my silence, but it was not received. I suppose Zach de la Rocha said it the best, "Silence can be like violence, sort of like a slit wrist". So, I must submit to my destiny, I can only submit my pinky promises to my publisher before I'm gone. I've been told that my ancestors must crucify me on camera to get rich as well as pay back the favors they traded for gifts that cannot be returned years ago.

I began looking at my options. I know my steps have already been directed by the king of kings. The grand architect is all seeing, all knowing, and ever present in my time of need. He has already prepared a banqueting table for me while in full view of my enemies. So, everyone can see. I submitted my memoirs to my publisher shortly after this revelation. Revelations seventeen through nineteen says it all for me and it sits well with my soul. After the initial content review, I was given a publishing contract. I subsequently learned that by publishing my life story means that I now own the movie rights, how appropriate to take my life back. I can only speculate how expensive that shift in power might just be. I was so thankful for the covid pandemic that required everyone to wear masks. I love myself and have never been sad in my own company. It was a fantastic life living on a yacht all alone on the ocean aboard sailing vessel Novocain, because I didn't feel a thing. But my publishing meant I would have to be in contact with someone.

About a month later I sold my 41-foot multihull "SV-Novocain" on Ebay to the highest bidder after a weeklong unreserved auction, unconcerned with the final selling price. These worldly possessions aren't actually mine. I'm merely a steward of things my king provides for me. He loves to see me doing amazing things for his glory. The grand architect always gives me the desires of my heart when it aligns with his will. I got what I want, again. The buyer paid me in bitcoin. During the sale the price of bitcoin was less than fifteen thousand dollars per bitcoin. I placed the asset into my digital wallet located in my phone. Upon delivery of my yacht and transfer of ownership I got onto a train and headed east towards my publisher to be close.

Bloomington Indianna was a fantastic town with plenty of open-minded people. Initially I stayed in an Air-B-N-B with the intension of heading to Florida as soon as I reviewed my published work. But, riding an electric unicycle throughout the town, I fell in love with the scenery of the colors changing in late September 2020 as well as the people. I loved how affordable things were after spending years in the slums of California and living on an island of trash in the bay area. I loved the bike lanes that were protected from traffic. I decided that I should become a productive member of society in this place. I put my resume out there and was approached by a dealership. Another amazing opportunity presented itself. I'm blessed beyond the curse and I know it. The anointing I have is real and cannot be washed off. As it would turn out I became an estimator for that dealership in town. I enjoyed my time there as well as the team members I worked with.

Although it didn't take long for a team member to develop jealousy motivated by years of seniority and the sense of entitlement. I believe she is a man hater; I don't know what happened to her before I met her, but it is so sad how she treats people. I've heard she beats her wife. Her disposition towards me could have been motivated by my professional skills encroaching upon her place in line to become the next shop manager. I noticed how evasive she became. It wasn't that hard to put the pieces together. She and the secretary there would be whispering to each other and seemed to act like cockroaches when the light turns on by the way they would disperse as I walked up. Apparently, hearsay is fun to gossip about. Drama queens are all the same. A few times as I walked up, I heard them say to one another, "Creep!". As well as the secretary saying to her, "that slime ball!" I thought to myself if they were talking about me, them probably, I'm covered in anointing oil. Nothing will stick. All the dirt and mud thrown at me slides right off and washes clean daily.

On October 6th, 2020 around two pm, the week my manager would be on vacation I noticed the general manager called her into his office with a few other men and closed the door. She was in there for about an hour talking with them. As I was doing my job, I noticed them all staring at me through the glass wall. It was fairly obvious, when I made eye contact with them their eyes averted. None of them could look me in the eye. They would simply look down at the ground. About twenty minutes after their meeting my senior publisher called me on my cell phone. She began discussing this book and the royalties. I excused myself as soon as she overheard that key word "royalties" from me and turned her chair to look at me. I walked outside to finish up the conversation. About ten minutes later I came back int the office, she asked me who I was talking to, I told her my publisher. She asked me about royalties, I said I can't talk about them because money isn't my motivator. Sorry, loose lips sink ships. That night I signed another contract for editing and publicity.

The next morning, the jealous coworker who called me a creep wasn't there at work. The secretary her best friend covered for her saying she had to pick up her wife since they were sharing a car owned by the dealership. Her own car was broken and she was driving a company vehicle, I heard later she got a new car for her help in my smear. I spy opportunity traded for integrity again. I think society should call those places "stealerships". I began to notice how nervous she acted as she came in late with her cell phone clutched in her hand and how she went straight to the restroom that was located next to the customer waiting area. She had been in there for over half an hour when a coworker was looking for her, I told him, "She is hiding in the bathroom". I couldn't believe I said that, but it just came out before I even thought about it.

As I was looking at my computer screen sitting behind my desk, I got a tap on the shoulder from the gentleman I had seen the day before who wouldn't make eye contact with me. Simultaneously I saw my coworker exit the bathroom, cell phone in hand recording.

The gentleman asked me my name and said he was a detective with the Bloomington police department. He told me to step up from my seat, while another officer hand cuffed me immediately. I saw my coworker smiling behind her camera phone with one fist raised in the air as her declaration of satisfaction. As I was lead outside, she followed. The detective placed me in the police car before asking me for I.D. He simply asked where my phone was. I told him it is on my desk, Samsung Galaxy Note ten plus. I saw his eyes light up as if he won the lottery. I know some people will do anything for money. I've never met a detective with a spine. I wasn't read my Miranda rights. As I was sitting in the police car, I noticed the entire dealership was outside watching with glee on their facial expressions. The detective came back from getting my phone and bag. He asked with excitement If I know what this is all about. I didn't know. I simply said, "I don't know, child support". He gasps as his jaw lowered and took two steps back as he clutched my phone and my journals taking them with him citing that Colley Wood, Texas had requested them to be used as evidence. I asked, "evidence for what?" He didn't say anything. While waiting I was approached by another officer, tiny tits I will call her. She asked where I had been. I replied, google said I traveled seven thousand two hundred thirty-two miles in 2020, twenty eight percent of the way around the globe, passing through four hundred fifteen cities, stopping in forty-nine different places. She asked if I was homeless, I replied, "no" I have an apartment, I just signed my lease.

I was taken to Monroe County Jail in Indianna and booked with sixteen third degree felonies. I asked what the charges were, the officers simply replied, "you already know", But I didn't. What could I have possibly done to acquire sixteen felony charges? I was processed into Monroe County jail even though I was there before eleven a.m., I wasn't given my first phone call until three a.m. the next day. I tried to call my publisher, but who would answer at that hour. It was probably part of their plan. I was locked in a cell under quarantine with only fifteen minutes every two days to make a phone call or take a shower. Still, nobody would tell me my charges. I'm pretty sure that official oppression is violation of my constitutional rights using qualified immunity. After a week of being incarcerated without being told why or any information, I was led to a virtual court room via zoom where I saw the judge on a screen. The judge had a smirk on her face as she asked me to sign an order of extradition to be taken to Texas to face these charges. I replied, "what charges?". She said she didn't know, I replied, phone records don't lie by omission, I used them to exercise my fourteenth amendment right to assert my ability to live free. She asked me how much money I had. I said "not much, I just gave it to my publisher. I'm under contract". Just then her eyes got huge as she scratched her head. She said she would appoint me a lawyer. I said "fine"

I wrote the lawyer a letter asking the details of my charges, after fourteen days I was presented with a misdemeanor charge for terroristic threat with a bond of five thousand for telling someone to pick out a photo for their obituary knowing we all die, I was again led to court. They asked me again to sign an order of extradition citing that they want me pretty bad and the governor of Texas was ready to extradite me if I didn't sign it, I wasn't surprised, I replied, my ex-wife Geneva is close family friends with him and others in the court system, I'm not surprised. But that statement seemed to surprise her. Phone records don't lie. The lawyer said if I sign it, they had fourteen days to pick me up, or I would be released. I didn't see what the difference was between signing and not signing, they can only hold someone for fourteen days anyways. I wasn't scared, I've nothing to hide. I don't use non-disclosure agreements and off shore bank accounts to live a double life in order to hide the truth and support the laundering of the elite's dirty money, so I signed the extradition order. As I was told, Texas only had a week to come get me.

Some could claim I was hiding as a fugitive from justice. But that's so far from the truth, I am a refugee from injustice, standing on my own two feet. That's the truest statement I can make about the situation. I write this knowing I never threatened anyone with bodily injury. I called Mr. Apple several times as well as his lawyer and said, "I'm ready when you are." Simply put, I believe the use of federal law is the threat that was made. In other words, my existence is a threat to the establishment. I expose the gang of cowards who wear blue costumes with shiny buttons who claim I deserve the treatment because of the hearsay and paid lies established by the oppressors who gave me my real name so long ago. I believe Federal law is very clear that as a united states citizen I am afforded certain unalienable rights as provided by my bill of rights as well as the constitution. I use the laws in place to threaten the law who hold positions of power at the state level. I hope to bring a confirmation to the statement that "small town equals big hell". Although they need not worry about revenge from me, I won't even piss on their face when their teeth are on fire.

I spent the next week incarcerated while meditating and reading expecting a change to take place. After the week came and went, I wrote the attorney again to ask why I'm not being released if they haven't come and picked me up yet. She informed me that I had extended their time frame by two weeks by signing the order. Again, more mediocrity in the legal department, because when there is that much money on the line all the lawyers involved will be paid off. A real lawyer would have advised me not to sign it since I only had a couple more days left. But I'm not scared. Nope, I'm not running from a fight, I am expecting it. As I suspected, in last minute fasion I was called on the intercom on October twenty seventh 2020 at 6:00 am, the corrections officer said, "roll it up, Texas is here to get you". I did so with much excitement. Down stairs I was met by two Tarrant County Sherriff's officers dressed in plain clothes. The officer who led me down stairs began to ask me about my charges, he seemed confused.

He saw my charges and said to the other two, "you are extraditing him for this?"

I spoke out of turn when I interrupted them all by saying, "Oh yeah, that's where they killed Kenedy on camera and tons of questions are left unanswered" The two Texas officers who had been excited a moment before looked at one another as if they had just seen a ghost. I saw the both of them drop their jaws simultaneously. Moments later I would be handcuffed wearing a lightweight jacket with the pockets cut out to hide the handcuffs that were now attached to the leather belt I was now wearing. I almost asked them if they would like me to autograph it somewhere for them, but I'm not giving them anything. The Monroe County officer began keeping a close watch on the two of them as if he was skeptical of their authenticity, as well as their motivation for putting me back on an airplane and heading back to Texas. It reminded me of the typical good cop bad cop routine, because the short stocky officer was acting proud of himself, bragging about traveling to Hawaii and even Alaska to pick up people for Tarrant County Texas. He kept trying to belittle me looking for a reaction. He even threatened to put me in shackles even though my behavior was exemplary. We got into the white dodge charger rental car and left the Monroe County jail. As we were driving through Bloomington the short officer asked me while laughing, "why did you stop here?" I simply replied, "My publisher is here in town". Both of the officers looked at one another in what looked like the onset of shock. Again, the short stocky officer began asking me if I had a mental illness, I replied "no".

He asked if I was suicidal, I simply said, "no". I stopped talking because I'm aware people who can be labeled with MHMR aren't given due process in Tarrant County at the Curry family justice center, and their rights are further violated. As we drove to the airport, I said nothing more. I sat in silence, praying for them both, I felt, no, I know, the grand architect already knows.

I was respectful to both of the officers, and even though I was given lots of looks of disgust by the airline staff while bypassing the TSA security checkpoint, I was steadfast in taking the high road, because there is a lot less traffic. During the plane ride, I was seated by the window and I enjoyed it. I got to see the light, I stared at the sun as it rose over the horizon in a new day. I'm unafraid. I wasn't sad. My life is for the glory of the lord, not my own. I kept praying, that's when I began to notice the tall officer who was sitting next to me began to bury his head in his hands for the rest of the duration of the flight. It almost looked like he was weeping. I felt the presence of my king was right there with me. I know only he is able to change the hearts of men. I must be seeing his handy work first hand. Once we landed, we were the last off the airplane. I expected to see media coverage because the court appointed lawyer in Indianna told me my arrest was all over the news in Texas. But to my surprise, I only saw one person waiting to see me. It was the mayor of Colley Wood's puppet. He was once an acquaintance of mine when we were in middle school. He lived down the street from once up a time a long time ago decades in the past. The puppet I'm referring to isn't worth mentioning his name, he is a very weird person who is good with computers and hacking. Michael didn't have social skills, so he went to a private school but remained best friends with the Mayor, Mr. Apple's son throughout high school and even after. I had no idea I was that interesting. I hope I get to ask him someday; does he follow Jesus that close? He had been stalking me for years. Everyone knows. As we made eye contact, he nodded his head and squinted his eyes as if to show how proud of himself and his actions he is. My hands were cuffed or I would have dusted my shoulders off, instead I simply smiled. I don't know if he could tell I was smiling because I was required to wear a mask. I was told by the short police officer that he would stop and get me a hamburger for lunch because the jail only had bologna sandwiches and it would be hours and hours before I could eat. My reply, "that's the for-profit prison complex for you, isn't it?" He looked away as if I he knows I speak the truth and it cuts like a knife.

After a short booking process and a quick arraignment for a five-thousand-dollar bond I was lead upstairs wearing a brand new but used green jumpsuit. I made a phone call to a bondsman knowing I had the cash in the bank to post that kind of bond. The next day I was arraigned again, this time on twelve additional counts of third-degree felony terroristic threat for the city of Colley Wood's gang in blue, as well as two counts of stalking for the mayor and his lawyer. I suppose they heard about my book. It's ironic isn't it. I was a thousand miles away for the past nine years. Is society that incredibly fake that the truth is so highly offensive? As soon as the magistrate saw me, she smirked and laughed just before she read me my charges in the virtual courtroom. I asked the judge presiding when I can expect my trial by jury. She said they wouldn't be doing trials until April of 2021 due to the pandemic; court had been shut down. As I was led back to my cell by the officer who was laughing, I asked if we could do the same thing again tomorrow. My bond was now set at one hundred sixty-five thousand dollars. That amount was higher than several capital murderers I met while in jail. Subsequently I was given my very own solitary cell on the top floor. I liked to think of it as my penthouse suite and I wasn't complaining. I had free rent, a bed that wouldn't sink in the ocean, three hot meals and I was able to read until my heart's content as well as write more. I wasn't required to make money to pay my ex-wife's required child support there by further supporting organized criminals.

The staff at the jail kept assessing me, I found out that I had high blood pressure, and they wanted to give me pills to correct the problem. But I refuse to take drugs, I know my blood pressure is elevated due to my incarceration. I also know I have king's blood flowing through my veins and the grand architect already knows my time and place of death, it cannot be changed by people. Instead, they put me on a diet tray with low sodium which I promptly traded every day to someone else who wanted fruit instead of cookies. I hope to stay salty and sweet for all eternity.

About a month later I was introduced to my court appointed attorney even though I wanted to represent myself, I wasn't allowed. Simply put, I've been told that doesn't happen in Tarrant County. It seems like a great way for Tarrant County Texas to maintain their ninety nine percent conviction rate they are so proud of. The court appointed attorney told me he had already met with the gang in blue of Colley Wood. He said the evidence doesn't hold much weight. He told me the charges were a result of a campaign led by the head of the church who is also the director of finance as well as a close friend of the governor. The woman I'm referring to is Geneva's best friend. She pays for everything and has been a stalker of mine for years who kept calling the police there. Initially the gang in blue told her, there is no threat present. But she kept calling back being well connected to Linda and Geneva as well as Mrs. Crocodile and the governor of Texas through the family whose name is on the side of the court house. I speculate she finally got someone to listen when I unexpectedly moved from the ocean and initially nobody could locate me. I suppose if you have a lack of real faith and only made of money then you must be easily scared because your existence is so fragile. I bet she is scared of her shadow in the dark now. Initially the lawyer told me the charges don't have much weight and would probably be no billed, I would only have to sit there for a year and wait it out. The attorney asked me what happened for these people to be so upset with me.

I replied, "using sex as a weapon isn't illegal yet, but conspiring is" His eyes squinted, I could tell he didn't like the truth as well as my response.

Then he said, "that sounds like a mental illness." I said "most gang stalking and gaslighting does just that, it's by design". "But phone records don't lie". "They provide details about means, motive, opportunity, malicious behavior, as well as manipulation for revenge".

He said with glowing eyes, "and you don't have a mental illness? "I said nope, I wanted to tell him to keep trying to protect a prostitution ring that uses cameras, but I believe everyone knows.

He said to me, "you've never been evaluated" I replied "I've never needed it" He said with a laugh, "well, we will see about that" I was happy. I thought to myself, keep trying, I literally get off on it.

I went back to my cell knowing he was paid very well with gifts that cannot be returned for his premeditated participation in the official oppression and smear campaign that exists against me here in Tarrant County Texas. I spent the next few months in maximum security incarceration without conviction. even though I was in solitary confinement I met many admitted capital murderers who had a lower bond than I did. Meanwhile I did my homework in the law library researching my charges and the specifics the law provides under the directives of the constitutions and the state laws. I learned so much, I wrote sixteen of my own motions for my trial by hand in three copies for each office to properly file them. All of my motions were muted by my court appointed attorney that I didn't ask for. I was reminded that Mrs. Crocodile's neighbor's name was on the side of the court house. Three weeks later I was brought to a virtual court room for a video plea. My court appointed attorney didn't show up. He refused to answer any of the letters I wrote, except for one. He sent me a letter saying he didn't answer phone calls from jail, and he would let me know when he was ready for me.

After eight months in county jail and two mental health assessments with no issues, I was brought to court and offered either one hundred sixty years of incarceration or probation for a guilty plea. I realized that when people with wealth conspire with people with power to oppress and silence someone by paying for lies under the alibi of social justice generated for entertainment, I should already be dead. Later I found out while I was incarcerated without conviction that Geneva supposedly had a stroke and that Linda bypassed the rule eleven court order in which she was not supposed to have any contact with our two boys. I suppose that means Geneva is in contempt of court. I can only guess Linda is going to great lengths to brainwash those two boys so she may cover for her own premeditated actions as well as keep them slaves so she may repeat the same level of torture and abuse I endured for her entertainment. I hope it makes them stronger, that's what it did for me.

I suppose that's the rhetoric provided by their logo, the square and the compass. I thought about it for a moment. I questioned my attorney in regards to my property that was seized as evidence, I asked him if I could get that property back because that was both my financials as well as my intellectual property and protected under the fourth amendment of the constitution to be secure in my persons, places, things, and papers. He assured me that whatever property was seized by the state as evidence would be given back to me and was located in the Tarrant County evidence and property room. If they saw the exculpatory evidence on my phone, I have kept for all these years then it would mysteriously vanish. Loose lips sink ships.

So, June 3rd, of 2021 I signed for deferred adjudication pleading guilty to terroristic threat public official. I know if the charges actually held any weight, then I would already be in federal prison. I also know with the four hundred thousand cases awaiting trial in Tarrant County, it would be at least four years before I would get a trial to be judged by twelve of my peers; if there were any who haven't seen my life already. If and only if, I wasn't mysteriously lost in the system much like the evidence against me would be. I am aware of the prejudice against me here in Texas made up for entertainment by cowards who cannot be honest, and instead use church as a tax shelter and an alibi. I am aware that people with wealth conspire with power to oppress the rest of us and have the nerve to say we are greedy, or that we deserve the treatment. If you don't know that also, you're blind. If you disagree with that statement, you are part of the problem. I believe its elitism, after all; I've already seen inside Muck's computer in August 2013. As I went into the court room of CDC1, I overheard the Sargent present talking to the court clerk about the possibility of a revocation hearing someday. Surely, he wasn't talking about me. I haven't even been pulled over in nine years. The timing was incredible. The usual judge was at lunch during this time. Instead of being seen by the highest judge in criminal court who is also next in line to become the district attorney, I would be seen by a different magistrate. I was told by my attorney that a special prosecutor was brought in by Colley Wood to prosecute me for these charges and a jury was on standby waiting. It sounded like more violations of constitutional rights by a gang of cowards. But I suppose those were all in vain, and more or less threats designed to intimidate and coerce me into not going to a lengthy trial. Trials are expensive and its well known that Tarrant County owes the state of Texas as well as the federal government millions and millions of dollars. Not to mention there are four hundred thousand cases awaiting trial and it would be almost four years before I would actually get a trial by jury.

In conditions of my probation, I was required to wear an ankle monitor with GPS, as well as not to leave Tarrant County, and not to come back to Colley Wood. I was also restricted from having any social media as well as never to come within a certain distance of the various tax shelters for the elite that everyone else knows as a certain church. I suppose those stipulations were mandated by the television "pastor" who is close friends with the Texas state governor as well as the grand master mason over the whole state of Texas. I felt no pain,

I don't have friends, I don't have family, just a few acquaintances, and I've never been happier. I know the church is fake, so why would I want to attend a congregation full of hypocrites? Thank you to my lawyer for muting my motions I filed with the court while awaiting trial. So sad the mediocrity I saw in a "Texas top attorney". I know the Law, I had to, because the "law" knew me before I was of age. I guess you could say it was a form of retributive punishment, or prosecutorial vindictiveness motivated by exclusivity of the family whose name is on the side of the court house and owns the justice center.

June 4th, 2021, just after a breakfast tray, I was led out of Tarrant County jail where I would check into the community supervision department and have an ankle monitor installed. During that process I wasn't given any information about my boundaries within the community. I was given an appointment for the following week to meet with my probation officer. I obliged. After being placed on GPS restriction I headed to the property and the evidence room to pick up my property and phone. The officer behind the window stated that there was no record of any property or evidence in my case held by the state. She thought maybe I was lying until I provided documentation that my property was seized. I called the attorney who represented me who told me he would file the motion required for a minimal fee of two thousand five hundred dollars, and there was no guarantee I would ever see it again. He replied, there is no record of my property as if he already knew.

I walked away from the court house with no money at all, no way to get anywhere, and not knowing what my boundaries are, as well as not knowing the current state of charge of the GPS monitor. I had no Idea when it would need to be charged next. I walked about a mile to a train station where I boarded the train and showed my release paperwork to get a ride to Richman's Hills, the city I was born in. From there I got onto a city bus using the same release paperwork to get a free ride. I got off the bus at a college campus where I randomly met an anonymous person who was legally blind. He helped me; he gave me good advice when he said, "no matter what, don't sit down, don't quit walking away or the police would pick me up." I will always believe that man was used by the king to speak to me. I know the grand architect speaks in mysterious ways.

CHAPTER 14

Purgation

I walked alone, with a brown bag containing my legal paperwork for two and a half miles to an old friend's house who was surprised to see me. I tried contacting him numerous times in jail. But I know every letter I wrote was read and scanned by the jail staff and put into my file. Everything I say can and will be used against me in a court of law. It was a glorious time to be reacquainted. He and his wife shared dinner with me. It was my favorite style of homemade pizza and salad with a cold glass of water. I hadn't seen him in almost nine years. I was thankful to see him again. The time was flying by. Around nine p.m. he asked me if he could give me a ride somewhere.

I politely replied, "no", "I would rather walk".

From his house I walked a little over three miles away wearing a backpack he had saved for me all these years. I tried to find my Half-brother and uncle's house. They are obviously the same person. But by the time I got close it was past eleven p.m. I hadn't seen or heard from him in years, so I didn't bother to look very hard. I kept walking another mile or more down towards the rail road tracks where I used to ride my dirt bike as a child. From there I walked East towards where my kids now live while in violation of court orders. I walked two and a half miles down the rail road tracks when it was almost two am at this point when my ankle monitor started vibrating continuously. The GPS unit was alerting me that I was close to a boundary. I immediately walked back from where I came about twenty feet when it subsided. I had nowhere else to go. So, I walked towards Duck's sister's house. She is the one with all the connections with the gang in blue because she helped set up the 911 phone and network system from the start while working for the phone company in the nineties. The time was probably close to three a.m. June fifth 2021 when I arrived on her front door step. I didn't want to say hello. I only needed to charge my GPS monitor and I remembered she had an outlet installed on the front porch of the house Duck had built for her free of charge for her participation in my smear. So, I sat on her front porch while I charged my ankle monitor while I kept a close watch of my surroundings. I almost caught an hour of sleep during that break.

Around four-thirty a.m. I started walking back the direction I came. My hips were so sore from walking so far already and blisters had begun forming on my feet. It felt like walking on broken glass through a desert filled with barbed wire. This would be the longest ten miles I would ever walk. Somehow, I felt in my spirit, it was making me stronger. I wanted to see if my grandmother was still alive. I missed her so much. That was the only refuge I could see on the horizon. I don't know how many calories I burned walking to my aunt's house. But now I was starving. Nobody was open and there was nowhere to turn. Although it wouldn't matter because I didn't have any money. As I kept walking, I saw a doughnut shop with workers inside although they weren't open for business yet. I've never done this before, but I've eaten manure for years. So, eating from the dumpster didn't scare me. So that's just what I did. Who cares about covid when you have type O-negative blood flowing through your veins? If you don't know yet, I believe I'm immune. Just behind the doughnut shop there was a dumpster surrounded by a brick wall to keep it out of the public's eye. I opened the side access door and peered into the dumpster where there was a clear trash bag sitting on top that contained at least a hundred of the day-old doughnuts. They looked to be simply surplus. There wasn't consumer trash in the same bag. It only contained pastries that looked and felt fresh still. I sat there for probably half an hour eating some sweet treats. I had a cinnamon roll first, then various cake doughnuts and followed them all up with a chocolate glazed with sprinkles. My cup was running over. I was gaining my strength. I needed the fuel and again I started walking. I walked blindly and into the unknown. I wasn't crying, I wasn't complaining, I was rejoicing. I know I serve a God who moves mountains for me to walk free. My king is so much bigger than my problems. He always makes beauty from ashes. I am thankful for being burned into another creation for his glory so we can all see.

I didn't know if Grandmother was still alive. She would be eighty-five years old by now. If she wasn't alive, her house might not be a refuge for me. But I had heard from the lord in mysterious ways, don't stop, don't sit down, keep walking. I made it half way when I was starving and thirsty. I stopped into a Whataburger to use the restroom and fill up a water bottle. Before I left, I prayed for the lord's favor upon my situation. I asked the manager of the location if I could have something to eat even though I had no money. I told her I just got released out of jail and had no money, but I needed something to eat. I looked her in the eyes with sincerity and humility as I was being completely honest. The manager was so gracious, she gave me my favorite burger without me even saying so. Moments later she brought out a Whataburger with bacon and cheese and a large fry with an empty cup for me to fill up with Dr. Pepper. I was given enough fuel to keep going. The lord is my provider, he uses people in the most unexpected ways. I enjoyed every bight as I sat in prayer thanking the king for his goodness and mercy, surely, they shall follow me all of my days. I continued on as my steps are directed by my king and my path is illuminated because he has already gone before me and made the way.

A few hours later I walked past the house I was born in; it looked the same as when I lived there. The school across the street had changed drastically. It had been completely remodeled. From there I followed the power lines as the crow flies and a few hours later I would cross Denton highway on foot through six lanes of traffic. My good aunt who is also a black sheep of the family was standing outside. Our eyes locked once I was about thirty yards away. She was so happy to see me. She exclaimed, "Oh my God!". I felt like the prodigal son. I learned my grandmother had passed. She died of a broken heart, and on her death bed she made a special request. She told my aunt that if I ever came back to Texas for her to help me in any way.

Three days later I had a job, I had a phone, I had a place to live, I had a car to drive, food to eat, Clothes to wear and I'm on my way to a better life close to where I was born. I'm blessed beyond the curse. God is good, all the time, I pinky promise his grace is enough for me. A few days later I filed a motion at the Tarrant County court house with supporting evidence that shows the detective in Colley Wood has my phone as well as my journals and kept it instead of turning it over for state's evidence. I speculate that it was sold to Linda for the value of my photos motivated to delete exculpatory evidence and resources in order to further oppress me. Technically speaking official oppression like that is only a Class "A" misdemeanor, but if it's paired with a conspiracy charge and a hate crime using qualified immunity to do so, then under the rules of criminal procedure it should lead to a whole slew of federal indictments for further trying to silence someone for shedding light into dark places for being a whistle blower as well as a game changer. Personally, I see the police as a gang as defined by the Code of criminal procedures as written in Vernon's Annumerated Codes of criminal procedures in Texas as well as under federal law. As many of my rights were violated in order to violate me, how could anyone who is watching the production in place see it otherwise? If someone wants to lie about me on camera, they should do it on a witness stand in a trial facing the penalty of perjury knowing real justice shouldn't cost a thing. Social justice should be enough to break the system as I have done with my king's help along the way. It's for his glory, not my own, I'm a nobody. After all, what is entertainment worth? Is it valuable enough for everyone to see we are all ruled by organized criminals and it's enforced by a gang of cowards who wear blue costumes with shiny buttons so blind sheep and boot lickers have someone to believe in and call when the lack faith in a broken system that's been slowly eroded by the mediocrity put in place by the ruling elite? I hope everyone can now see how money is simply a tool of slavery.

I'm quite literally dying to meet my King. I know He's waiting for me. I feel it coming soon, and it makes me so happy. We all get what we have coming. Why should I lift a finger to help a world full of fools and slaves who treated me the way you did? I think the slavery that is coming is probably well deserved. I'm the strongest slave. I've been a slave to slaves my whole life. The best slaves don't even know. That means after I'm sodomized on camera, the world will know a whole new form of slavery. Mental sodomy. Unless somehow it goes both ways, first, we all become slaves. Mercy isn't up to me. I simply watch as a unicorn, knowing sometimes in life, you don't know what you've got until it's gone. All my haters are actually just fans.

Being put on a pedestal for entertainment's sake feels like the opposite of falling. I rejoice, knowing my King needed the large audience for some reason, and I trust His plan. He used my life in a big way, and I don't really understand it. It's simply not my burden. The real King is my judge, not the "grand worshipful master" at the most secret lodge in Texas, who also claims that "judge" position as his appointed day job as well as his name on the side of the courthouse. No way. That's Mrs. Crocodile's next-door neighbor. He bound her into that years ago when her first husband mysteriously died. There is no such thing as a free lunch.

I'm so thankful I finished my work before I died, because my loose lips always sink ships.

I'm already a dead man walking thankfully. Everyone knows what happens to people who write down events that take place in my family's cult. I do. That's exactly why I did. So, everyone else can learn. What do I have to fear? I live fully every day, knowing each day alive is a gift. Surely goodness and mercy shall follow me all the days of my life. I'm finding my own way as my King leads me back home. Only after confirming for everyone that money won't bring happiness, I've learned in this life that's simply a test of salvation, and I'm stronger now. I know all the cowards who were used to procure lies on camera to smear me will face death all alone. We all will. I suggest they chose a photo for their obituary, because tomorrow isn't guaranteed. Thank you to everyone, from the people who told me to the people who said it in silence, as well as the people who didn't know I was listening and reading lips, for your help to get here. Thanks so much for all the forgiveness that was extended to me for all those years. I say it all stems from Grace. It's no wonder there is so much hate in this society because they breed themselves and are required to do so by the breeding in place. I will often wonder if I helped them usher in my ancestor's New World Order, or if I stood in the way, as a patsy who was strong enough to enjoy the attention. Oh well, I will always be blind, and I am just fine with that.

My ancestors' cult is simply human trafficking, trying to create concubines through codependency and hand out social justice. When it's done at the highest level, I suppose the appropriate alibi is entertainment. I suppose that means maybe we are ruled by criminals. I'm not allowed to break the system that's in place and designed for me to fail. I'm a nobody. I think bigger. I've already seen the poorest people are so poor, all they have is money. Their life choices to procure wealth are simply not my burden to bear. Real wealth isn't having more; it's actually needing less. I see money is a curse and prevents me from seeing my King's hands work. It is easier for a camel to pass through the eye of a needle than for a rich man to enter into heaven. I need less of the world and more of my King. That's where I'm headed now, if anyone wants to continue following.

My mansion in heaven is waiting, and I long to be in His presence. Don't hold me hostage here anymore. This life is only a test. Death is only the beginning. I'm finally happy now, because I have learned how to learn. I learned how to be happy regardless of my situation. I'm finding my own way doing wheelies everywhere I can, knowing my time is gone in any moment, I'm happy to die, because I've been raised in a sewer by rats and surrounded by fools who actually believe I am one also. I guess that makes me the king of fools. I can only trust it's by my King's design. Everyone knows, you are who your friends are. That means I'm not a nobody; I'm nothing in this life. I look forward to being seated next to the king of kings in the next life after I ride the white horse on the horizon into a battle for eternity and freedom for all those who believe in the second coming.

I saw the bigger picture so long and was commanded to keep quiet. If you are a hater I have and now own, I'm not even sad for you. Burn me like that cigarette, and I'll happily give you cancer while I smile back at you, because mercy isn't up to me. I see a longer list than the Kennedy curse. But who's counting?

Thanks for taking some of your precious time to read this in its entirety. I'm thankful to have left something for my little unicorns to find along the way that will speak volumes to them because they lived it also. I pray that you learn how to see more clearly, through my own learning; the world could and should be different if we all saw wolves wearing sheep's clothing, trying to turn people into money right before our very eyes. The choice is yours, stand for something, or fall for anything. What's your integrity worth? Money is just paper with art and man-made for all of us to believe in. I see it as a curse. Serve God or serve money, nobody gets to do both.

Printed in the United States
by Baker & Taylor Publisher Services